Making a Daily Advancement

Making a Daily Advancement

Mike Lawrence

Dedication

For my wife Debbie

Acknowledgements

I wish to acknowledge the kindness of the late W. Bro. Bernard Cordell, the late W. Bro. Rev. Canon Leonard Tyzack, the late W. Bro. Geoff Goode, and many other brethren, who, over the years, have presented me with Masonic books that have helped my research greatly.

First published 2018

ISBN 978 0 85318 556 7

Published by Lewis Masonic

an imprint of Ian Allan Publishing Ltd, Addlestone, Surrey KT15 2SF.

Printed in Malta.

Visit the Lewis Masonic website at www.lewismasonic.co.uk

Contents

About the Author

Bro. Michael Lawrence PM, PZ, PProvDepGSwdB
Cornwallis Lecturer 2009
Colin Dyer Memorial Lecturer 2010
Member of the East Kent Provincial Debating Team 2011

Michael spent much of his working of his life in Local Government; he joined Freemasonry in 1994, and in 1996, was appointed the Manager of the Folkestone Masonic Centre. His first Masonic article was published 1998 and he presented his first Masonic lecture in 2001. During the next thirteen years his lectures raised over £10,000 for charity. By 2013, he started to write a regular blog and in 2015, he realised that over the years he had enough material for several books. His first book, *I Greet You Well*, was published by Lewis Masonic, and contained a dozen of his most popular lectures.

His writings are not full of fanciful and romantic imaginations, but simple and to the point with the sole purpose of promulgating the many facts and historical events overlooked by those who wish to take Freemasonry along a path it was never meant to tread.

Taking early retirement in 2016, he now writes a regular blog at:

http://freemasonsareus.wordpress.com/

You can visit and like his Facebook page at:

https://www.facebook.com/pg/freemasonsareus/

You can tweet him or ask him a question at:

https://twitter.com/Freemasonsareus/

Foreword

'There is nothing new under the sun', a late lamented friend would always say to me, and it is true, most things appear just to be there until we, or somebody else, discovers or finds them. The same can be said about Freemasonry, it's all there, the history, the documents, albeit sparse, it is there, and all we have to do is to look in the right places to find it. And that is all I seem to have done since joining Freemasonry in 1994, that is, to search in those places feeding on the information that I gleaned and endeavouring to make that daily advancement in Masonic knowledge. Fortunately, or unfortunately depending on your stance, the reading spawned writing, the writing grew into lecturing and suddenly I found I had the makings of several books.

Another statement I can also categorically say, without any fear of contradiction, is that despite all the books, essays, lectures and articles I have read or listened to, I am no nearer to discovering the origins of this wonderful and noble science than I am ready for a journey to the moon. It is true to say that we all have our pet theories, that we often expound upon when called to do so, but there is never that true conviction in our words and we end up almost talking ourselves out of our long-held views because we cannot prove them, or another theory seems more attractive.

Perhaps it's the absurdity that pushes us on to seek for something that is probably staring us all in the face yet just manages to evade capture; that keeps the writers writing, the lecturers lecturing and researchers researching, and ever may it be so. Yet we do not all join this fraternity for that reason, for as the Great Architect made each of us different, so each of us gets something different from the Craft. It's true to say that the percentage of men that actively participate in reading Masonic books is very small and perhaps its more an indictment on the Craft that most of a member's time is taken up learning ritual by rote, rather than leaning the meaning of the ritual they are speaking, but that's a different issue.

I have found it no better with the Masonic knowledge in general of established members, particularly when I overheard a conversation about a very 'high up' and 'important' Mason. 'Yes, he holds 18 Degrees, has a dark blue apron and wears three different jewels', went the discussion.

I smiled inwardly, knowing that these two Master Masons had several years' membership between them and should have known better. it saddened me to think that they associated the terms 'high up' and 'important' to the number of degrees one may have taken, the colour of one's apron and even more upsetting, the number of jewels one might wear. I realised at this point exactly what may have been meant by the words in the Charge that admonishes us to '...endeavour to make a daily advancement in Masonic knowledge'.

Another example I read was written by a well-known Masonic writer, who explained how his journey into Freemasonry began on the night of his Initiation when a noose was placed around his neck. Noose! A noose is a knot which is used to hang people; we employ a cable-tow or running noose which demonstrates submission and symbolically acts as a restraint, sadly the term 'noose' changes the whole ethos of the Initiation ceremony and the whole symbolic meaning of the cable tow.

I was about to start this next sentence with the words 'We all know that...', but that is where I am wrong. In fact, we do not all know and unless things are explained to us, like the two brethren I overheard, we will continue to remain in such ignorance. Other ways we perpetuate such ignorance is when a learned, or rather not so learned Brother, who in a well-meaning manner, actually imparts incorrect information to an inquiry. For the record, let me state quite categorically that there is no disgrace in not having an answer. A simple 'I'll follow that one up for you', or 'Can I come back to you on that one', will be a sufficient answer to give anyone.

So how do we, as a fraternity of likeminded men, combat this ignorance and satisfy the challenge of that Charge? Well if we take the trouble to look, there are several mediums we can use and here are the five most popular: the Internet, magazines, books, Lodges of Research and not forgetting Provincial libraries, all viable areas to extend our knowledge. But whatever medium suits you, understanding Freemasonry and satisfying the advice given us in the Charge, will take some effort on our part. You will readily recall the famous picture of Christ with the lantern, standing at the door; the door has no handle and therefore must be opened by the person that seeks knowledge, rather than the person that has the knowledge. So, by purchasing this book, you are seeking to extent your learning.

Hopefully, you will find this book informative; however, you will not find anything new or original, but rather a collection of informative pieces to increase your knowledge, thoughts to consider, humorous stories drawn from my many years as a Freemason and a look at other Orders. It is something any of us could do and I take no credit for doing something which I consider as my hobby. Some men fish, others play golf; I read and write.

Oh! And by the way, the Brother with the 18 Degrees was a Knight or Sovereign Prince of the Rose Croix, a Christian Order classed as one of the Knighthood Degrees, which all Master Masons that have a belief in the Trinity, are eligible to join.

His dark blue apron was by virtue of the fact he holds a Provincial office.

As for his jewels, the first was his Royal Arch Chapter Jewel, worn by all Companions of the Holy Royal Arch. The second was a Charity jewel, which he purchased himself after donating a minimum of £25 to the Masonic Trust for Girls and Boys. The third was his Lodge Centenary jewel, which he also purchased.

Like so many instances in everyday life, things in Masonry are not always what they may seem!

M.L.
Folkestone
November 2017

Introduction

Welcome to my new book designed to help you make a daily advancement in Masonic knowledge. Surprisingly, during your Masonic career, that Charge is never rescinded and whatever lofty rank you achieve, whatever additional Degree you may take, it is your duty to study the science of Freemasonry, so that you may personally develop a deep and meaningful understanding of exactly what is expected of you. So, if you are an Entered Apprentice or a Grand Lodge Officer, this book is for you and helps you to create a platform from which to begin in earnest, a regular study schedule.

The book is set out in a day-to-day date format and you can choose to start on the day you receive the book or at the beginning. Personally, I would strongly advise you to commence your study on the day you receive the book and continue day by day. No doubt you will be tempted to read through the book quickly, as there are many interesting items, but if you truly wish to make that daily advance then perhaps, if you read the article for the day, you may be inclined to research the topic a little further; much of this you can do online. You may even wish to make a list of subjects you wish to look at deeper and there are many books and online resources you can research.

So if you can, approach each day with the knowledge that it will contain something historic, an explanation of a term often heard but misunderstood, a humorous story which may prompt you to record your own, something thought-provoking or some information about the different Degrees. Whatever it is, I really hope you enjoy the beginnings of your new study programme, and remember it isn't a race; Masonic knowledge comes through the slow and steady approach and the retention of each new subject you cover.

January

1st Happy New Year and welcome to the start of your daily advancement. Did you know that the first Masonic exposure was published in an anonymous letter printed in *The Flying Post or Post Master*, issue No. 4712, dated 11-13 April 1723. It was in the form of a catechism and was given the title *A Mason's Examination*, by Robert Freke Gould when he reprinted it in the *History of Freemasonry.* Although an exposure, the document runs in a similar pattern and is themed in the same manner as several other catechisms of the day. It has a wonderful description of Freemasonry, hopefully valid some three hundred years later:

> *It is indeed agreed on all hands, the Masonry, the most substantial Part of Architecture, is of singular Use or Ornament; that Free Masons are no prying inquisitive Busiebodies, but honest industrious Persons, who desire only to excel in their own Profession; that the Worshipful Society are no innovators in Religious Affairs, no perjured Plotters or Conspirators against the establish'd Government; that they in no way interfere or clash with any other Society or Corporation, however dignify'd or distinguish'd; for all which excellent Qualifications, a reasonable Person would be willing to pay their Persons, their Lodges, their Constitutions, all due Respect and Honour.*

2nd I was recently reading a copy of an application to Grand Lodge for a warrant of a new lodge dated the year 1849. Amongst other things, I was somewhat dismayed at the detail explaining when the new lodge would meet, which was always on the night of the full moon on certain appointed months.

It appears that lodge meetings of old would always be held on the night of a full moon and I always considered it had something to do with the moon being one of the Three Lesser Lights, which we are told, governs the night.

After some research, and much to the dismay of our many researchers who associate our rituals with cosmic science, this did not have that significance at all. It was done purely to provide some light for inebriated brethren to find their way home after the meeting. Street lighting, as you know, had yet to fully adorn our thoroughfares.

What this does show however, is that Freemasonry is often practical and pragmatic, not all symbolic. In real terms we find the simplest of practices has a simple explanation.

3rd The First, Second and Third regular steps taken by all Freemasons have been part of our ritual from as early as 1724, when it was first recorded. The *Grand Mystery of Free-Masons Discover'd* (1724), and the *Institution of Free Masons* (c.1725), asks the same question:

Q. How many Steps belong to a right Mason?
A. Three

A Mason's Confession (c.1727) reproduces a rough drawing of three set of feet/shoes, standing at right angles and placed on three parallel lines, indicating three steps, while the Wilkinson MS (1727) and Pritchard's *Masonry Dissected* (1730), both mention the Candidate taking three steps towards the Master before taking their Obligation. *Three Distinct Knocks* (1760), indicates that only one step is taken in the First Degree, two in the Second and so on.

Therefore, I have given just a brief glimpse of a practice we see at every meeting, yet often never realise the custom is almost three hundred years old. As for the symbolism of the steps, I can find no explanation in any of the old catechisms, MSS or exposures.

4th A rather strange quasi-Masonic society sprang up in 1740, called or rather known as 'the Mopses'. Founded by the Duke of Bavaria not long after Pope Clement XII issued a Papal Bull condemning Freemasonry and forbidding any practices of its rites by good Catholics, it also established itself in France. The Order was an imitation of Freemasonry, but also included women.

Their emblem was a dog depicting fidelity and love, and the term 'Mops' was said to be German for pug-dog.

Coincidentally, there does not appear to be any connection between the term 'Mopses' and the onerous but practical task given to the junior initiate of taking the mop and bucket to erase all designs traced on the floor of the Lodge by the Tyler, with chalk or charcoal.

5th Temple, or lodge room? What word do you use to describe the room where you meet? First of all, let me point out that you can use either word and there is no right or wrong word, or official direction, so let us take a quick look at both terms.

The room where we meet is representative of two places, i.e. King Solomon's Temple (hence the Worshipful Master occupying the Chair of King Solomon) and an Operative Mason's workshop (hence the Warrant, the working tools of an Operative Mason, the *Book of Constitutions* and the Volume of Sacred Law).

The term 'temple' invokes thoughts, to the uninitiated, of worship or adoration, whereas 'lodge room' indicates a place of business.

My own preference is the term 'lodge room', but this is because I have always seen how the general public view or perceive Freemasonry and I feel the term 'temple', adds to that wrong perception. However, I have noticed a distinct change in that perception when I have used the term lodge room, adding that it is the place where Freemasons conduct their business.

It may just be that I have spent over twenty-five years discussing Freemasonry with non-members and experience has shown me the less complicated we make discussions, the easier it is to break down those prejudices.

6th I once saw a Visiting Officer, step forward during the investiture of the Tyler, and remove the sword which, by lodge tradition, had been placed diagonally across the V of SL, and slide it to rest on the pedestal.

Apart from being very bad manners, tradition dictates that if that is the practice and tradition of the lodge, then there is absolutely nothing wrong with the placing of the sword in that position.

There has never been any ruling issued by Grand Lodge and all too often, we base our judgement on the system of Freemasonry we practice ourselves, never thinking that other systems have their own traditions, usages and practices.

We must also accept that promotion to high office in Freemasonry is not based upon one's knowledge of the Craft and although we must show respect to Senior Officers, they are by no means infallible. In most cases, if a Senior or Visiting Officer finds something amiss at the meeting he is attending, he will raise the matter at a later point rather than draw attention to the matter and affect the flow of the meeting.

7th I have always taken the time to spend a few minutes talking to the Tyler, whom I consider to be one of the most important Officers of the lodge. Normally an elderly Senior Past Master, I find them full of wisdom and humorous stories of the many incidents that have occurred during the preparation of Candidates.

Like the time a Candidate produced a carrot and asked what part of the ceremony would it be used, or the time a Proposer forgot to tell his Candidate to wear black socks and he subsequently wore white.

Tyler's have a knack at putting the Candidate as ease and coping with all manner of situations, for which most carry a small bag containing all the necessary or extra items he may be called upon to use in the event of a mishap or unforeseen incident.

I remember with great fondness the Tyler who so readily helped prepare me, and put me at ease, when I was initiated. If I recall he was well in his nineties, yet he eloquently explained the process and sent me into the lodge, quietly confident and at ease.

So please, do not pass your Tyler without spending a moment to talk with him, greet him well and show him the respect he deserves as a Senior Member of the lodge. It will make his day, and prove to him that although outside the lodge, he has not been forgotten.

8th We are introduced to the Seven Liberal Arts and Sciences in the Second Degree, but if we go back in time to about 1390, we may read the earliest Masonic reference in the Regius MS:

Grammar is the first science I know,
Dialect the second, so I have bliss,
Rhetoric the third without nay, (doubt)
Music is the fourth, as I you say,
Astronomy is the fifth, by my snout,
Arithmetic the sixth, without doubt,
Geometry the seventh maketh an end,
For he is both meek and hende, (courteous)
Grammar forsooth is the root,
Whoever will learn on the book;
But art passeth in his degree,
As the fruit doth the root of the tree;
Rhetoric measureth with ornate speech among,
And music it is a sweet song;
Astronomy numbereth, my dear brother,
Arithmetic sheweth one thing that is another,
Geometry the seventh science it is,
That can separate falsehood from truth, I know.
These be the sciences seven,
Who useth them well he may have heaven.

9th Pendent to the corners of the lodge carpet are four tassels; these are meant to remind us of the four cardinal virtues, namely: Temperance, Fortitude, Prudence, and Justice, the whole of which, tradition informs us, were constantly practiced by a great majority of our ancient brethren. Here we examine Fortitude.

In Latin, Fortitude is pronounced *Fortitudo* meaning courage or bravery. In visual art it is often shown as a marble column.

The Emulation Lectures of the Three Degrees explain Fortitude thus:

> *Fortitude - Is that noble and steady purport of the soul, which is equally distant from rashness and cowardice; it enables us to undergo any pain labour, danger, or difficulty, when though necessary, or deemed prudentially expedient. This virtue, like the former, ought to be deeply impressed on the breast of every Mason, as a fence and security against any attempts which might be made either by threats or violence, to extort from him any of those Masonic secrets he has so solemnly engaged himself to hele* [pronounced hail], *conceal, and never improperly reveal; the illegal revealing of which might prove a torment to his mind, as the Compasses were emblematically to his body when extended to his naked left breast at time of his Initiation; alluding to the Pectoral.*
>
> First Lecture, Sixth Section.

Fortitude therefore gives us endurance; endurance to undergo pain, peril or danger and should impress on a Freemason's mind the importance of safeguarding against any illegal attack that may be made, by force or otherwise, to extort from him any of those valuable secrets with which he has been so solemnly entrusted and teaches him to let no dangers shake, no pains dissolve the inviolable fidelity he owes to the trusts reposed in him.

It symbolises more than physical courage, as it also represents moral courage that all Freemasons must have in showing the strength and ability to make a decision based upon their own moral convictions and stick to it regardless of the consequences. The Mason must exhibit the highest moral and ethical principles in their life and standby those principles when society looks unfavourably upon those principles.

10th The 'Fixed Lights of the Lodge', originally represented by three windows, were situated in each lodge and referred to three of the four cardinal points on the compass, namely East, South and West. Symbolically, light for these three points guided the workmen to and from labour, there being no sun light emanating from the North. In his article, 'The Symbolic Lights', Bro. Widley Atchison explains:

> *A lodge has three symbolic lights; one of these in the East, one in the West, and one in the South. There is no light in the North, because King Solomon's Temple, of which every lodge is a representation, was situated so far north of the ecliptic, that the sun and moon, at their meridian height, could dart no rays into the northern part thereof. The North, therefore, we Masonically term a place of darkness.*

The three cardinal points, or 'fixed lights', also represented the Master, in the East, the Senior Warden in the West and the Junior Warden in the South, who when combined as the principal officers of the lodge, light up the way for the speculative Mason to complete his labours.

11th Before you were Passed to the Degree of a Fellowcraft, you were asked the following test question, 'Where were you made a Mason?' and you answered, 'In the body of a lodge, just perfect and regular'. When therefore is a lodge considered to be 'Just'?

A Lodge is considered 'Just' when the Volume of Sacred Law lies open on the Master's pedestal. In March 1877, the Grand Orient of France made alterations to its Constitutions which excluded, amongst other things, the Volume of Sacred Law from its ceremonies, this meant that their lodges could no longer be considered 'Just' and this action transgressed one of the most important Landmarks of the Order. In December 1877, a special committee of the Grand Lodge of England was appointed to consider the matter and submitted their report to Grand Lodge on 6 March 1878. Subsequently, the Grand Lodge of England withdrew all recognition from the Grand Orient of France.

Thus, Freemasons who are members of lodges constituted under the Grand Lodge of England are not at liberty to attend any such lodge constituted under the Grand Lodge of the Orient, known as an irregular Grand Lodge.

12th I often think about an elderly Brother whose love for the Craft was ever present and evident in his conduct, both in and out of lodge. He was perfectly crafted in the ritual as each word and phrase he spoke was perfectly presented, timed and delivered with small nuances whereby it gave the listener the moment needed to absorb the point being presented.

His humour was legendary and always welcomed and I recall how on one occasion, he gently chided our very pedantic Secretary while delivering the Second-Degree Tracing Board lecture, for when he announced, '…and Scripture informs us that there fell on that day, on the field of battle and on the banks of the Jordan, forty and two thousand Ephraimites...' He halted, looked straight at the scrivener's table and asked rather mischievously, 'Brother Secretary, will you take their names as read?' Needless to say, Brother Secretary saw the funny side of the remark.

13th There has always been some doubt as to whether Horatio Nelson was a Freemason. Here is the information I found.

In 1839, an article in the *Freemasons Review* claimed that Lord Nelson and his servant, Tom Allen, were Freemasons, but the writer provided no further evidence. In his work, *History of Freemasonry in Norfolk*, Bro. Hamon Le Strange, said that among the furniture of the Lodge of Friendship, No.100, at Yarmouth, there is a stone bearing an inscription commemorating the foundation of the Lodge of United Friends, No.564, on 11 August 1797; on the reverse side, an inscription reads:

In Memory of Bro^{r}. V^{t}. Nelson
of the Nile, and of Burnham Thorpe, in Norfolk,
who lost his life in the arms of Victory,

in an engagement with
ye Combin'd Fleets of France and Spain,
off Cape Trafalgar, Oct. 21, 1805
Proposed by Bro^{r}. John Cutlove

At the Masonic Hall, Reading, there is a framed print with a representation of a banner carried at Lord Nelson's funeral. It bears the following inscription:

> 'We rejoice with our Country but mourn our Brother.'

Beneath the banner we read the following inscription:

> 'Banner carried by the York Lodge, 256, at Lord Nelson's Funeral.'

I think it fair to assume that Bro. Nelson *was* a Freemason and despite no corresponding evidence, i.e. date of Initiation etc., he should be recognised as a member of the Craft.

14th I was asked by a newly appointed Deacon if, during his year of Office, he would be used to carry commands and messages as mentioned during his investiture. I commended his enthusiasm but advised him that in our own lodge, the Deacons are seldom called upon in this manner, although I have visited a lodge where it is the custom to use of the Deacons in that way.

I recall on one occasion a document had to be signed in open lodge, the Secretary had previously given the document to the Master prior to the meeting. Upon signing, the Master gave it to the Senior Deacon who delivered it to the Senior Warden. The Senior Warden gave it to the Junior Deacon who took it to the Junior Warden. The Junior Warden returned it to the Senior Deacon who returned it to the Secretary…or something like that.

Even the DC on the evening became confused and we all quickly realised why Deacons are seldom employed in that capacity.

15th Those of you that are familiar with the Lectures will be aware that they are delivered in catechetical form, i.e. a series of questions and answers delivered in rote or formulaic manner. These earliest of proven Masonic ritual aide-memoires are written in this form, and that system of learning by rote has persisted since that time.

Whereas we all enjoy listening to well-learnt ritual, I often feel we lose the spirit or message contained therein; as in many cases the practitioner is often more concerned with effective delivery than the meaning of his word and to some extent this is worrying, as we are all known at times to judge a Brother on his ritual delivery, rather than his character. We also frequently miss opportunities to discuss the deeper meaning of our ritual; so many lodges are concerned with ritual perfection they ignore the very essence of what lessons are being taught.

Therefore, a Brother can spend his entire Masonic career delivering word perfect ritual, but failing to heed the lessons taught therein. This may make him popular among his brethren, but in a life time, their association with the ritual is fleeting, as Freemasonry is more concerned about the immortality of the soul.

So, the next time you hear or deliver a piece of ritual, consider the message. Be true to yourself by trying to live in the same manner you are teaching the brethren who are listening and expecting to heed your words.

16th In an organisation that is exclusively male, I was curious to examine why we refer to our first lodge as our 'Mother Lodge'.

The late Terence Haunch suggested that the use of feminine terms in respect of Masonic lodges may perhaps be no more than recognition of the female generative principle, i.e. Mother Earth, Mother Country, Mother Tongue, etc. Interestingly, the German preference for the male principle, i.e. 'Fatherland' does not extend to Masonic use, and the same descriptive English term is used.

Individual Masons using the term 'Mother Lodge', are indicating that it was that lodge that gave them Masonic birth. Also, in the Masonic sense, a Mother Lodge is one that produces its own offspring, so therefore becomes a parent, in the same manner when it sponsors a new lodge, it is known as a 'Daughter Lodge'.

17th In these days where much of our time is taken up with family and business matters, it can often be the case that we are unable to attend to our Masonic duties. Whereas we should never diminish the responsibility we have to our lodge, particularly where we may hold an Office, attendance should not be to the detriment of the more important and consequential areas of our life. The beauty of a fixed calendar means that our lodge meetings can be scheduled well in advance and important family events or business matters can be appropriately diarised where possible.

However, if the case arises where you know that you will be unavoidably detained, then your apologies should be sent, immediately, to the Worshipful Master, via the lodge Secretary.

The practice of passing on one's apologies via another lodge member or somebody else that might be at the meeting is quite improper. The summons to attend lodge is sent by command of the Worshipful Master, therefore it is to him, via the lodge Secretary, that you should send your apologies.

18th Have you ever considered joining another Order? There are a series of additional Orders, often known as Side-Degrees, which Master Masons, by virtue of the Degree they have already attained, may join. However, some Degrees require that you are also a member of the Holy Royal Arch.

Many brethren have asked why this is so and my answer is quite simple; under the English Constitution, the Holy Royal Arch is recognised as being the completion of the Third or Master Mason Degree. You will recall that at the close of the Third Degree ceremony, our Master Hiram had been slain, and the secrets he had held, died with him and because of this, substitute secrets were provided.

The colourful story of the Holy Royal Arch revolves around the freedom from bondage of the children of Israel, and the permission granted them to rebuild the Temple. This culminates in the discovery of those lost secrets in a vault, found by chance, when workmen begin to prepare the ground for the foundation of the Second Temple.

The lodge room that we have come to know is transformed to represent the Sanhedrin, with a representation of the vaulted chamber where the secrets were discovered, at the centre. The regalia is totally different in colour, and includes a sash and jewel. The apron is the same style as the Craft Apron. The Officers are also different, with the three Principles, two Scribes and three Sojourners replacing the Master, his Wardens and Deacons.

Its message is clear and simple, peace on earth and goodwill to all men and I would strongly advocate to all new members that practise Freemasonry under the English system, that membership of the Holy Royal Arch completes the story of Craft.

19th The Secretary's Toast, like so many of our customs, seems to have been lost in the fog of antiquity that surrounds the origin of so many of our practices and usages.

Quite possibly it originated as one of the ways of honouring distinguished brethren and like the more formal toasts accompanied by 'Masonic fire', it is probably no more than a harmless relic of the drinking customs of a convivial age such as are to be found in other societies, outside Freemasonry.

It consists of a series of whispered phrases passed in turn from the Secretary to his neighbour on the left and thence round the whole table. As these are completed each Brother in turn announces the name and number of his Mother Lodge.

The word 'Drink' is then passed softly from one to another and when all have done so, the Secretary says aloud 'Drink all' and all drink again, culminating in a form of salvo with firing glasses that completes the procedure.

Another old custom seldom used these days in our rush to get through the Festive Board.

20th In general everyday living, as well as in Freemasonry, we employ symbols to communicate a message. For example, enter any building site and you will be met with simple, yet colourful signs to remind us to wear safety equipment, or warn us of what dangers lay ahead. Regardless of language, the symbol or sign is set to denote something relevant to what we are doing. In the case of entering a building site, the symbols pertain to wearing hard hats, safety glasses and boots, etc., and we are left in no doubt.

Freemasonry being a progressive science, also employs symbols to denote something relevant to what we are doing. Like entering a building site, each Freemason upon entering a lodge room will immediately recognise simple symbols relevant to him, i.e. the Square, the Level, or Plumb Rule, to name the obvious. There is no shortage of teachings on how we apply these symbols to our lives but not all symbols are explained to us so eloquently. Each Freemason is allowed to study and arrive at a conclusion of how each symbol is relevant to his life; ever remembering that each symbol is applied to our lives in the moral sense, a guide to a code of conduct or level of behaviour, befitting the title Master Mason.

Such well-mannered behaviour and good conduct is the true sign of every Freemason and the goal for which each of us strive. Otherwise, what is the purpose of our membership?

21st In these days of electronic communications – emails, texts and other mediums – here is a salutary warning to all would-be practitioners and a timely reminder of the devastating effects of predictive texts.

I recently received an important email advising all members of the lodge, General Purposes Committee, that a meeting was to be held.

The email included a rather curious Agenda item at No.6, which read: 'The Master Elect will discuss next year's offenders'. The term 'offenders' should have read 'Officers' and we all had a good laugh at the 'typo'. However, I was later to learn that the Brother Secretary was a retired Police office.

22nd The Sign of Fidelity, which is not a mode of recognition, is given by placing the right hand on the left breast with the thumb extended. I have often been asked how to discharge this sign and I must confess I have heard varying opinions on the subject. From my own research, I have learnt that in the Emulation system, the sign is dropped and not drawn or cut. The same applies to the Sign of Reverence – also not a mode of recognition – which is given by placing the right hand on the left breast with the thumb hidden.

However, as each lodge has its own traditions, usages and customs, one should always, in the first instance, seek guidance from your lodge Director of Ceremonies, who will gladly give you advice regarding the practices of your lodge.

23rd One of my all-time favourite quotes by Joseph Fort Newton is the following:

> *The secret of Masonry, like the secret of life can be known only by those who seek it, serve it, live it. It cannot be uttered; be felt and acted. It is in fact an open secret, and each man knows it according to his quest and capacity. Like all things worth knowing, no one can know it for another, and no one can know it alone.*

I illustrated this some years back after I was invited to present a lecture on how to develop one's Masonic understanding, knowledge and career. At the close of the lecture, I issued a small pamphlet I had prepared for each of those present, entitled 'How to succeed in Freemasonry without really trying'.

I duly distributed the pamphlet, only to have almost every recipient in the lodge room complain that the pages were blank.

Of course they were blank; to succeed in Freemasonry you must be pro-active, you must, as Joseph Newton prescribed, 'seek it, serve it, live it'.

24th There are many different Orders that a Master Mason can join based upon his interests, tastes and beliefs. Here is a simple guide.

For example, once you have taken the three Craft Degrees you are eligible to join:

The Holy Royal Arch
The Mark Master Masons
The Ancient and Accepted Rite (Rose Croix)*
The Order of the Secret Monitor
Societas Rosicruciana in Anglia*
Royal Order of Scotland*

A Master Mason who is a Companion of the Holy Royal Arch is eligible to join:

Red Cross of Constantine*
Knights Templar and Knights of Malta*
Order of Athelstan

A Master Mason who is a Mark Master Mason is eligible to join:

Royal Ark Mariners

A Master Mason who is a Companion of the Holy Royal Arch and a Mark Master Mason is eligible to join:

The Allied Masonic Degrees
Royal and Select Masters

Order of Knight Masons

Members of the Order of Secret Monitor are eligible to join:
The Order of the Scarlet Cord

A member of the Societas Rosicruciana in Anglia is eligible to join:
The Royal Order of Eri*

A member of the Royal and Select Masters is eligible to join:
The Order of the Silver Trowel

A member of the Knights Templar and Knights of Malta is eligible to join:
The Order of the Knights Beneificent of the Holy City*
The Order of St Thomas of Acon*
Holy Royal Arch Knight Templar Priests*

A Holy Royal Arch Knight Templar Priest is eligible to join:
The Order of Holy Wisdom*

Orders that are marked with a star (*), require the Candidate to be a Trinitarian Christian. For details of any other entry requirements or further information, please contact the appropriate Order.

25th Have you ever heard non-Freemasons or the uninitiated, referred to as the 'profane'? You will not hear it used very much these days, but it was taken from two Latin words, *pro* meaning 'in front of' and *fanum* meaning 'the temple'. When conjoined the term means 'those in front of or outside the Temple'.

The 21st century meaning from the *Oxford English Dictionary* is a bit more explicit and is defined as, 'not relating to that which is sacred or religious and/or of a person not respectful of religious practice'.

I think I am glad the term is seldom used, as in these climes it almost sounds offensive.

26th You are all familiar with the peculiar manner the date is written on our Grand Lodge certificates; in fact, during its presentation we are told:

> *The year of Initiation is, however, shown as AL, that is Anno Lucis, or the year in the era of Masonic Light which precedes the Christian era by four thousand years.*

So to compute the year of your Initiation, just add four thousand years.

But there are other date variations used in different Masonic systems and here are just a few examples.

In England, the Order of the Royal and Select Masters use 'A. Dep' which is *Anno Depositionis*, the year of the deposit and of the completion of the Temple, 1000BC, while the Royal Ark Mariners use 'A. Dil' which is *Anno Diluvii* referring to the year of the deluge, 2348BC.

In America, the Ancient and Accepted (Scottish) Rite use *Anno Mundi*. Irish Craft certificates use the term *Anno Laotomiae*. The Knight Templar certificates formerly used the term *Anno Ordinis*, while for many years the English Royal Arch certificates used *Anno Salutis*.

Believe it or not, there are at least another half dozen examples in use in the many Degrees that fall under the Masonic banner.

27th How often or how many times have we heard a Brother proposing a toast with the word 'Bumper'? For example, 'Brethren, join me in drinking a bumper toast to...' Well, the term 'bumper' originally referred to a leather cup, which, at a later date, came to mean any individual drinking vessel. The shape was that of a squat mug, but came to refer to any glass or drinking vessel. In the Masonic setting, the English exposure entitled *Jachin and Boaz* (1762), the Candidate is instructed to 'take a bumper' to drink with.

Likewise, there neither appears, as one might think, a connection with the association of the term 'bumper' and the banging of the glasses on the table, although an exposure published in France in about 1740, refers to the drinking vessels as 'cannon'.

Therefore, these days when using the term 'bumper' in proposing a toast, its meaning is that the proposer of the toast is in fact encouraging enthusiasm in the bestowing of the toast on the recipient, for which we should all be happy to comply.

28th One side Degree which many brethren join in their early Masonic career is the Mark Degree. Famed for its rather relaxed attitude, the humour often overshadows the important message of the Degree, which is from Psalm 118:22 – 'The stone which the builders refused is become the head stone of the corner'. Students will quickly recognise that this enigmatic verse is really a Messianic prophecy and is evident from the fact that Christ Himself applied it thus.

Many Mark Master Masons wrongly consider their Degree to be the completion of the Fellowcraft Degree, probably because of this opening exchange at the door of the lodge.

> Brother Inner Guard goes to and opens door and addresses the Tyler: *Whom have you there?*
> Brother Tyler replies: *Brother A.B. who has served his time as an Entered Apprentice, worked in the quarries as a Fellow Craft and is now desirous of becoming a Mark Master Mason to qualify him to preside over a Lodge of Operative Masons.*

And after his obligation he is told:

> *In former times it was custom in all Fellow Craft Lodges for each Fellow Craft to choose a mark by which his work might be known to his Overseer*

The ritual, like that of the Craft, is allegory and one has to be a Master Mason to Advance to the Degree; therefore it is classed as a separate and distinct Degree, exclusive of the Craft System and governed by its own Grand Lodge.

In 1856, there was a brief attempt to propose a resolution that the

Degree be accepted as 'a graceful addition to the Fellow Craft Degree' but the resolution was not confirmed.

29th I attended a lodge where they did not use Tracing Boards; they carried out the custom of literally drawing the requirements of each Degree on the floor. Apart from being quaint, the process I felt, added unnecessary time to the ceremony.

The drawing process reminded me of the early days of Freemasonry, before the advent of Tracing Boards, when it was the Tyler's duty to draw the lodge, initially using chalk and later charcoal, tape and clay. At the end of the evening, the onerous task of cleaning the floor always fell on the youngest initiate, possibly as a demonstration of his Obligation of secrecy.

As this simple process became more difficult, possibly because of the intricacies of the symbols, so the designs were painted on linen, canvas, oil-cloth and even on slabs of marble, all which could conveniently be rolled up and stored until the next meeting. Eventually, the designs were transferred onto boards, which became even easier to display, to move and to store.

There is no formal or specific design for the style authorised by Grand Lodge, other than the fact that is must display the elements of the Degree which is contained in the ritual.

30th Despite how often we use, learn and repeat our ritual, we still tend to forget that we are using modern English, in the form, language and style, of that which was used some two hundred years ago, and in some cases earlier. Also, the likelihood of some of the words now meaning something different is a fact, as well as many of the terms are not only archaic, but have been forgotten or never used in 21st century vocabulary.

In his book, *A Glossary of the Craft and Holy Royal Arch Rituals of Freemasonry*, A.C.F. Jackson suggests that there is a distinct difference in the style of the Craft and Holy Royal Arch rituals. He goes on to say how the Craft ritual is more direct and uses words derived from the Anglo-Saxon language, whereas he feels the Royal Arch ritual has a greater reliance on the many syllabled romantic languages.

If you consider the language of the Craft, it gives away its age for we know the English language developed from the West Germanic dialect of the Angles, Saxons and other Teutonic tribes, who invaded England in the 5th and 6th centuries and later developed as the medieval Old English language of the Cathedral builders.

The Royal Arch ritual on the other hand, being a much later product, contained the artistic or English romanticism literary style that was used in England at the end of the 18th century.

31st All Freemasons have their own ideas as to where Freemasonry originated. In my own opinion, and having discussed these theories with many individual brethren, I have found that most beliefs rely entirely on thought rather than actual study, as many have confessed to me they favour popular ideas merely because they are essentially, 'a good idea' 'plausible' 'attractive', and basically, flatter the Craft. Having said this, several of the most eminent scholars of the 20th century brought forward some excellent theories that very few Freemasons have heard.

The Transitional Theory – Harry Carr
The Original Birth Theory – Eric Ward
The Theory of Conspiracy to Fellowship – Frederick W. Seal-Coon
The Religious Base Theory – Colin Dyer
The Rosicrucian Theory – A.C.F. Jackson
The Associate Theory – A. Geoffrey Markham
Monastic Origins – Cyril N. Batham
The Darwinian Concept – Cyril Richard S. E. Sandbach
The Age of Enlightenment Theory – Michael Spurr
The Royal Society Theory – Michael Baigent

Strange, not a Knight Templar amongst them!

If you really want to develop your Masonic knowledge, I recommend you read these articles as they will certain help broaden your own knowledge base and give you a greater understanding of the complexities of how, why and where Freemasonry originated.

February

1st The drama of the ritual of the Holy Royal Arch is set in Jerusalem, immediately after the return of the children of Israel, from the Babylonian captivity, when Zerubbabel is preparing to rebuild the city and the Temple.

The Chapter represents the Grand Sanhedrim whose deliberations are interrupted by the arrival of three sojourners from Babylon who ask to be permitted to assist in the rebuilding work. They are instructed to clear the ground of Solomon's former Temple in order to receive the foundations of the new Temple. In doing so, they discover a hidden vault which they break open and enter, inside the Principle Sojourner discovers a scroll, which is the lost volume of the sacred law and a pedestal on which is inscribed the name of the Most High, which as biblical history tells us, was never uttered and therefore its true pronunciation was lost. Additionally, inscribed on the pedestal are the names of the three Grand Masters. They immediately report their discoveries to the Sanhedrim and are instantly rewarded by being constituted members of the Chapter.

However, like the Craft, the story is purely allegorical, as historically; the three Principals and Scribes could not have been in Jerusalem at the same time.

In Ireland and many of the Grand Chapters in America, the legend is not that used in England and Scotland, but is concerned with the repair of Solomon's Temple under Josiah, but the intent of the ritual is the same, which is to lead the Companion, without transgressing the bounds of religion, to contemplate the nature of, and his relationship with, his God whatever his religion may be.

2nd Here's an amusing poem, author unknown.

Ten Master Masons, happy, doing fine;
One listened to a rumour, then there were nine.
Nine Master Masons, faithful, never late;
One didn't like the 'Master', then there were eight.
Eight Master Masons, on their way to heaven;
One joined to many clubs, then there were seven.
Seven Master Masons, life dealt some hard licks;
One grew discouraged, then there were six.
Six Master Masons, all very much alive;
One lost his interest, then there were five.
Five Master Masons, wishing there were more;
Got into a great dispute, then there were four.
Four Master Masons, busy as could be;
One didn't like the programs, then there were three.
Three Master Masons, was one of them you?
One grew tired of all the work, then there were two.
Two Master Masons with so much to be done;
One said 'What's the use', then there was one.
One Master Mason, found a brother - true!
Brought him to the Lodge, then there were two.
Two Master Masons didn't find work a bore;
Each brought another, then there were four.
Four Master Masons saved their Lodges fate;
By showing others kindness, then there were eight.
Eight Master Masons, loving their Lodges bright sheen;
Talked so much about it, they soon counted sixteen.
Sixteen Master Masons, to their obligations true;
Were pleased when their number went to thirty-two.
So we can't put our troubles at the Lodges door;
It's our fault for harming the Lodge we adore.
Don't fuss about the programs or the 'Master' in the East;
Keep your obligation by serving even the very least.

3rd There are three distinguishing characteristics found in the breast of every good Freemason, these are Virtue, Honour and Mercy. With regard to Virtue, we are taught:

> *In reading the history of ancient Rome, we find that the Consul Marcellus intended to erect a Temple to be dedicated to Virtue and Honour; but being prevented, at that time, from carrying his design into execution, he afterwards altered his plans, and erected two Temples, contiguous to each other, so situated that the only avenue to the Temple of Honour was through that of Virtue; thereby leaving an elegant moral to posterity, that Virtue is the only direct road to Honour. Virtue is the highest exercise of, and improvement to, reason; the integrity, harmony, and just balance of affection; the health, strength, and beauty of the soul. The perfection of Virtue is to give reason its full scope; to obey the authority of conscience with alacrity; to exercise the defensive talents with fortitude, the public with justice, the private with temperance, and all of them with prudence; that is, in a due proportion to each other, with a calm and diffusive beneficence; to love and adore God with an unrivalled and disinterested affection and to acquiesce in the dispensations of Divine providence with a cheerful resignation. Every approach to this standard is a step towards perfection and happiness, and any deviation therefrom has a tendency to vice and to misery.*

4th I found it interesting to say the least, that despite early references to Mason's marks and the occasional or isolated passage or mention or the term 'Mark', there is no record of the Degree of Mark Master or Mark Degree being conferred before 1 September 1769.

On that date, Thomas Dunckerley made several brethren Mark Masons in a Royal Arch Chapter, after which the Degree quickly spread across England, Scotland and Ireland being worked in both Lodges and Chapters.

Confusion arose after the Union of 1813, when a Chapter in Aberdeen granted a Warrant to six of its members, resident in London, authorising them to meet in London. Of course, the Aberdeen Chapter had no such authority and was challenged by the Supreme Grand Chapter of Scotland who eventually suspended the Chapter. But problems deepened because the irregular Mark Lodge had Advanced many English Masons, several of considerable distinction.

As one would imagine, their actions were noticed by Grand Lodge, particularly as Lord Leigh, Provincial Grand Master of Warwickshire, was installed as the Master of a Mark Lodge in 1855. The following proposal was therefore put forward on 5 March 1856: 'That the Degree of Mark mason is not at variance with Craft Masonry, and that it be added thereto, under proper regulations.'

It being deemed that the Mark Degree was '...a graceful addition to the Fellow Craft Degree...'

During the following three months, much deliberation was given to the proposal and at the June communication it was moved and carried that the proposal not be confirmed.

This decision had obviously been expected as the Grand Lodge of Mark Master Masons was formed within the same month on 25 June 1856, with Lord Leigh as its first Grand Master.

5th In 1792, the Grand Lodge of the Ancients agreed that a Brother should be nominated annually, from each of the lodges under their jurisdiction, from whom nine 'Excellent Masters' would be chosen. Their function was to visit lodges and promote a uniformity and preservation of ceremonial practices and to report back to Grand Lodge or the RW Deputy Grand Master. They were known as the 'Nine Worthies'.

A special medal was struck for them to wear during their year of Office and passed to their successor. The appointments ceased at the time of the Union in 1813, the medals recalled and can now be seen in the museum at Freemasons', Hall.

The term 'worthies' was by no means new. In 1584, Richard Lloyd, the English Romance writer, published *A short discourse of the most renowned actes, and right valiant conquests of those puissant Prince called the Nine Worthies*, these were: Joshua, Hector, David, Alexander, Judas Maccabaeus, Julius Caesar, Arthur, Charlemagne and Guy of Warwick. (Guy of Boulogne was sometimes substituted for Guy of Warwick.)

Shakespeare only mentions five worthies; Pompey, Alexander, Judas, Hercules and Hector. However, in 1592, Lloyd writes of, *The Nine Worthies of London*, who were, Sir William Walworth, Sir Henry Pritchard, Sir William Sevenoke, Sir Thomas White, Sir John Bonham, Christopher Croaker, Sir John Hawkwood, Sir Hugh Calverly and Sir Henry Maleverer.

6th Another early exposure of 1724 called *The Whole Institution of Masonry* appears to be a shorter version of a 1725 exposure entitled *The Whole Institutions of Free-Masons Opened* and the much later, *Dialogue between Simon and Phillip* (1740).

It consists of an exchange of about fifteen questions, but to demonstrate it worth, we read in the final exchange the following:

> *Q) What posture did you receive your Secret Words in?*
> *A) Kneeling with square and Compass at my Breast.*
> *Q) What were you Sworne too?*
> *A) For to Hold and Conceal.*

Bearing in mind these exposures were generally written, in many cases from memory, the accuracy of the ceremony at this point is still fresh even after nearly three-hundred years.

7th Lecture One Section Seven gives us a wonderful, yet simple explanation of how we should conduct ourselves as an Entered Apprentice:

Q) In what degree in Freemasonry were you initiated?
A) That of an Entered Apprentice.
Q) How long should an Entered Apprentice serve his Master?
A) Seven years is the stipulated time; but less will suffice, if found qualified for preferment.
Q) How should he serve him?
A) With Freedom, Fervency, and Zeal.
Q) Excellent qualities; what are their emblems?
A) Chalk, Charcoal, and Clay.
Q) Why?
A) Nothing is more free than Chalk; the slightest touch leaves a trace. Nothing more fervent than Charcoal; for when properly lighted no metal can resist its force. Nothing more zealous than Clay, our mother Earth; she is continually labouring for our support. Thence we came, and there we must all return.

8th In the late 17th and early 18th-century London, it was not only the Freemasons that had secrets and signs as proved by this piece found in the *Tatler*, Issue 26, dated 17 June 1709:

But my reason for troubling you at this present is to advise you of a set of people who do assume the Name of Pretty Fellows; they even get new Names and they have their Signs and Tokens like Free-Masons...

So who was it that had signs and tokens like Freemason's? Groups like:

The Most Ancient, Honorable and Venerable Society of Adams, meeting at the Royal Swan, Kingsland Road.

The Loyal and Friendly Society of Blue and Orange, meeting at the Kouli Khan's Head, Leicester Field.

The Ancient and Joyous Order of the Hiccolites, meeting at the Sun Tavern, Fish-Street Hill.

The Very Honorable Order of Cabalarians, meeting at the Magpie, Bishopsgate Street.

...and you thought the Society of Free and Accepted Masons, who met at the Goose and Gridiron, was a one-off organisation?

9th What is the significance of the Valley of Jehoshaphat? The term is mentioned twice in the Bible:

Joel 3:2: *I will also gather all nations, and will bring them down into the valley of Jehoshaphat, and will plead with them there for my people and for my heritage Israel, whom they have scattered among the nations, and parted my land.*

Joel 3:12: *Let the heathen be wakened, and come up to the valley of Jehoshaphat: for there will I sit to judge all the heathen round about.*

The Sloane MS No 3329 (c.1700) mentions the word 'Valley':

Q) What is a just and perfect or just and Lawfull Lodge?

*A) A just and perfect Lodge is two Interprintices two fellow craftes and two Mast*ers *more or fewer the more the merrier the fewer the Bett*er *Chear but if need require five will serve that is two Interprintices two fellow craftes and one Mast*er *on the highest hill or Lowest Valley of the world without the crow of a Cock of the bark of a Dogg.*

But it is not until 1723, in the first Masonic Exposure, *A Mason's Examination*, we read:

Q: Where were you made a Mason?

A: In the Valley of Jehoshaphat...

Masonry Dissected (1730), brings them both together when it says:

Q. Where does the Lodge stand?

A. Upon Holy ground, or highest Hill or lowest Vale, or in the Vale of Jehosaphat, or any other secret Place.

From this point on the term becomes more regular, but we have no further explanation as to why the place was used or introduced into the ritual other than the biblical reference that it was the place that the heathen will be judged.

10th Some humorous Graces I have heard at Festive Boards over the years:

Our *Heavenly Father, we thank you for*
this food, and humbly request that
you perform a miracle and remove
the calories from the dessert.

Thank you for teaching me gratitude with this delicious bread and meat.
Thank you for teaching me patience while waiting 'til we to eat
Thank you for teaching me faith, expecting food and never having doubts.
Thank you for teaching me suffering by providing these Brussels sprouts.

We thank the Lord for what we had,
If there had have been more we would have been glad.
But as there wasn't such a lot,
We thank the Lord for what we got.

11th What are the formal wine takings at the Festive Board that we enjoy after the meal and how should we conduct ourselves?

The formal toasts list, which is provided annually by the Provincial Office, is taken after the meal and includes:

The Queen

The Grand Master
The Grand Lodge
The Provincial Grand Master
The Provincial Grand Lodge
The Worshipful Master
The Initiate
The Guests and Visitors
The Tyler's Toast

For formal toasts the procedure is as follows, each Brother, when requested, stands to join the proposer in wishing health and well-being to the recipient. Etiquette dictates that the recipient of the toast, if present, remains seated and does not respond by drinking their own health.

12th I wish I had a pound for every time I attended a Masonic meeting and heard almost every Senior Officer or visitor in that lodge, prompt an Officer as he stumbles with his words. Well, in my mind, such behaviour is rude, uncalled for, and un-Masonic and the least possible way one can encourage better ritual delivery.

The fact remains that we will all forget words or make a mistake, but it is incumbent upon the DC, or whosoever is designated to prompt the Officer, to ensure he has a pre-arranged signal to assist that Officer in the event he forgets his words.

It is not the responsibility of any other Officer or visitor to prompt and the only way to stop this practice is for the Director of Ceremonies to announce to those assembled, prior to the meeting, the manner Officers will be promoted in his lodge, and any further help is unnecessary. That instruction will put an immediate stop to this practice.

13th The Regius MS, acknowledged as the earliest Masonic document, was written in Chaucerian English verse, the reason why it is often referred to as the Regius Poem. The term *poem* is used rather loosely as the 794 lines are very irregular in rhythm rather than accepted poetry.

It is also referred to at times as the Halliwell MS, because in 1840, James Orchard Halliwell was the first publisher. Halliwell was not a Freemason, but was intrigued by the moral disciplines contained in the document.

It was written at a time when the Catholic or Universal Church was the religion of the realm and contains, like many later pre-reformations MS, Trinitarian influences which were late expunged from Freemasonry by the distinctly Presbyterian Anderson and other early Protestant Masonic characters that attempted to make Freemasonry deistic therefore confirming that Freemasonry was not a religion, but rather a perspective on the nature of God.

14th I was at a meeting some years ago when a Grand Officer was saluted with the Grand or Royal Sign while the lodge was still in the First-Degree.

The salutation of Grand Lodge Officers should always be made in the highest Degree which the lodge is to be opened and the corresponding salutation for that Degree, given with the advised number of times.

In respect of the Grand and Royal Sign, I was taught that the habit of slapping the thighs on the downward motion is not part of the sign.

15th The term 'Deacon' is an ancient word which in both Latin and Greek means servant, messenger, as well as guide and instructor. In the early days of Freemasonry, there were no Deacons in English lodges, the change came about 1813. However, it does seem to have definitely been a Scottish tradition.

The office is now classed as a regular and statutory office and brethren must be appointed to fill the office each year, usually by progression from Inner Guard. But the same applies, other than the Immediate Past Master, no office is yours by right and progression through the lodge offices can only be earned by diligent duty, good attendance and hard work.

Both the Senior and Junior Deacons wear the same jewel, a dove bearing an olive branch, the figure is illustrated at the top of their wands. Some lodges have permission to use another emblem which is Mercury or Hermes, both signifying messengers.

With regard to the Deacons wand of office, it is neither a walking stick nor a prop, but part of the insignia of his office and should be carried as such. Therefore, when you perambulate around the lodge, please do not drag it around like it is some sort of incumbrancer; hold it about six to eight inches off the ground, in your right hand which should form a right angle with your body.

As a general guide to the role of the Deacons, your early attendance is of paramount importance, not to prop up the bar by seeking refreshment from any labour that you have yet to perform, but as an officer of the lodge, to meet and greet visitors.

The key to any successful year is regular attendance at your Lodge of Rehearsal, studying the ritual and ensuring good communication between you and any of the Candidates entrusted to your care.

16th

Some brethren believe our ritual developed from the processions, pageants or tableaux performed by the medieval Guilds and which were referred to as sacred dramas or miracle plays. These were staged on wagons and drawn in procession through the streets of the town. During such times, records show us that in Norwich the Mercers, Drapers and Haberdashers presented 'the Creation', the Grocers 'Paradise' and the Smiths 'David and Goliath'; whilst at Hereford the Glovers depicted 'Adam and Eve', the Carpenters 'Noah's Ark' and the Tailors 'the Three Kings'.

Many compare our own ritual drama with this type of practice, and it is not too far from the imagination to consider that some Masonic legend could well have developed from a miracle play which found its way through some stonemason's fraternity that enacted the building of King Solomon's Temple.

But this is purely fanciful imaginings and not fact as the introduction of the significance of King Solomon's Temple to Freemasonry, was an early 18th century innovation and not the result of some medieval practice.

17th The Orange Order is a strongly Protestant society established in 1779 in Ulster and often associated with Freemasonry. Since its inception, the highly religious and sectarian Order has spread to England, Scotland, Australia, Canada, United States and Africa where they were inspired by Ulster missionaries.

Its name is a tribute to the Dutch-born Protestant King William of Orange, who defeated the army of Catholic King James II in the Williamite–Jacobite War (1688–1691). Its members wear orange sashes and are referred to as Orangemen.

The Loyal Orange Institution has a series of Degrees whose emblems include the square and compass, King Solomon's Temple, a rainbow and a dove with an olive branch, to name but a few, but as previously mentioned there is no connection to Freemasonry whatsoever and such sectarian Orders are not recognised by the United Grand Lodge.

18th The Ancient and Accepted Rite, known to many of us as Rose Croix, is the mainstay of the Christian Degrees that are available and worked in many of our lodges throughout England. To be eligible for membership, one has to be a Trinitarian Christian and Master Mason. It is recognised by United Grand Lodge of England as being consistent with the English Masonic system.

Originating in France and once known as the Scottish Rite, it actually has no connection with Scottish Freemasonry in that sense. The rite was established in England in 1845 and the governing body is known as the Supreme Council of Grand Inspectors-General.

The Rite consists of thirty-three Degrees, the first three being that of Craft Freemasonry. The next fourteen are conferred by name only, in a Lodge of Perfection. The fifteenth and sixteenth are conferred in the

Council of Princes of Jerusalem. The seventeenth is conferred in the Lodge of Knights of the East and the West. The eighteenth Degree is conferred in a ceremony known as the Second Point. The nineteenth to the twenty ninth are conferred nominally during the thirtieth Degree, and are conferred upon those that have served as the Most Wise Sovereign, by members of the Supreme Council, with the thirty-first to the thirty-third Degrees, being worked in full, again by the Supreme Council. Members of the thirty-first to the thirty-third Degrees are recruited by selection. In England, only seventy-five persons can hold the thirty-third degree at any one time.

19th Pendent to the corners of the lodge carpet are four tassels, these are meant to remind us of the four cardinal virtues, namely: Temperance, Fortitude, Prudence, and Justice, the whole of which, tradition informs us, were constantly practiced by a great majority of our ancient brethren.

Here we examine Prudence. In Latin, Prudence is pronounced *Prudentia* meaning to act with wisdom. In visual art it is often portrayed as a female with a mirror in her right hand and a snake in the left hand.

The Emulation Lectures of the Three Degrees explain Prudence thus:

> *Prudence – Teaches us to regulate our lives and actions according to the dictates of reason, and is that habit of mind whereby men wisely judge, and prudentially determine, all things relative to their temporal and eternal happiness. This virtue ought to be the distinguishing characteristic of every Free and Accepted Mason, not only for the good regulation of his own life and actions, but as a pious example to the popular world who are not Masons, and ought to be nicely attended to in strange or mixed companies, never to let drop or slip the least Sign, Token, or Word, whereby any of our Masonic secrets might be illegally obtained; ever having in recollection that period of time when he was placed before the Worshipful Master in the East with his left knee made bare and his bent right foot formed in a square, body erect with the square,*

right hand on Volume of the Sacred Law, alluding to the Manuel.
First Lecture, Sixth Section Six

When acting with prudence, the Freemason shows his ability to govern and discipline himself by the use of reason, sagacity or shrewdness in the management of his affairs, skill and good judgment in the use of his resources and caution or circumspection as to danger or risk to himself, his family and his neighbour.

Therefore, the Freemason regulates his life and actions agreeably to the dictate of reason enabling him to judge, consider and determine wisely on all things relative to his present, as well as his future happiness implying not only caution, but also the ability to judge in advance the probable consequences of one's actions.

These characteristics should be habitual and demonstrated in Lodge, but more important when abroad in the world. Prudence in not given, but gained through thought, study and circumspection. It brings the Freemason closer to his God and reminds him to reflect upon the moral and social consequences of his activities and his relationship to his Creator.

20th For those of you that have never heard the Tyler's song, here is a version I found on-line. It is sung, at the close of the Festive Board, prior to the Tyler's toast.

'Are your glasses charged in the West and South?' The Worshipful Master cries.
'They are charged in the West!' 'They are charged in the South!' Are the Warden's prompt replies.
'Then to our final Toast tonight your glasses freely drain; Happy to Meet, sorry to part, happy to meet again.'

Chorus: Happy to meet, sorry to part, happy to meet again.

'Did you hear the Toast in the West and South?' The Worshipful Master cries.

'It was heard in the West!' 'It was heard in the South!' Are the Warden's prompt replies.
'To all poor Masons of the Craft relief from want and pain: Happy to meet, sorry to part, happy to meet again.'

Chorus: Happy to meet, sorry to part, happy to meet again.

Now your work is done in the West and South the night is waning fast,
the Worshipful Master is moved to say, 'This Toast shall be the last'.
'Goodnight, God speed and once again repeat the farewell strain: Happy to meet, sorry to part, happy to meet again.'

Chorus: Happy to meet, sorry to part, happy to meet again (repeat).

21st The term 'lodge', often spelt *logia, logge, loygge, luge and, ludge*, it is an old French Gallic word meaning 'hut' and which appears to have different meanings in England and Scotland. In both countries, a lodge was used to designate a mason's workshop that was generally erected in connection with all building operations.

Hence, we read in the Vale Royal Abbey building accounts of 1278, carpenters were paid to erect lodges. The same goes for mason's lodges and workshops at Catterick Bridge in 1421, Kirby Muxloe Castle in 1481 and so on. Then we have details of repairs to mason's lodges at Beaumaris Castle in 1330 and Westminster Abbey in 1413.

The lodge was in fact a workshop where masons cut, dressed and carved stone and it would be fair to say that they would also have taken their permitted breaks within its walls, as at the lodge attached to York Minster in 1370 and St Giles, Edinburgh in 1491.

It is also most likely that here, within its walls, questions affecting the masons trade were discussed along with, difficulties experienced during work, techniques, grievances and without doubt, superstitions, fables and stories passed down from the beginning of English squared stone building.

22nd *The Institution of Free Masons* (c.1725) is an exposure, probably from part of a similar group of two others of the same age. It bears a similar title, but has a much greater content that the other two. It was purchased from a dealer in about 1905, by Bro. A. F. Calvert and ultimately sold on to Bro. Douglas Knoop in 1941. Its authenticity again can be verified by some of the questioned asked.

One of the most amusing parts of the said document is the clumsy way it suggests how you might know another Freemason:

> *You must whisper Saying thrice, the Mr, Fellows of the Right Worshipful Company whence I came greet you well…*
>
> *Then the other will answer, God greet you well, the Mr, Fellows of the Right Worshipful Company whence you came…*
>
> *and then*
>
> *How do you do Brother? & drink to each other & ask, In what Lodge were you made a free Mason?*

Can't say I would feel comfortable doing this today!

23rd We frequently refer to lodge customs and where to open the Volume of Sacred Law is another variation I have often seen.

For example, some lodges use Psalm 133, the blessing of unity, for the First Degree, Amos 7:7, the Lord with the plumb-line, for the Second Degree and Ecclesiastes, the death of man, for the Third degree. Other lodges use Ruth 2, for the First Degree, Judges 12, for the Second Degree and Genesis 4:22 for the Third Degree.

In 1760, an English exposure entitled *Three Distinct Knocks* give 2 Peter, for the First, 1 Judges 12, for the Second and 1 Kings 7, for the Third Degree. Whereas the French Exposure *Reception d'un Frey-Macon* (1737), tells us that the Entered Apprentice took his Obligation on the Gospel of St John.

Having explained these variants, you will realise that there is no actual official ruling or guidance on the matter and many lodges open the V. of S.L., as and where it falls open and have no concern as to the page it opens at in relation to the Degree.

24th During the first fifty years of Freemasonry, there arose several problems from a group of London Irishmen who were not made welcome in the wealthier lodges containing bankers, other professionals and aristocrats. The other issue that arose was the Irish Freemasons practised the Holy Royal Arch, something ignored by the established Grand Lodge.

In 1751, The Grand Lodge of the Ancients were set up and dubbed the original Grand Lodge, the moderns and as you can imagine both Grand Lodges immediately began to vie for position.

For example, one Grand Lodge began to establish lodges aboard warships, while the other founded military lodges. One started a school for girls; the other created a school for boys. One cultivated lodges in the provinces, while the other developed links and lodges in Scotland and Ireland. Both cultivated links with the American colonies. The rivalry continued for over sixty years until a Union of the two Grand Lodges was negotiated and The United Grand Lodge of England was formed on 27 December 1813.

25th The words, 'hele', 'conceal' and 'reveal', first appeared in that form in Prichard's *Masonry Dissected* (1730), when it says: 'I will Hail and Conceal, and never Reveal....'

Prior to that we find the words mentioned in other, earlier Masonic documents, and later in the form mentioned in 1730. For example:

The Edinburgh Register House MS (1696), says:

'...to heill and conceall...'

The Chetwode Crawley MS (c. 1700), says:

'...Hear and Conceal...'

The Sloane MS, (c. 1700), says:

'...heal and Conceal or Conceal and keep secrett...'

The Kevan MS (*c.*1714-1720), says:

'...to hear & Conseal...'

The *Grand Mystery of Free-Masons Discover'd* (1724), says:

'...Hear and Conceal...'

The *Institution of Free Masons* (*c.*1725), says:

'...hide & conceal...'

The Wilkinson MS (1727), says:

'...heal & conceal...'

Three Distinct Knocks (1760), says,

'...always hail, conceal, and never will reveal...'

Jachin and Boaz (1762), says:

'...always hale, conceal, and never reveal ...'

Another example of the evolution of our ritual.

26th What is the convenient room adjoining the lodge that is referred to during the test questions leading to the Second Degree?

The convenient room adjoining the lodge is of course the Tyler's room, that small antechamber generally situated in the north-west corner. This is where each Candidate undergoes the preparation for his entry into Masonry. In not so well-appointed buildings, any room situated near the lodge room can be used. It is also here we find the Tyler or Outer Guard, generally in the form of an experienced, mature Brother who cheerfully puts us at ease as he helps us prepare. Armed with a drawn sword, his role is symbolically to keep off all intruders and Cowans to Masonry.

27th These days, so many lodges have opted to use battery operated or electric candles, instead of the wax or oiled filled types. However, regardless of the fact that I am a staunch traditionalist, I always thought this was a good move.

Not so long ago, I attended a meeting where the wicks of the oil filled candles had been adjusted so crudely that a thick black haze covered the whole of the lodge room. The trouble was that there was nothing that could be done and by the time the Candidate retired, one could hardly see from East to West.

Apparently, there was one benefit from the issue that night, the bar steward advised me later that the sale of cold beer had doubled.

28th The signs held during the Prayers or Obligations differ from system to system, but here is a brief guide.

With regard to the Opening and Closing of the lodge, all assembled brethren will stand, with the sign of the Degree, Penal Sign in the Third. The Sign of Reverence is given for prayers offered during the conferment of the Degree. The Candidate for Initiation is not expected to give the Sign of Reverence '...when the blessings of Heaven are invoked upon the proceedings' for he has yet to be taught the sign.

The signs held during the Obligations do vary. During the First-Degree Obligation, the Entered Apprentice Sign is held. During the Second-Degree Obligation, the Sign of Fidelity Sign is held. During the Third-Degree Obligation, the Penal Sign is held.

With regard to the timing of the discharge of the sign, it is generally cut at the end of the Obligation. However, some systems prefer the sign to be cut after the Candidate has sealed his Obligation.

Always remember, that every lodge has its own customs and every Director of Ceremonies have their own way of doing things. Therefore, be observant in what you were taught in your Mother Lodge and remember that in Freemasonry, there is not always a right or wrong way, as long as what is being done is within the spirit of our ancient landmarks.

29th Looking at the development of Freemasonry in the early 1700s, what induced people to join a lodge?

In a similar sense, religious historians have asked the same, seeking to explain why men became Quakers or Methodists, while others remained in the Church of England. Some might argue it was an accident, for example being in the right place at the right time. No doubt George Fox or John Wesley had great persuasive testimonies which effected people's beliefs; others may have joined because of a family connection, following in father's footsteps for example. But the question remains, why would men join a body whose fundamentals were in part, secret at the time of joining, and whose rites were not known until he had bound himself by an oath?

In the 17th century, more than any other period, men were definitely preoccupied with the pursuit of secrets and we use as an example: alchemy, astrology, Rosicrucianism and the biblical Apocalypse, to name but four.

However, 18th century poet Goronwy Owen, expected to find the 'hidden wisdom of the ancient druids', when he joined, while William Stukeley states in his autobiography that 'curiosity led him to be initiated into the mysteries of masonry, suspecting it to be the remains of the mysteries of the ancients'.

In 1730, perhaps Pritchard's *Masonry Dissected* summed up the reasons in the following question:

Q) *'What do you learn by being a Gentleman Mason?'*

A) *'Secresy, Morality and Goodfellowship.'*

March

1st Throughout his existence, man has fought hard to be closer to his maker by tempering his actions, controlling his thoughts, serving his fellowman and striving for perfection. The Society of Free and Accepted Masons is no more than an extension of that idea.

The signs, symbols and phrases we use to help us to reflect on our relationship with our God, have merely been lent to us, that we as Freemasons, may try to follow the paths of those ancient peoples by striving for higher ideals. Ever remembering that the whole ethos of our art is to love our God and serve our fellow man; two of the greatest principles found in all of the world's major belief systems.

So just remember, the next time you hear the Charge, it is not Freemasonry that is time immemorial, it is our usages and customs that are.

2nd Dr Robert Crucefix was born in 1797, initiated into Freemasonry on 16 April 1829, and became Master in 1833. In 1834, he was instrumental in establishing and editing the *Freemasons Quarterly Review* and established a movement for aged Freemasons which became the foundation for the Royal Masonic Benevolent Institution. At the time, he fought for an 'Asylum for Worthy and Decayed Freemasons' while his opponents preferred a system of annuities, but his persistent determination carried the project through.

In 1836, he was appointed Junior Grand Deacon, but was suspended for six months by the Board of General Purposes in 1839, through a complaint that he had allowed 'intemperate language' to be used at a meeting where he was presiding; the suspension was confirmed by Grand Lodge in June 1840.

Known for being outspoken, he responded with a strongly worded letter to the Grand Master which was published in the *Freemasons Quarterly Review* along with some editorial comments and observations which were deemed improper. Crucefix was summoned to attend a special Grand Lodge meeting on 30 October 1840, to show just cause why he should not be expelled from the Craft. He attended and condescended to offer a full unreserved and humble apology, which was accepted by those present.

The building of the Asylum commenced in 1849, but Crucefix died the following year and never saw the amalgamation of the Asylum charity with the Annuity Fund.

He is also known for his involvement in establishing the Ancient and Accepted Rite in England. After writing to the American Supreme Council in 1845, their response was to appoint him the first Sovereign Grand Commander of the Supreme Council 33° for England and Wales and it is from this patent, that all subsequent members of the Council derive their authority.

3rd All salutes, unless a Brother has disabilities preventing him from doing so, should be taken in the standing position.

A salute is a Masonic sign, and that sign is considered to be one of the secrets of the Degree. In all ceremonies in any Degree, the Candidate is informed: '...it is in this position that the Secrets of the Degree are communicated...'

Therefore, the position alluded too cannot be met in the seated position.

4th The Premier Grand Lodge did not initially recognise the Holy Royal Arch as part of Freemasonry, although some of their members were exalted in separate Chapters. The Grand Lodge of the Antients argued that the Holy Royal Arch was the fourth degree and could be worked in a lodge under the authority of the lodge warrant.

In 1766, some members owing allegiance to the Premier Grand Lodge set up the first Grand Chapter and exalted as the First Principal of the

Order, Lord Blaney, the then Grand Master of the Premier Grand Lodge. This caused problems because it was felt such an action would imply recognition of the Order, so somebody tampered with the Charter of Compact, the document setting up the Chapter and altered the date to 1767 and put the letter P in front of the words Grand Master, implying that at the time of his exaltation Lord Blaney was a Past Grand Master and by this date they claimed he acted in a private and not an official capacity.

But whatever the intrigue, recognition of the Royal Arch was essential to the Union of the two Grand Lodges and this was achieved in 1818 by the somewhat ambiguous wording of the Preliminary Declaration of the *Book of Constitution*, which states: '…pure Antient masonry consists of three degrees and no more, namely the entered apprentice, the fellowcraft, and the master mason, including the Supreme Order of the Holy Royal Arch…'

5th

A Mason's Wife
By Robert Pinkerton

From active Masons, resolute,
Our wives and families we salute;
We surely know the price you pay,
Who sit alone while we're away.

No high degrees on you conferred,
In Lodge, your name is seldom heard;
You serve our cause though out of sight,
While sitting home alone tonight.

Masonic papers list our names,
Awards are given, fit to frame;
But yours is absent...you who strive,
To keep our fortitude alive.

You are part of every helpful deed,
On your encouragement we feed;
Without your blessings, how could we,
Continue acts of charity?

And so, this poem, we dedicate,
To every Master Mason's mate;
And offer our undying love,
Rewards await in Heaven above.

6th As with many things in Freemasonry, there has been much conjecture regarding the significance of the letter 'G'. Many arguments have been put forward to explain its symbolism, but in general, we have no hard of fast rule as to its origin purpose or use.

Harry Carr advises us that in the first instance, the orientation of the letter should be readable from East to West, although this does vary across Freemasonry in general, with some lodges not depicting the letter at all.

An early reference to the letter 'G' is found in Pritchard's, *Masonry Dissected* (1730), which says:

Q. Why was you made a Fellow-Craft?
A. For the sake of the Letter G.
Q. What does that G denote?
A. Geometry, or the fifth Science.

And:

Q. When you came into the middle, what did you see?
A. The Resemblance of the Letter G.
Q. Who doth that G denote?
A. One that's greater than you.
Q. Who's greater than I, that am a Free and Accepted Mason, the Master of a Lodge.
A. The Grand Architect and Contriver of the Universe, or He that was taken up to the top of the Pinnacle of the Holy Temple.

Interestingly, it was Jesus who was taken to the top of the Holy Temple. Matthew 4: 1-11

Therefore, according to this exposure, the letter G is either Geometry, or the fifth Science or The Grand Architect and Contriver of the Universe or He that was taken up to the top of the Pinnacle of the Holy Temple.

7th The Mark Degree has its origins in the practice of stonemasons choosing a unique mark for themselves, which was displayed on a stone that they had worked upon and would identify that particular craftsman who had completed the work. The marks were also used to identify each mason when claiming their wages. Therefore, one of the first parts of the ceremony is for the Candidate to choose his mark, which is registered in the lodge registration book.

In a similar fashion to Craft Masonry, each new member for Advancement, progresses from apprentice to Master, but unlike Craft, there is one ceremony. Therefore, during the course of the evening, the Candidate moves from Mark Man to Mark Master Mason in the same ceremony.

The ceremony is based upon allegory and tells the story of a crucial piece of stone, produced by the Mark Man, which is discarded because its form is not recognised by the three Overseers. The building of the Temple comes to a halt for the want of the stone and a search is made to recover the stone amongst the rubble. Hence the ethos of the Degree which is summed up in Psalm 118:22 - *The stone which the builders refused is become the head stone of the corner.*

The Degree contains messages for the discerning Mason which demonstrates that the wisest of men can be mistaken and the weakest can display greater perseverance than the strongest, that the insignificant have the potential for distinction – and that we all have a part to play in Life. Like Craft Masonry, there is no historical accuracy in the ritual which also uses King Solomon's Temple as a vehicle to accentuate the salient points of the Order.

The regalia has a colourful apron, in the style of a Craft apron and a breast jewel featuring the keystone, which plays an integral part in the ceremony and which represents the discarded stone.

8th The second known Masonic exposure was published in 1724, it was an anonymous twelve-page pamphlet entitled *The Grand Mystery of Free-Masons Discover'd.*

The second edition of the same pamphlet in 1725, has A. Moore ascribed as its publisher, and included two additional letters, signed by *Verus Commodus* concerning the *Society of Freemasons* and the *Society of Gormogons.*

The origin of the pamphlet was described in the Preface, thus:

> *The piece having been found in the Custody of a Free-Mason, who died suddenly, it was thought proper to publish it in the very Words of the Copy, that the Publick may at last have something Genuine concerning the Grand Mystery of Free-Masons.*

As a matter of interest, the Ancient Noble Order of the Gormogons was a short-lived 18th century society which was formed by expelled Freemason, Philip Wharton. It left no records or accomplishments to indicate its true goal and purpose. It is believed from the few published articles that the society's objective was to ridicule Freemasonry.

During its brief existence, it was accused of being a Jacobite-leaning group and there is some evidence of such an association, since the first known Grandmaster was the Chevalier, Andrew Michael Ramsay, a Jacobite of strong convictions.

According to its surviving by-laws, it appears to have been a charitable organisation and there are some surviving pendant badges, bearing their sign.

9th I was recently reading an article by the late Harry Medoza, who referred to a 1768 reference to the position of the apron flap, which as we know varies from system to system. It says: 'The master undid the flap off my apron, which was fastened to my waistcoat button, and told me that in the quality of a master, I was at liberty to let it fall down.' (Indicating the flap was up prior to being given the said permission.)

Unfortunately, I have not been able to find the original reference dated 1768. *Solomon in all his Glory*, was published in March 1766 and *The Freemason Stripped Naked*, August 1769.

But whatever the case, the reference is clear in its position of the apron flap, although no reference is given to the Degree.

10th I find it truly amazing as to some of the pieces of information you come across during one's daily advancement in Masonic knowledge. For example, I was reading about the famous Goose and Gridiron Ale-house in St Pauls Churchyard near to the West End of the Cathedral.

Apparently, the name was a corruption, or parody, on the arms of the Swan and Lyre, a musical society which also met at the ale-house. After the fire of London, the tavern was rebuilt, and the sign writer made such an appalling job of the sign that some local wag termed it 'the Goose and Gridiron' and that name stuck.

11th The Order of the Secret Monitor, although believed to be of Dutch origin, mainly arose in America where any Mason who had received the Degree could confer it upon another Mason. Brought to England in about 1875, a Grand Council was formed in 1887, with the ritual being extended and two further Degrees being added.

There were however some early problems as the Grand Council of Allied Masonic Degree, who had also been granted licence from America, continued to confer their version of the degree. For over thirty-seven years, both Orders were conferring the Degree until 1931, when C.W. Napier became both Grand Supreme Ruler of the Order of the Secret Monitor and also Grand Master of Allied Degrees.

It was Napier that was instrumental in forming the agreement to transfer all rights of the Degree to the Grand Council of the Order of the

Secret Monitor and the Degree was subsequently removed from the Order of the Allied Masonic Degrees.

12th Masonry, we are told is a progressive science.

Science is a noun; meaning the methodical process of study, that builds, collates and organises knowledge in the form of logical explanations which are often proven in practice or predicted in theory.

Progressive is an adjective; in the Masonic sense, meaning continuous, developing, and ongoing.

When brought together, the meaning becomes the continuous process of studying and collating Masonic knowledge in an understandable form. The scientific subject of our study is philosophy, the understanding of man's place in the natural order of society and in the pursuit of truth, which is the simplest definition of science.

Therefore, Masonic science comprises of three main elements, the search for truth, the gathering of knowledge and the development of self. So, we seek to understand what it is, how we can use it, how it can benefit mankind and its place in society.

The next time you hear the Worshipful Master say, 'Masonry being a progressive science…' you will know that he is not referring to the progress we make from an Entered Apprentice to Master Mason, but the continuing pursuit of self-development and knowledge of the purpose of Freemasonry.

13th Legend has it that since 1882, a woman has been in attendance at every Third-Degree ceremony carried out at my local Masonic Centre, in Folkestone. According to a Centenary Festival Booklet, it was in 1882, that W. Bro. F. H. Field presented the Lodge with a set of Emblems of Mortality imported from Zululand.

In 1895, another lodge was inaugurated on the same premises to cater for the professional classes who at the time felt it below their status to be part of the other lodge, who at that time was made up mainly of builders.

However, I was reliably informed by the late Bro. Peter Eagle-Bott, that among these professionals were a number of eminent Consultant Physicians whom upon examination of the relics, identified their sex, thus the legend was born.

This legend was later confirmed to me in a letter from two forensic anthropologists who examined the said emblems.

The Emblems of Mortality are part of the lodge paraphernalia used in the Third-Degree story to help illustrate the untimely demise of that chief Architect Hiram Abiff. They are symbols used purely to remind us of our own mortality.

14th I remember the humour of an elderly and well respected Brother, who in my own mind, was the epitome of Freemasonry for his conduct was always exemplary, his manners impeccable, his ritual word perfect and humour always the toast of the lodge.

I recall one evening when he was called upon to present a recently Raised Master Mason with his Grand Lodge Certificate. As you are aware, there is a no formal ceremony for the presentation, however there are guidelines on specific details to be included.

The Brother was received enthusiastically and proceeded to display his remarkable knowledge of the origin and design of the certificate. As usual he had us all spellbound and he proceeded to the section that explains the three pillars, he went on:

> *...the outstanding feature of the design is, as you will notice, three pillars, each with its corresponding base. The one in the centre, like the Worshipful Master's pillar in the Lodge, is of the Ionic Order adopted by Masons as an emblem of Wisdom and has reference to Solomon, King of Israel, and his wisdom in building, completing and dedicating the Temple at Jerusalem to God's service. The pillar on the left, like that of the Senior Warden's, is of the Doric Order, emblematical of strength, such as the strength of Hiram, King of Tyre in supporting King Solomon*

with men and material. The right-hand pillar, like the pillar of the Junior Warden, is of the Corinthian Order, the emblem of beauty...

At that point the Brother halted, looked to the South, directed his comments to the Junior Warden and remarked, '...although I don't know what happened in Brother Jones' case' and calmly continued the presentation.

15th Our Order has been founded on three grand principles namely Brotherly Love, Relief and Truth. Here we look at Brotherly Love.

The term 'Brotherly Love' extends to the manner in which we treat each other which should be in a most respected, courteous and helpful manner. By this means, we should support a Brother in all of his laudable undertakings, keep his lawful secrets when entrusted to us and support his character in his absence as well as his presence.

The Emulation Lectures of the Three Degrees explain Brotherly Love thus:

By the exercise of Brotherly Love, we are taught to regard the whole human species as one family, the high and low, the rich and poor, created by One Almighty Being, and sent into the world for the aid, support, and a protection of each other. On this principle Masonry unites men of every country, sect and opinion, and by its dictates conciliate true friendship among those who might otherwise have remained at a perpetual distance.

First Lecture, Sixth Section Six

Therefore, Masonry teaches the immutable law of the Brotherhood and the Order strives to unite and conciliate all mankind into this true Brotherhood, men of every race, nation, creed, the high, the low, the rich, the poor, the burdened, the distressed, it is incumbent on every Freemason to soothe the unhappy, to sympathise with them in their misfortunes, to be compassionate with them in their miseries, and to restore peace to their troubled minds wherever possible.

16th 'So mote it be', heard frequently at the end of Masonic prayers literally means 'So it is required' or 'So it must be', like the word, 'Amen'. The phrase appears in the last stanza of the famous Halliwell or Regius MS., which is Freemasonry's earliest document dated c.1390: 'Amen! amen! so mot hyt be! Say we so all per charyte'

More recently, the term has been adopted by neo-pagans who use it in a similar way in their rites and ceremonies.

A.C.F. Jackson explains that the term 'mote' is an Anglo-Saxon word with three different meaning and in the Masonic setting when coupled in the phrase 'So mote it be' simply means 'So let it be'. *(A Glossary of the Craft and Holy Arch Rituals of Freemasonry)*

17th Many early students of Freemasonry were quick to associate our origins with the ancient Greek or Eleusinian mysteries, for example, the known fraternity of Dionysian Architects. (Dionysus was the Greek name for Bacchus, the god of wine)

Dionysian artificers and priests were responsible for the erection of temples and other buildings and were associated with the possession of secrets and mysteries, connected to that trade. In this sense, one can liken the knowledge of raising a perpendicular, building a span across two perpendiculars all based upon two uprights and a lintel, as being at that time, a mystery.

However, any such connection or similarity to any form of Freemasonry is purely coincidental and there is absolutely no evidence to prove any association.

18th In the lodge rooms of old, ceremonies were carried out with the brethren seated around a large table, which, as numbers grew, became totally impractical; as did the small rooms in taverns and inns which the innkeeper made available for the meetings. As the transition to the use of assembly rooms and eventually purpose-built lodge rooms progressed, so did the evolution of the lay out of the lodge room itself and the implements and paraphernalia which originally stood on the table, were moved around the lodge

One such item is the 'derrick' from which the smooth ashlar hangs. Many of us are familiar with it being placed on or at the side of the Senior Wardens pedestal, but in some Lodges, it is placed at various other points, and on other occasions is can carry the rough ashlar.

It is believed that the 'derrick' was introduced to illustrate the lifting device we know as the 'Lewis' and no more than that. In a similar vein, we are not really sure why the rough ashlar was consigned to the Junior Wardens pedestal and smooth ashlar consigned to the Senior Wardens pedestal.

Other than as a demonstration to show the progress of man from his primitive state to his final years, where his constant acts of piety and charity shine through the once rough exterior, I can find no other reason at this stage for the ashlars being prescribed to these positions.

What we do know is that lodges that continued to use hired rooms tend to have smaller, more manageable versions of these items which have to be packed away after each meeting.

19th The first Grand Master appointed in 1717 was Anthony Sayer, although very little is known about him. We know he was a gentleman, as he did not work for a living and that he was a member of the lodge which met at the Apple Tree Tavern; although there is no record of him being Master. In 1719, he served as Grand Senior Warden after which he became Tyler of the Old Kings Arms Lodge No.28, which met at Charing Cross. A record of this time, reports he had fallen on hard times and was assisted out of the Charity box. Later he was to receive some financial aid from Grand Lodge.

The *Evening Post* reported his death in 1742 and stated that 'the funeral was attended by a great number of that honourable society of best quality'. He was laid to rest in St Paul's Church, Covent Garden, where his widow was buried just a few months earlier.

20th A newly appointed DC who was about to rehearse his first Initiation, was a little confused as to how or who would take the poniard from the Inner Guard to the Worshipful Master. I reassured him that he had seen it done many times before, but had probably not fully noticed how it happened. I have seen this done in two or three different ways, but conclude this is the easiest.

After the Inner Guard vouches that the Candidate is properly prepared, the Worshipful Master instructs the Deacons to attend the Candidate. As the Candidate stands at the door of the lodge, the Inner Guard presents the poniard to the Candidate, as he does with the Square, in the Second Degree and the Compasses, in the Third Degree. The Junior Deacon then steps forward to attend the Candidate as the Senior Deacon places the kneeling stool in position. Meanwhile the Inner Guard retains the poniard.

The Candidate is led to the kneeling stool and assisted both up and down by the Deacons. At the conclusion of the prayer, and the exchange with the Worshipful Master, the Senior Deacon removes the kneeling stool and collects the poniard from the Inner Guard. As the Junior Deacon leads the Candidate at the start of his perambulations, the Senior Deacon follows discreetly and hands the poniard to the Worshipful Master before taking his seat.

Some lodges wait for that part in the ceremony when the poniard is shown to the Candidate and at that point the Inner Guard brings the poniard to the Worshipful Master, awaits it use and returns with the poniard to his seat.

Either way is perfectly acceptable.

21st In Masonic legend, the three ruffians who murdered Hiram Abiff were, Jubela, Jubelo and Jubelum. These were first referred to in Samuel Pritchard's *Masonry Dissected* (1730), however, they were not named until the exposure, *Three Distinct* Knocks, which was published in 1760 and *Jachin and Boaz,* in 1762.

However, William Preston does not mention their names in *Illustrations of Freemasonry* (1772) and George Oliver, that zealous Masonic writer of the mid-19th century, wrote that their names were not known; neither do they appear in any of other printed ritual that began to appear in England at that time.

From Capt. WM. Morgan's 1827 *Exposition of Freemasonry*, we read the fate of the three.

> First, Jubela *'O that my throat had been cut across, my tongue torn out, and my body buried in the rough sands of the sea, at low water mark, where the tide ebbs and flows twice in twenty-four hours, ere I had been accessory to the death of so good a man as our Grand Master, Hiram Abiff!'*
>
> Second, Jubelo *'O that my left breast had been torn open and my heart and vitals taken from thence and thrown over my left shoulder, carried into the valley of Jehosaphat, and there to become a prey to the wild beasts of the field and vultures of the air, ere I had conspired the death of so good a man as our Grand Master, Hiram Abiff!'*
>
> Third, Jubelum *'O that my body had been severed in two in the midst, and divided to the north and south, my bowels burnt to ashes in the centre, and the ashes scattered by the four winds of heaven, that there might not the least track or remembrance remain among men, or Masons, of so vile and perjured a wretch as I am; ah, Jubela and Jubelo, it was I that struck him harder than you both. It was I that gave him the fatal blow; it was I that killed him outright.'*

22nd Undaunted by their initial problems and the Craft's refusal to acknowledge the Degree, the Grand Lodge of Mark Master Masons has gone from strength to strength and to date the Degree has spread throughout the world where English Craft has taken root.

Interestingly, in Ireland, the Mark Degree is conferred within Royal Arch Chapters as a prerequisite to the exaltation ceremony. In Scotland, the Degree can be worked in Craft Lodges, and in America, the Mark is the first of four Degrees received within the Royal Arch Chapter.

Finland, Greece and Cyprus, for example have formed their own Grand Lodges, but France, Germany, Spain and the Netherlands work under the London Headquarters.

In 1871, some fifteen years after the establishment of the Mark Grand Lodge in England, the Degree of Royal Ark Mariner was adopted and added a further dimension to the history of the Degree.

23rd What actually was it that the Tyler of old drew on the floor of the hired room of the Ale-house, where the lodge met? Well, to begin with it was nothing as detailed as the tracing Board designs that we are familiar with today.

Primarily, the drawing was a visual aid where the Master teaches the initiate or Candidate for advancement certain aspects of Freemasonry; in particular the Degree which is being worked. Some old records suggest that it began with a simple boundary in the shape of a square, or double square. Geometric symbols were added like a square, circle, triangle or pentagram, with the addition astrological figures like the Sun, the Moon and the Stars. Then there were pillars, ladders, squares, compasses, Levels and plumbs, etc.

By the end of the 18th century, permanently painted illustrations were becoming more popular and the preferable option.

24th If, like me, you are particularly inquisitive with regard to the words we repeatedly use during our ritual, then hopefully also like me, you follow up your inquiry to learn more of their meaning or origin.

For example, before we join Freemasonry, we know by a natural inclination and preconception, that Freemasonry is secret. However, to what degree that secrecy extents we, at that time, have little or no knowledge. So you can imagine on the night of being raised to the Third Degree I heard the following:

> *I further solemnly engage myself to maintain and uphold the five points of Fellowship in act as well as in word; that my hand, given to a Master Mason, shall be a sure pledge of brotherhood; that my feet shall travel through dangers and difficulties to unite with his in forming a column of mutual defense and support; that the posture of my daily supplications shall remind me of his wants and dispose my heart to succor his weakness and relieve his necessities, so far as may fairly be done without detriment to myself or connections; that my breast shall be the sacred repository of his secrets when entrusted to my care - murder, treason, felony, and all other offences contrary – to the laws of God and the ordinances of the realm being at all times most especially excepted.*

It was only when I re-read the ritual that I realised that 'murder, treason, felony, and all other offences contrary – to the laws of God and the ordinances of the realm' were not *accepted*, as the Worshipful Master pronounced, but *excepted*, meaning that I can support a Brother *except* in cases of 'murder, treason, felony, and all other offences contrary – to the laws of God and the ordinances of the realm'.

One simple mispronunciation can give the totally wrong meaning.

25th The ceremony of the Holy Royal Arch begins with the return of the children of Israel from their Babylonian exile or captivity.

The Babylonian Captivity, or Babylonian exile, is the name typically given to the deportation and exile of the Jews of the ancient Kingdom of Judah to Babylon by Nebuchadnezzar during the 6th century BC. This event coincided with the destruction of the First Temple of Jerusalem.

After the overthrow of Babylon by the Persian Empire, in 537 BC, the Persian ruler, Cyrus the Great, gave the Jews permission to return to their native land, and more than 40,000 are said to have availed themselves of the privilege, as noted in the Biblical accounts of Jehoiakim, Ezra, and Nehemiah.

The Persians had a different political philosophy of managing conquered territories than the Babylonians or Assyrians: under the Persians, local personages were put into power to govern the local populace.

The actual return of the first forty thousand exiles was led by Zerubbabal, followed by a second group of about six thousand organised by Ezra. This second body of exiles had been invested with royal powers and succeeded after great difficulties in helping to establish the post-exilic Jewish community.

26th There is a difference between the knocks given in various parts of the ceremony.

The single knock given by the Worshipful Master at the opening of the lodge calls the brethren to order. The single knocks given by the Worshipful Master at other times signifies the end of a specific part of the ceremony or the close of a specific agenda item.

Other distinct knocks the Worshipful Master may use are specific to each Degree and will be used according to strict convention and identify the degree the lodge is working in at any given time.

The only means of communication between the Worshipful Master and the outside world when the lodge is at work is by the Tyler. During parts of the ceremony when the Tyler responds to certain knocks, he confirms two things, a) that he is present at the door of the lodge, and b) that he is fully aware which degree the lodge is currently working in, a necessity for any late comer.

During the ceremony, late comers are announced by a single knock given by the Tyler. This is classed as an alarm rather than a report and signifies that there is a Brother without, seeking admission. However, lodge traditions and other systems dictate other meanings for the single knock.

27th Did you know that the heart, hand, badge sign, also known as breast, hand, badge and heart, apron, glove, is technically a salutation, not a sign. Possibly alluded to in documents of the early 18th century, the first real mention or description of the salutation can be found in two exposures of the 1760s, *Three Distinct Knocks* (1760) and *Jachin and Boaz*, (1762), which have the following:

> *...holding your Left-hand up, keeping it square; then clap with your Right-hand and Left together, and from thence strike your Left-Breast with your Right-hand; then strike your Apron...this is done altogether as one clap...*

According to my research, I can find no real reason for the salutation and its unusual manner and no symbolism attached to it.

28th The Order of the Secret Monitor consists of Three Degrees, these are:

Secret Monitor – First Degree
The legend is related of the extraordinary story of David and Jonathan and the Candidate is instructed as to action that should be taken if a Brother is about to do anything which might prove harmful to his own well-being; the ceremony teaches friendship and fidelity.

Prince – Second Degree
The ceremony centres on the Book of Samuel and tells how Saul sought the life of David; although David had once spared Saul's life. It also tells of the different actions used to thwart the efforts of the jealous King Saul.

Supreme Ruler – Third Degree
This degree is one of Installation pertaining to the Kingship of David and is concerned with headship of the Conclave.

29th Laurence Dermot was a journeyman painter who was born in Ireland in 1720, and initiated in Dublin in 1740. He became Master in 1746 and in that same year became a Royal Arch Mason. He arrived in London in about 1748 and joined a London lodge.

At the age of thirty-two, he was appointed Secretary of the newly formed Grand Lodge of the Antients; an office he held for almost twenty years when he was appointed Deputy Grand Master in 1771. He held the office of Deputy again in 1777, and from 1783 to 1787.

A remarkable Freemason, who despite his vocation as a painter, could speak some Latin and Hebrew and he produced the renowned *Constitutions* of the Antients which he titled, *Ahiman Rezon*, meaning 'the secrets of a prepared Brother'.

By about 1863, he became a wine-merchant and presented the Grand Lodge with the Grand Masters throne as well as giving much of his property, prior to his death, to the charity fund.

Sadly, his death, in 1791, went unrecorded in his Grand Lodge's Minutes, but it must be said he was a remarkable man who once claimed that the Holy Royal Arch was 'the, heart and marrow of masonry' and did much to encourage its development.

30th The tradition of preparing the Candidate for the First Degree, took a strange turn at a lodge where I acted as Tyler many years ago. You are familiar with the first part of the preparation of an initiate, which is to divest him of all metal substances. The depriving of metal and metallic substances prior to entering the lodge room derives from the story of the building of King Solomon's Temple, where we read in I Kings 6:7 that:

And the house when it was in building, was built of stone made ready before it was brought thither: so that there was neither hammer nor axe nor any tool of iron heard in the house, while it was in building.

Compare with Deuteronomy 27:5

And there shalt thou build an altar unto the Lord thy God, an altar of stones: thou shalt not lift up any iron tool upon them.

Exodus 20:25

And if thou wilt make me an altar of stone, thou shalt not build it of hewn stone: for if thou lift up thy tool upon it, thou has polluted it.

Joshua 8:31

As Moses the servant of the Lord commanded the children of Israel, a it is written in the book of the law of Moses, an altar of whole stones, over which no man hath lift up any iron...

So there was a definite instruction in the building of the altar which continued in the erection of the Temple and the same theme thus continued in the Craft story.

Can you therefore imagine when I discovered that the right-hand slipper used in the next part of the preparation of the Candidate had a metal buckle and further enquires indicated that the same slipper had been in use for over fifty-five years.

It would therefore appear that according to the ritual, the ceremony of all initiates in living memory is void, for we read:

...to evince to the Brethren that you neither had money nor metallic substance about you, for if you had, the ceremony of your Initiation thus far, must be repeated.

Needless to say, when I pointed out the problem, new slippers without buckles, were purchased forthwith.

31st One of the reasons I have discovered as to why men became Freemasons, suggests that they had an interest in architecture. In the 1723 *Constitutions* Anderson himself commented on the Gothic style saying it was 'a barbarous product of the Dark Ages' and praised the various Italian architects of the Palladian style.

While in York, antiquary Francis Drake and his contemporary Edward Oakley, both leading Freemasons of the 1720s, commented on the giving of lectures on architecture and geometry in the lodge. In fact, Drake claimed that in London lodges and other parts of the kingdom, lectures on the same were given at every meeting.

Evidence of one such lecture delivered in 1723 by Dr. William Stukeley, still survives in the British museum and is entitled, 'The Roman Amphitheatre at Dorchester'.

While other contemporary lodge minutes tell us that at the Old King's Arms Lodge, Master Martin Clare read part of the 'Architecture of Palladio', 'to which the Society were very attentive'. Similarly, George Payne presented a lecture about the 'Manner of Building in Persia'.

So even if we consider that Drake's assertion that lectures 'on the same were given at every meeting' were an exaggeration, his remarks do at least suggest that architecture played a somewhat small part in the early Grand Lodge meetings.

This is somewhat confirmed as late as 1735, when William Smith claimed in his book *A Pocket Companion for Freemasonry*, the importance of a knowledge of architecture by Freemasons.

April

1st In Freemasonry, depending what degree we are in, we use different appellations, i.e. 'Great Architect of the Universe', 'Grand Geometrician of the Universe', 'The Most High' etc., but have you ever wondered why?

Primarily, the significance of these terms used is that we can corporately engage in the common ceremonies regardless of our own belief system.

The terms used are those employed in much of the 17th century when the whole nature of God, as the Creator of the world and the planets were subject to continuous investigation and it is to that period, we need to look to understand just what these churchmen and scholars meant by using these descriptions.

The early Masonic documents from 1696-1730 shed no light on this issue and as late as 1760, lodges were opened in the name of 'God and St John'.

The renowned Masonic historian, Neville Barker Cryer, sees no great significance in the name changes and believes the terms were naturally introduced when it was intended to introduce a Brother to the progress he had made in the Science, the specific message of the Degree and a guide to further contemplation of his God.

2nd Native to China, the skirret is a white rooted, long forgotten vegetable probably brought to England by the Romans.

Freemasons recognise the term as one of their working tools and describe it as an implement which acts on a centre pin, whence a line is drawn to mark the ground for the formation of the intended structure.

The term was first used by Richard Carlisle, in his 1825 work a *Manual of Freemasonry*, to describe the Working Tools of the Third Degree.

3rd In general, annual lodge subscriptions become due on the date appointed in the By Laws of the lodge. The fee set in the By Laws, although subject to change as per the appropriate procedure, has in general, been calculated to ensure its covers the complete annual running costs of the lodge itself.

These calculations are self-explanatory, and any good Treasurer will ensure he remains within the projected expenditure forecast in the previous fiscal year. However, some brethren inadvertently omit to ensure their own subscription fees are paid on time, thus occasionally forcing the Treasure to adjust his expenditure accordingly.

Most Treasurers will always ensure there is a positive balance to cover late fees, but why should he? Sadly, it then becomes the unnecessary, onerous and occasionally embarrassing task of the Treasurer to remind late-payers, when it is incumbent upon every individual member to pay his subscriptions on time.

So many Treasurers find this part of their office disconcerting and to aid this problem, many lodges have now reduced the period of expulsion from the lodge for non-payment of fees, from one year to three months. At the same time and to avoid personal embarrassment, they have put into place plans for fees to be paid by Standing Order, on a monthly basis. So brethren that have had difficulty in the past paying a one-off fee, can now break it into smaller and more manageable payments.

This adjustment to the time frame for payment also prevents outstanding membership fees accruing for more than a year; bearing in mind that Grand and Provincial Lodge fees must be paid per member on the lodge roll, regardless of whether or not the members have paid their fees.

4th The story of our ritual and its formation must begin somewhere and the drama of the Holy Royal Arch culminating in the Principle Sojourner, being emblematically lowered into a vault, is no exception to this.

Here are some interesting similarities with contemporary writings.

The Ecclesiastical History of Philostorgius, who was born 368 AD, was translated and published in 1669, in a book entitled, *Solomon's Temple Spiritualised.* The book records that the Roman Emperor, Julian the Apostate, ordered the rebuilding of the city of Jerusalem, during the course of which a cave was discovered by a workman who was lowered by rope into the vault. He discovered a perfect square and in its centre, a column upon which was found a book wrapped in fine linen cloth; the first words being 'In the beginning was the word'. The book was the entire Gospel of St John. This verse incidentally played a very important part in the early Holy Royal Arch ceremony, but was dropped during the 1835 ritual revision.

Robert Macoy, in his book *A Dictionary of Freemasonry*, reports of the finding of a vault in the ruins at Yucatan, where the explorer, Stephens, recorded the following: 'The only way of descending was to tie a rope around the body and be lowered by the Indians…' As you can see, it is not beyond the realms of anyone's imagination to understand where the allegorical story originated.

We can also find references to the discovery of a law-book during repair work that was being carried out on the Temple in 2 Kings, 22 and 2 Chronicles, 34. Many commentators identify the book as Deuteronomy, the fifth book of the Bible. Both books record the fact that Hilkiah the Priest, '…finding the book of the law that the Lord had given Moses'.

5th

Here is a point of interest; some years back a Brother mentioned to me that the Master of his lodge had met with an unfortunate accident, which had claimed his life. As he was Senior Warden at the time, he asked me whether he would have to step into the Master's Chair prior to his Installation or would another Master be appointed to take the Chair. The answer to both questions are no!

In the event of such a catastrophe, the Senior Warden, or in his absence the Junior Warden, or in both their absences, the Immediate Past Master, or in his absence, the Senior Past Master shall act as Master in summoning the lodge until the next Installation meeting.

However, the Immediate Past Master, or in his absence, the Senior Past Master of the lodge shall take the Chair.

In the event that no Past Masters of, or in, the lodge are present, then the Senior Warden, or in his absence the Junior Warden shall rule the lodge.

During this situation, neither Warden can occupy the Master's Chair, nor can Initiations take place, nor Degrees conferred, unless the Master's Chair is occupied by a Brother who is a Master or Past Master of the Craft.

6th Coming under the jurisdiction of the Grand Lodge of Mark Master Masons, the Degree of the Royal Ark Mariner first came to prominence in Bath, in 1790, after which there are several references to the Degree. After some difficulties, the Degree was revived in 1816, at which point it was placed under the protection of the Mark Grand lodge, although it has no historical connection with the Mark Degree.

Minutes from a Grand Lodge of Royal Ark Mariners dated 1871, claim that a Grand Lodge was formed in the year 1772, but there appears to be no reliability to this fact.

Consisting of one Degree, for which one has to be a Mark Master Mason to qualify, the ceremony reminds the Candidate, who is to be Elevated, of the providence and mercy of God, telling the story of the great deluge. The Candidate is taught the importance of family strengths and that out of chaos, mankind can survive if all adversity if faced together.

Analogies are drawn between the dangers of the flood and the dangers of life, and Candidates each are reminded of how they should strive to reach the Ark, the haven of rest, as the Ark is momentarily symbolised as the Ark of salvation.

7th There seems to be some confusion over the origins of the office of Tyler. I have heard many an authority try to prove that there is some connection with the encampments of the Knights

Templar, who according to an old French book, entitled, *Proc des Templier*, advises us that they posted a sentry on the roof of the building to guard against eavesdroppers.

In French, the words 'to tile' are *tullier*; and it is from this, a thin association is drawn. However, the theory collapses when we study the subject a little closer.

From the minutes of Lodge No.39 (Erased 1751), which met at the Swan and Rummer, Finch Lane, London and dated 10 March 1731, we read:

> *Br. Johnson be desired to attend to gard the Lodge every Lodge night, and that he be allowed eighteen pence and one pint of wine for his attendance.*

From the minutes of Lodge No.163 (Erased 1810), which met at the *Two Black Posts*, Maiden Lane, London, and dated 22 June 1738, we read an instruction for:

> *...Bro. doorkeeper to lock up all aprons.*

And the portrait of Andrew Montgomey, dated 1738, and clearly entitled 'Garder of ye Grand Lodge'.

Therefore, it is obvious the term 'Tyler' was a later innovation and no inference or connection can be made to the practises of the Knights Templar.

8th Apparently, according to some Masonic students, the Craft signs are, and have been known, to various followers of the Islamic prophet Muhammad and have been well received in Egypt, Libya, Turkey, India and Malaya. It has also been claimed that the Freemasonry we practice is no more than a copy of their ancient rites as practiced by Saladin.

Legend has it that Saladin was initiated into the Order of Chivalry by Richard Coeur de Lion and in return, Saladin initiated Richard into the Lower Dervish Degrees and that Richard, in turn passed those signs and secrets to his knights, including Templars, who passed them onto to the men who built the churches and cathedrals.

Oh, that the origins of Freemasonry were that simple!

Sadly, there is absolutely no credible evidence in existence to prove the theory and no vehicle to show how the signs or secrets were passed on. The days where many Freemasons believed that the source of Freemasonry lay with the Knights Templar have long since ceased and have been academically disproved.

9th We have often heard quotes or references from the oldest recognised Masonic document which is the Regius MS., dated 1390. It was written just over 300 years after the Battle of Hastings, which saw the start of an unprecedented, almost frenzied programme of castle and cathedral building.

What is also interesting is that the Regius MS appears to be a copy of an even older document because it speaks of an already established Craft, which is a full grown working organisation.

There are definitely two other rarely referred to documents, which were specifically written for working masons.

The London Regulations for Masons (1356)

In 1356, to end a violent conflict between mason hewers and mason layers (or setters) the London authorities, acting on behalf of the King of England, Edward III (1312-1377), drew up special regulations to organise the craft of stone construction. Those corporate rules were strengthened during the following century, with the creation of a Company of Masons of London in 1481.

The York Ordinances (1370)

Titled 'York Minster Masons' Ordinances', it is part of a series of manuscripts written on parchment which are presently held by the library of the cathedral; and was written in old English; as reproduced in *The Fabric Rolls of York Minster*, in a book published in 1859.

The ancient capital of the kingdom of Northumbria is the seat of the cathedral and Metropolitan Church of St Peter in York (usually called York Minster), the largest religious building in the western world; dominated by three towers, one of them 200 feet high. The cathedral is renowned for the purity of its architecture, the richness of its facades and the quality of its sculptures. Its dimensions are also considerable: its length is 518 feet, its choir height, 102 feet. It has the widest nave in Europe.

10th After the self-styled revival of Freemasonry in 1717, the number of lodges grew rapidly, and it is estimated that almost one hundred lodges established themselves in the first decade.

The trouble was, that before the 1st century was out, there also began to appear rival Grand Lodges. This was due much to the poor leadership as much as anything else, but changes and innovations took their toll.

There was the York Grand Lodge, the Grand Lodge of all England, the Grand Lodge South of the River Trent, the Supreme Grand Lodge, to name but four.

One of the first issues was caused by a paragraph in Andersons *Constitutions*, titled 'Concerning God and Religion'; these days, an important part of our stance, but then, very offensive to the majority of mid-18th century Freemasons, many of whom were Trinitarians. This was followed by a series of exposures, when certain unscrupulous men published sensitive material which led to irregular lodges being formed and degrees being conferred for money.

From a few other references, we also learn of other innovations which caused problems:

The Installation of the Master was in some cases abolished or omitted.

The Third Degree was remodelled.

The symbolism of the preparation of the Candidate was changed.

The passwords and signs of the First and Second Degrees were reversed.

Aprons were reversed, worn upside down.
Some other long practiced usages and traditions were dropped or changed.

The 1784 *Book of Constitutions* tells us that, 'Some variations were made to the establish forms, more effectively to debar clandestine activities and their perpetrators, from the Lodges'.

Troubled times from the first one hundred years of Freemasonry, solved only by the Union of 1813.

11th In Scotland, the word 'lodge' was used to describe an organised body of masons associated with a particular town or district. In the Schaw Statutes of 1598 and 1599, we read that 'Edinburgh shall be the first principle lodge and Kilwinning the second'. From the St Clair Charters of 1601 and 1628 we learn of other territorial lodges at St Andrews, Dundee and Glasgow to name but three.

These lodges carried out certain official duties of a trade nature, including the regulation of Apprentices, keeping records of the reception and entry of Apprentices, the admission of Fellowcrafts, assigned marks to members.

Other duties also included settling disputes between Masters and their servants, ensuring no Cowans were employed, ensuring Masters did not employ Apprentices or Journeymen of other Masters, collecting funds by way of fees and fines, relief of the distressed, feasting at the expense of the Candidate and conferring the Mason Word on qualified members.

12th I was asked recently to explain the origin and symbolism of the 'All Seeing Eye' and its relationship to Freemasonry. Firstly, we must recognise that the symbol is not Masonic at all, but it was used by the Egyptians to represent Osiris, also known as 'The Eye of Horus'. Secondly, I consider its introduction to Freemasonry more of an innovation than an original teaching.

I can find no reference to the subject in any pre-1772 exposures or ritual aide-mémoires. In fact, it was William Preston who first referred to it when he wrote:

> *...and although our thoughts, words and actions may be hidden from the eyes of man, yet that All-Seeing Eye, whom the sun, moon and stars obey, and under whose watchful care even the comets perform their stupendous revolutions, pervades the inner recesses of the human heart, and will reward us according to our merits.*

Therefore, in this sense, the 'All-Seeing Eye' is that of God.

13th *The Great Priory of the United Religious, Military and Masonic Orders of the Temple and St John of Jerusalem, Palestine, Rhodes and Malta*, is the official title of the Order better known to us as Knights Templar and Knights of Malta.

The earliest known minute or reference to Masonic Knights Templar in England was in Portsmouth 1777; the degree was worked in a Royal Arch Chapter. However, it was not until 1791, that a Great Priory or Grand Conclave was formed with seven other Encampments, with Thomas Dunckerley, installed as Grand Master.

Based on, but not to be confused with, *The Poor Fellow-Soldiers of Christ and of the Temple of Solomon*, also known as the Order of Solomon's Temple, the Knights Templar or simply as Templars, and it was a Catholic military order recognised in 1139 by Papal Bull *Omne Datum Optimum* of the Holy See. The Order was founded in 1119 and active from about 1129 to 1312. The Masonic Order and the contemporary Knights Templar International or Knights Templar UK, have no connection.

A Candidate for this Masonic Order must hold a belief in the Holy Trinity and be a Royal Arch Mason. In England, the Degrees within the Order are:

Knight Templar
Knight of St Paul or Mediterranean Pass

Knight of St John of Jerusalem, Palestine, Rhodes and Malta

Like all Masonic Orders, the Degrees and traditional history are based around highlighting the message and ethos of the Degree and are not necessarily historically accurate.

Additionally, there developed a popular myth that the Knights Templar were the founders of Craft Freemasonry, but good research has proved that like many theories, in was based on fanciful ideas designed to appeal to one's vanity, rather than historical accuracy.

14th In 1887, John Lane produced a fascinating work entitled *Masonic Records* (1717-1886) which detailed every lodge that had been established by the First Grand Lodge from 1717 to 1886. These records have enabled the early history of Freemasonry, in a particular place, to be readily traced and provides information about individual lodges.

Lane was born in 1843, and was initiated into Jordon Lodge No.1402 in 1878, becoming Master in 1882. His second edition ran from 1717 to 1895, whereupon he presented the copyright to Grand Lodge and was appointed Past Assistant Grand Director of Ceremonies.

Known for other Masonic works, he became a member of the Quatour Coronati Lodge No.2076, in 1887. He died in December 1899.

In 2003, the Centre for Research into Freemasonry and Fraternalism, working with the Library and Museum of Freemasonry, produced a database adding lodges that came into existence after 1894.

15th The Holy Royal Arch is based around the building of the second Temple. The Second Temple, known to us as the third, or Grand and Royal Lodge, was reconstructed and stood between 516 BC and 70 AD. During this time, it was the centre of Jewish worship, which focused on the sacrifices known as the *Korbanot*.

King Solomon's Temple was destroyed in 586 BC when the Jews were exiled during the Babylonian captivity. Construction of a new temple was begun in 535 BC and completed in 516 BC, with its dedication in 515 BC. As described in the Book of Ezra, rebuilding of the Temple was authorised by Cyrus the Great and ratified by Darius the Great.

The Romans destroyed Jerusalem and its second Temple on 4 August 70 AD, ending the Great Jewish Revolt that began in 66 AD.

16th I notice that at lodge meetings held on hot summer days, the DC occasionally announces that the brethren have the Master's permission to dispense with gloves. This naturally begs the question 'where is it stated that gloves are part of our regalia?' And furthermore, if it can be shown that they are an essential part or our regalia, where is the authority given for the Master to make the change?

If we refer to the Grand Lodge Proceedings during and after the Second World War, on 3 September 1941, the MW Pro Grand Master stated that 'whilst it was regrettable that anything which has a Masonic symbolism should be dispensed with, he felt it was justified in the case of the wearing of gloves, in the national interest because of the use of clothing coupons'.

In a discussion held at Grand Lodge on 4 December 1946, after the removal of wartime restrictions, the MW the Grand Master stated, 'white gloves are a part of our regalia'.

On 7 June 1950, it was stated:

> *The Board has also given consideration to the wearing of white gloves at Masonic Meetings, and now recommends that, from the 1st January 1952, it shall be left to the discretion of the Master of each Lodge to decide, after duly considering the interests of the members generally, whether to request that they be worn.*

The subject was again dealt with in the Proceedings dated 10 June 1964: 'Enquiries are often made of the Grand Secretary as to the correct procedure to be observed in the wearing of gloves during Lodge meetings.'

The recommendation of June 1950 is repeated and a further recommendation of the Board states:

> *If gloves are worn they should be worn [at all times] except: (i) By the Candidate for the three degrees. (ii) By the Master Elect when actually taking his Obligations on the V.S.L. There is no objection to E.A.'s and F.C.'s wearing gloves when not actually being passed or raised.*

17th

What do Edward VII, Winston Churchill and Oscar Wilde have in common with comedian Jim Davidson, cricketer Clive Lloyd and the Duke of Edinburgh?

If the Royal Society dates from about 1665 and is the oldest Society in the world – which is the second oldest?

For what organisation did Hitler, as part of his invasion plan, raise his infamous *Sonderfahndanglist GB* or rather 'Special Search List Great Britain' which contained some 3,000 entries including the names, addresses of buildings, and companies associated with those names and addresses, from the same organisation?

Which organisation has groups meeting in every part of the known world, where of course, the Government of that land will allow?

Which organisation's origins have been connected with such ancient mysteries of that of Isis and Osiris of Egypt, Mithras of Persia, Adonis of Syria, Dionysus, Eleusis and the dreams of the Grecian mythologists, the Druids, and more latterly with the Roman Collegia, the Comacine Masters of Italy, the Steinmetzens of Germany, the French Compagnonnage, medieval Trade Guilds, the Knights Templars and even the monks of Henry's dissolved monasteries?

Of course, the common answer to all these questions is Freemasonry.

18th

What are the informal wine-takings at the Festive Board that we enjoy during the meal and how should we conduct ourselves?

As a general rule, the informal wine-takings taken during the meal is when the Master generally takes wine with the following:

His Wardens, with whom he rules the lodge
Grand Lodge Officers or special visitors
Visiting Masters
The new Initiate on his first night
The Officers of the lodge or those that helped with the ceremony that evening
Past Masters of and in the lodge
Members of the Holy Royal Arch
The Master's personal guests

These informal wine takings require the recipient to respond by standing and taking wine in the same manner of mutual respect. However, be aware that certain lodges follow their own traditional procedures.

19th Why do we use the term 'free-man' or 'free-born' when speaking of the qualification of membership, particularly when serfdom and bondage no longer exist in this country? The Section One, Lecture One explains:

> *It alludes to that grand festival given by Abraham at the weaning of his son Isaac, when Sarah, Abraham's wife, observing Ishmael, the son of Hagar, the Egyptian bond-woman, teasing and perplexing her child, remonstrated with her husband saying, 'Put away that bond-woman and her son, for such as they shall not inherit with my son, even with Isaac.' She spake as if endued with a prophetic spirit, well knowing that from the loins of Isaac would spring a great and mighty people, such as would serve the Lord with freedom, fervency, and zeal; and fearing that if the two youths were brought up together that Isaac might imbibe some of the slavish principles of Ishmael, it being a general remark in those days, as in the present, that the minds of slaves were less enlightened, and more contaminated than those of the Free. This*

is the reason that Freemasons give why all men should be free-born; but, in the present day, slavery being generally abolished, it is considered that if a man be free, although he may not be free-born, he is still eligible to become a Freemason.

20th Have you ever wondered what the hidden mysteries of nature and science are?

As a rather loose and certainly not exhaustive guide, modern day science falls into four categories: 1) Natural science which studies the material universe. 2) Social science which studies people and societies. 3) Formal science which studies logic and mathematics. 4) Applied science which studies engineering and medicine.

The science that Freemasonry refers to, is the social science category, that being philosophy. Science itself is the study of nature and behaviour of natural things and the knowledge we obtain from them. Therefore, our studies concern ourselves with the hidden mysteries of Masonic science.

From a non-Masonic point of view, Freemasonry lends itself to all manner of imaginations from secret signs to Initiation ceremonies, and a non-Masons understanding cannot evolve past that stage. Freemasons however, by virtue of their own studies, learn and understand the wisdom in its teachings, the lessons in its symbolism and its use, as a society, to the world in general.

The whole art of Freemasonry being the transfer of that knowledge into one's thoughts, deeds and actions for the benefit of society at large and the development of self.

21st The lodge room where Freemasons meet, we know is representative of King Solomon's Temple; however, the room where Companions of the Holy Royal Arch holds its convocations is representative of the Great Sanhedrin.

The Great Sanhedrin was an assembly of Jewish judges who constituted the Supreme Court and legislative body of ancient Israel. In total, there were seventy-one Sanhedrin members. During the period of the Second Temple in Jerusalem, prior to its destruction in 70 AD, the Great Sanhedrin would meet in the Hall of Hewn Stones in the Temple during the day, except before festivals and Shabbat.

22nd I have often queried why the Craft in general, appear not to 'fire' after the loyal or Queen's toast. DCs have explained that it is because Her Majesty is not a member of the Craft; however, in one sense this reason seems to contradict the reasons for the tradition.

The tradition of Masonic firing takes its rise from a convivial custom, practiced prior to the formation of the Craft; the act of 'firing' is the completion of the toast and in part honours the subject of whom the toast is being offered. Firing is intended to be a hearty, enthusiastic, noisy salute and should be given with proper zest.

Firing is not a secret act or part of our modes of recognition and in that sense, can be carried out with ladies or non-members present. Likewise, the room does not have to be tyled, and the waiting staff may continue to attend to the diners during the formal toasts, although it is occasionally suggested that some discretion need be shown to avoid surplus noise.

23rd There are three distinguishing characteristics found in the breast of every good Freemason; these are Virtue, Honour and Mercy. With regard to Honour, we are taught:

Honour, may justly be defined to be the spirit and supererogation of Virtue; the true foundation of mutual faith; and the real intercourse by which the business of life is transacted with safety and pleasure. It implies the united sentiments of Virtue, Truth, and Justice, carried by a generous mind beyond those mere moral obligations which the laws require, or can punish the violation of. True honour, though a different principle from religion, is that which produces the same effects; the lines of action although drawn from different parts, terminate in the same point. Religion embraces Virtue, as it is enjoined by the laws of God; Honour, as it is graceful and ornamental to human nature. The religious man fears, the man of Honour scorns, to do an ill action; the latter considers vice as something beneath him; the other as something which is offensive to the Divine Being. A true man of Honour will not content himself with the literal discharge of the duties of a man and a citizen; he raises and signifies them to magnanimity: he gives, when he may, with propriety refuse; and forgives, where he may with justice resent. The whole of his conduct is guided by the noblest sentiments of his own unvitiated heart; a true moral rectitude of the uniform rule of his actions; and a just praise and approbation his due reward.

24th Consider the sentiment of this poem, author unknown.

If Providence your lot hath blest,
In peace and affluence to rest,
Let not your mind contracted be,
Nor scorn the abodes of poverty.

When you behold in abject state,
A brother crushed by fortune's fate,
Lend him your aid, his wants to free,
And you shall honour Masonry.

When o'er the list of human woes,
You find the tear of grief overflows,
The widow's moan, the orphan's sigh,
Your help shall honour Masonry.

Where discord reigns with direful sway,
The balm of reasoning their display;
Show to the world a conscience free,
And you shall honour Masonry.

Your time shall pass serenely on -
While conscience dictates, right is done:
Your hoary locks shall honoured be,
If you've regarded Masonry.

When life's tempestuous scenes are o'er,
And nature's calls require no more,
In heaven you'll take your last degree,
If you have honoured Masonry.

25th Following the Union of the two Grand Lodges in 1813, there was still a certain amount of friction between lodges, and as a result Lodge No.31 of Liverpool was suspended and subsequently erased. However, the lodge, along with two others, formed 'The Grand Lodge of Free and Accepted Masons of England According to the Old Constitutions', and was made up of twelve lodges, with the addition of a further nine. It was also known as 'The Grand Lodge in Wigan'.

Surprisingly, the last Grand Master was elected as late as 1886 and he was a member of the Lodge of Sincerity, one of the original three lodges. In 1913, the Grand Lodge returned to the United Grand Lodge of England and its members were re-Obligated.

26th The evening was set; three extra rehearsals had taken place and all the offices of the lodge felt that this night's Installation would be one of the best and most efficient we had ever held.

The Representative of the Right Worshipful the Provincial Grand Master duly took his place and was appropriately saluted. The Worshipful Master thanked his Officers, and the Master Elect was obligated. The Inner Workings took place and were word perfect.

The members filed back in and the salutes in the Three Degrees given. The investiture of the Officers began, first the Wardens, followed by the Chaplain, Treasurer, Secretary, and then the DC.

Dear Brother DC, an old and respected Past Master of the lodge, stood with great dignity in front of the Worshipful Master. You could see the pride on his face at the exemplary way the ceremony had progressed so far. He stood there knowing that he had been asked to act in that office for one more year.

'Worshipful Master', he called, 'Whom do you appoint Director of Ceremonies?'

The new Worshipful Master, a keen amateur dramatist, halted for effect, slowly looked at the DC, but before he could draw a breath, he was totally upstaged. The DC had had a serious wardrobe malfunction and before the Master could continue, the DC's trousers inadvertently dropped to his ankles.

27th

The Degrees of the Order known to us as the Knights Templar consist of three degrees:

Knight Templar

The Degree celebrates the actions of a band of knights who, in 1118, were granted refuge in the confines of King Solomon's Temple by Baldwin II, king of Jerusalem. The Candidate is reminded that after periods of warfare and pilgrimage, penitence and meditation prepare him for the Christian Knighthood, and he is proclaimed a Knight of the Temple.

Knight of St Paul or Mediterranean Pass

This Degree was founded to commemorate the battle of 1367, involving the Knights of St John of Rhodes when crossing the River Offanto, which ran red with the blood of their enemies. Their victory ensured the knights could pass all parts of the Mediterranean coastline without molestation.

Knight of St John of Jerusalem, Palestine, Rhodes and Malta

This Christian Knighthood Degree celebrates the long history of the Knights of Malta, their repeated battles with the infidel and their progress from leaving Jerusalem to their final home on Malta. The ritual has an esoteric meaning, mainly that of the mystical resurrection.

28th Surprisingly, nobody really knows why, in 1815, Euclid's 47th Proposition became the emblem adopted for the collar jewel of a Past Master. Anderson had previously claimed that it was the 'foundation of all Masonry, sacred, civil and military' and it was used on the frontispiece of his 1723, *Book of Constitutions*.

The theorem was actually attributed to the revered Pythagoras; the mathematician and philosopher who was born *c*.570 BC in Samos, Greece and not Euclid, who resided in Alexandria, Egypt and who was born *c*.350 BC.

Over the years, Masonic students have tried to make parallels between the mathematical formulae and Freemasonry, and have considered it to be the perfect representation of the Craft Three Degrees, i.e. the two smaller squares resting on the legs of the right-angled triangle representing the Entered Apprentice and the Fellowcraft respectively; while the square on the hypotenuse, which is equal to the square on the other two legs, represents the Master Mason Degree.

29th The term 'cable' appears several times in our ritual and it seems to imply a different meaning on each occasion that it is used.

The first occasion it is used is in the Initiation ceremony where coupled with the word 'tow', it symbolically represents a restraint, of no specific length, which would prevent or hinder any attempt by the Candidate to rush forward during his reception into the lodge, should he be tempted to do so.

The second use of the term is also in the Initiation ceremony and is coupled with the word 'length', e.g. '…and buried in the sea at low water or a cable's length from the shore…' indicating a specific measurement, which is not stated.

A 'cable's length' is a unit of marine measurement, defined by the *Oxford English Dictionary*, as about one hundred fathoms or one-tenth of a sea mile; the earliest non-Masonic reference being 1555. In the Masonic sense, it implies that whatsoever is buried at a 'cable's length' would be irrecoverable.

The third reference is during the Obligation of a Master Mason when he promises to, '...pledge myself to...answer and obey all lawful Signs and Summonses sent to me from a Master Mason's Lodge, if within the length of my Cable Tow and plead no excuse...' However, again no specific distance is stated.

This reference is really a modern symbolic allusion to one of the oldest of the operative regulations, which required the medieval mason to attend his 'assemblies', except in sickness, or 'in peril of death'.

Nowadays the term simply means that one promises to attend the lodge, if it is in one's power to do so, regardless of any distance.

30th Here are a series of questions and answers, which remind Companions of the Holy Royal Arch, where they are and why they were there. The Candidate acts out the drama as one of the Sojourners.

Q) Where are we?
A) In Jerusalem!
Q) Where did we come from?
A) Babylon, the captivity now being over!
Q) Who allowed us to come back to Jerusalem?
A) Cyrus, the King of Persia!
Q) Who are we?
A) The Grand Sanhedrim!
Q) Who sits at the head of the Sanhedrin?
A) Zerubbabal, Haggai and Joshua!
Q) Who are they assisted by?
A) Scribes, Ezra and Nehemiah!

Q) What did Cyrus give us permission to do?

A) To rebuild the Temple at Jerusalem!

Q) What did we do to help the reconstruction?

A) We hired three workmen (Sojourners) to clear the ground in order to receive the foundations. They made a discovery of great importance which they immediately conveyed back to us.

Q) What did they discover?

A) The name of the True and Living God Most High. Which was lost through the untimely death of Hiram Abiff!

Q) What was the reward for the industry and fidelity of the workmen?

A) They were made members of the Grand Sanhedrin!

May

1st Was Freemasonry influenced by early English Druidism, I was once asked, and to be truthful for a brief moment I was stuck for an answer. For example, our Officers and perambulations can be said to imitate the worship of the sun. The Master, Senior and Junior Wardens all represent the position of the sun at crucial parts of the day, the rising, the meridian and the setting. The Candidate always follows its path; from East to West and our religious feast days also coincided with the summer and winter solstice. Therefore, there can be said to be similarities, but this is because of the sun itself. Man's life through the ages has been totally dependent on the cycle of the sun and the warmth it brings; therefore, it has been incorporated into the belief systems of many groups.

However, by far the best argument I have heard for a connection with Druidism, is the origin of the term 'Mason'. For the Druids of the British Isles, 1st May was the second most important holiday of the year. It was on this day that the festival of Beltane was held and among other traditions, dancing round the May pole heralded the return of summer and new growth. Druids were therefore known as the sons or May or May's Sons (Masons).

Merely an observation and no more.

2nd In the Masonic setting, the very first use of that well-known adjective, 'speculative' can be found in the Cooke MS. (*c.*1425), where it says, referring to Prince Edwin, the legendary youngest son of King Athelstan: 'For of speculatyf he was a master and he loved welle masonry and masons.'

Plot's *Natural History of Staffordshire* (1686), speaks about the Order being spread across the nation and loosely describes how a Candidate is admitted and clearly refers to an operative mason. But he then goes onto say: '...but some others they have (to which they are sworn after their fashion) that none know but themselves...' – indicating two types of mason.

Anderson's *Constitutions* (1723), refers to Free and/or Accepted Masons, also signifying two types of mason.

But the word 'speculative' is not officially used again in English Freemasonry until over three hundred years later when, in 1757, in a letter written by the Deputy Grand Master, he refers to operatives and speculatives, and then again by Preston in his *Illustrations of Masonry* (1775).

From that point on, the word 'speculative' becomes commonly used to describe Freemasons and thus every time we hear the Working Tools delivered, we hear the words: 'But, as we are not all operative Masons, but rather free and accepted or speculative...'

3rd Here is a most wonderful piece of allegorical ritual used in the Degree of Royal Master, Royal and Select Masters and relates to an alleged discussion between Hiram Abiff and Adoniram.

> Adoniram: *Grand Master Hiram Abiff, when shall I receive the Master Word?*
>
> Hiram Abiff: *My worthy Companion Adoniram, I do not know if you will ever receive it, for according to an agreement entered into between Solomon, King of Israel, Hiram, King of Tyre, and myself, the word cannot be given until the Temple has been completed, and then only in the presence and with the assistance of all three.*
>
> Adoniram: *But, Grand Master Hiram Abiff suppose that one of those three, even you yourself, should be removed by death. How should I receive it then?*
>
> Hiram Abiff: *Companion Adoniram, death is a subject which admits of no levity when mentioned by mortal man. The young may die, the old must die, and the wisest knoweth not how*

soon. None can escape that inexorable doom. The youngest entered apprentice upon the chequered pavement below dwells ever in the shadow of death; while the invisible hand extends equally over King Solomon on his ivory throne. We walk upon the ashes of generations who have gone the way before us, to which our ashes must in turn contribute, and our bodies crumble into dust. The very air we breathe is but the sighing of spirits once mortal, now clothed in immortality. It is not for me, Companion Adoniram, to hope to escape the common doom of man, but when I die the Word will be buried there. Companion Adoniram, death terminates the labours of a man. Henceforth generations may build and occupy, but he will not be there. The thoughtful brain, the skilful hand, the sinewy arm are alike useless and superfluous in the grave, where there is neither work, nor device, nor knowledge, nor wisdom. The most gifted of mortal kings thus meditates 'The dead know not anything: their love, their hatred, their malice, their envy, is forgotten! Neither have they, henceforth, a portion in anything that is done under the sun. What an incentive is this to an industrious use of our faculties, that we should labour diligently to complete that inner temple for God's eternal praise, and finish our task ere the Sabbath of eternity sets in; and be ready to sleep in peace, as the night cometh when no man can work. My work, Companion Adoniram, is not finished, though I have laboured faithfully and long; but when I die the Word will be buried there. Companion Adoniram, it is through the gate of death that we enter into a place of refreshment and rest, and receive the rewards of our labours. The supreme Master of the Universe, before whom we bow in humble adoration, and whose all-seeing eye has marked our labours in the Lodge below, promises to spread before us in that Sublime Lodge above all the joys and glories of an Eternal Sabbath. After the strong hand of death has levelled all in the humiliation of the grave, the Almighty hand of the Supreme Master will prevail, and exalt every Brother to the glorious companionship of that undissolving Lodge. There the designs upon the trestle board will be seen completed. There the adoration of the twelfth hour will be the everlasting joy. There the noontide of bliss will eternally shine. And there the scales of doubt and darkness will fall from our eyes, and the wise purposes of the Divine Architect will be displayed in all their splendour. With this light of faith beaming upon me, I can say 'O death, where is thy sting? O grave, where is thy victory?' My hope, Companion Adoniram, rests in that Higher Lodge to which I am advancing; but when I die the Word will be buried there. Ah!! What have I said, what done? More than I ought, I fear. Still, I rely on your secrecy and fidelity as a Craftsman. Assure me that my trust will not be in vain.

Adoniram: *I assure you.*

4th If you are a student of Freemasonry in general, and its many associated and appendant Degrees, you will hear from time to time, a word that you are unfamiliar with. One such word is 'Heredom', for example: Rose Croix of Heredom or The Heredom of Kilwinning.

The etymology or meaning of the word is actually lost, but that does not mean that many have put forward fanciful and varying definitions. Here is a list of the more popular definitions I have found:

From Herodium, a castle built by Herod
From Highrodiam, a Masonic Degree practised at Gateshead in 1746
From Harodim
From the Greek *hieros* (holy) and *domos* (a house)
From the Latin word hoeredum, meaning heritage
From Heroden, the name of a mountain in Scotland

Whatever the term means, when used in association with Masonic Degrees it implies, 'Rulers or High Masonic Dignitaries'.

5th The Degrees we practice under the jurisdiction of various Grand Lodges, Conclaves, Councils and Encampments, are recognised as being regular. There are however, several quasi- or pseudo-Masonic bodies admitting men and women, which although honourable, are deemed irregular and not recognised. Among them we find Co-Masonry, the Order of the Eastern Star and the Order of the Mechanics.

As Freemasons under the United Grand Lodge of England and its associated Orders, we are positively discouraged from fraternising with these groups or attending meetings on any pretext, and such attendance or involvement with them can place our own membership in jeopardy.

If you intend visiting an unknown lodge, particularly while on holiday, please ensure you discuss your planned visit with your lodge Secretary who will give you concise instruction and correct advice as to its regularity or if it is recognised by Grand Lodge.

6th Records regarding the early days of Freemasonry are not only sparse but often unreliable and as that great Masonic scholar Harry Carr would infer, that as much of our proceedings were based on secrecy, so any published material of the late 17th or early 18th century must always be viewed with suspicion, as the author would generally be looking for monetary gain.

Similarly, the reliability of Anderson's minutes of the formation of Grand Lodge has also caused some concern. Written some six years after the alleged formation of Grand Lodge, we are, as many historians agree, reliant on a second-hand version of events, as it is believed that Anderson was not actually present at the formations meeting.

In these minutes, which we are all familiar with, Anderson tells us that there were four lodges that met at the Apple Tree Tavern to choose a Grand Master and to form a Grand Lodge, *pro-Tempore in due form*.

Forty years later in 1763, a book entitled *The Complete Freemason or Multa Paucis for lovers of Secrets*, stated that there was six lodges, not four, that took part in the meeting.

There is in fact, no real evidence to suggest either record is accurate;

however as with most things, we weigh up the information and form our own opinion.

7th The words, 'It proves a slip' is a phrase that has survived from early Masonic documents, but appears to allude to a theme, which seems to have disappeared from our ritual. The original theme was death, decay or corruption, and resurrection; nowadays we concentrate on the first and the last.

Looking at the old references we find the following:

Graham MS (1726) says:
'…takeing a greip att a finger it came away so from Joynt so to the wrest so to Elbow…so one said here is yet marrow in this bone…'

Prichard's *Masonry Dissected* (1730), says:
'...when Hiram was taken up, they took him by the Forefingers, and the Skin came off, which is called the Slip...'

'Le Catechisme des Francs Macons,' (1742), says:
'…one of them took hold of the body by a finger, and it came away in his hand. Another did the same...and then taking him by the wrist it came away...he cried out...which signifies among the Masons 'The flesh falls from the Bones'.

L'Ordre des Francs-macons Trahi, 1745, says:
'La chair quitte les os, ou le corps est corrompu...' (The fresh parts from the bones or the corpse is rotten.)

Masonic historians strongly argue that there is a mnemonic link between the first part of the Master Mason's words and the terms 'Marrow in the bone' or 'rotten to the bone'.

8th With the exception of the Craft system, the Royal Order of Scotland is by far one of the oldest Orders as evidence suggests that the Order was practised in London as early as 1741. Using a charter granted him in The Hague, William Mitchell set up the Order in Edinburgh in about 1753 and in July 1767, this body was later to become the Grand Lodge of the Royal Order of Scotland.

Interestingly, their history tells how the King of Scots was the hereditary Grand Master and a seat is kept vacant for him at all Provincial and Grand Lodge meetings. Unlike the Craft system, the Order has no private lodges as the Provincial Grand Lodge is the lowest tier of the organisation. Today there are some eighty-eight Provinces in many parts of the world.

Membership is highly prized as it is by invitation only and each Candidate must have been a Master Mason for at least five years. The Order offers two Degrees which are the Heredom of Kilwinning and Knighthood of the Rosy Cross.

9th English records suggest that Accepted Freemasonry has been practised since the late 16th century but according to Anderson by the early 18th century, the Craft had been sorely neglected.

However, the late 17th and early 18th centuries saw the development of Gentlemen's Clubs and these may well have formed the basis for the so-called revival in 1717.

At the time, *The Spectator* told its readers that:

> *...little nocturnal assemblies founded upon eating and drinking where men are thus knit by a love of Society, not a spirit of faction, and do not meet to censure and annoy those that are absent, but to enjoy one another...there may be something very useful in these little institutions and establishments.*

These clubs, like the early lodges, met in ale-houses and coffee shops and we must consider ourselves fortunate, as without these early clubs, Freemasonry may well have remained permanently neglected.

10th At the turn of the 19th century, the Grand Lodge according to the Ancients accepted the idea of reconciliation and drew back from the position it had held and after sixty-three years of bitter resentment, sought amends. In the same vein, the Grand Lodge, daubed the Moderns, also saw wisdom in the same.

The reconciliation took place on St John's Day, 27 December 1813, at Freemasons' Hall, where both Grand Lodges filed in, side by side, and clasped hands across the altar.

At that point, the Articles of Union were read and the Duke of Kent, who was Grand Master of the Ancients, retired, and the Duke of Sussex who was Grand Master of the Moderns was duly elected as Grand Master of the United Grand Lodge of England.

Both Dukes were blood brothers, being sons of reigning monarch George III, and the rest? The rest, shall we say, is history and since that date the Craft has grown to the position in society that we see today.

11th There are five main Scottish Statutes and Charters, which help us understand the development of the Masons trade in Scotland. These are:

The Seal of Cause, 1475
The Schaw Statutes, 1598
The Schaw Statutes, 1599
The Sinclair Charter, 1601
The Sinclair Charter, 1628

There is a general belief that non-operative Freemasonry developed first in Scotland, however there is little evidence to suggest this.

It is a fact that individual lodge records have existed in Scotland since the 17th century, and this is earlier than any lodge we have in England. However this only goes to prove that the admittance of non-operative masons in their lodges was actually later than the admittance of Accepted Masons in England.

12th Can you recall when you were made a Fellowcraft and stood in the south-east part of the lodge and the Worshipful Master informed you that in the previous Degree, you were '...acquainted with the principles of Moral Truth and Virtue...'?

What exactly were the principles of you were acquainted with?

Briefly, moral truth means that we know that something is right or wrong, whereas virtue relates to us using that knowledge to ensure we actually do what we know to be right.

Both can be brought together under the heading of ethics. Ethics is fundamentally related to what kind of person we ought to be, or strive to become. There is a definite link between what kind of person or character we are, and the moral character and virtue we show. We can think of one's moral character as primarily a function of whether we have, or lack, various moral virtues and vices.

The virtues or vices that make our moral character are typically understood as dispositions to behave in certain ways. For instance, an honest person is disposed to telling the truth when asked, but we are unlikely to think that an individual, who tells the truth to his friends, but consistently lies to his wife or parents, possesses the virtue of honesty.

Our understanding of moral truth and virtue or the application of ethics in our daily lives is based upon what society accepts, and as we are encouraged to regulate our actions by the divine precepts of the V. of S.L. and to be exemplary in the discharge of our civil duties, so we already have knowledge of the principles of Moral Truth and Virtue.

However, knowledge and actions are two different things; the true Freemasonry is one who having knowledge of the definition of acceptable behaviour, applies that knowledge, without hesitation, to his daily actions.

13th Here are just a few observations regarding the changing of Tracing Boards.

Generally speaking, it is the Junior Deacon who has the responsibility to change the Tracing Board for the opening and closing of each Degree. This does however differ depending upon lodge custom.

During the Installation, when the office of Junior Deacon has been vacated, the responsibility for changing the Tracing Board will fall upon the Director of Ceremonies or his assistant.

It is permissible to present the Second-Degree Tracing Board without allowing the Candidate to restore himself to his personal comforts, although not advisable.

In many lodges, members are expected to stand during the explanation of the Second Degree Tracing Board, in strict Emulation it is insisted upon.

The exact time for the Deacon to leave his seat and change the Tracing Board in any Degree is when the Junior Warden has finished speaking and sounded his gavel.

However, as with all matters of Masonic etiquette, local usages, customs and traditions are strictly adhered to and in many cases there are no rights or wrongs. Needless to say, the main objective of the ritual, ceremony and perambulations is that they should be carried out with the dignity due to the office, and with decorum and solemnity.

14th The five orders of architecture were identified as early as 1562, in a book by Giacomo Barozzi da Vignola, who wrote about classical architecture.

The book identifies the five orders as Tuscan, Doric, Ionic, Corinthian and Composite with each part subdivided into other parts, all illustrating the styles of the colonnade arcade, arcade with pedestal, individual pedestal, entablatures and capitals.

Joseph Gwilt in *The Encyclopaedia of Architecture* explains the term 'order', thus:

> 'An Order in architecture is a certain assemblage of parts subject to uniform established proportions, regulated by the office that each part has to perform'.

The origins of the five orders are thus:

> The Doric order originated on the mainland and western Greece and is the simplest of the orders.
>
> The Ionic order came from eastern Greece and its origins are

entwined with the little known, Aeolic order.

The Corinthian order is the most ornate of the Greek orders and is characterised by the slender fluted column with ornate capitals decorated with two rows of acanthus leaves and four scrolls.

It was the Romans that adapted all the Greek orders and developed two others, which were modifications of the Greek orders, but they were not named or formalised as Tuscan and Composite, until the Renaissance period. Therefore, the Tuscan order was a very plain design, with a plain shaft, a simple capital, base, and frieze, and the Composite order is a mixed order, combining the volutes of the Ionic with the leaves of the Corinthian order.

15th Along with the advent of the paper dining table cover, which has replaced the more traditional table cloth, a new art form has developed, namely, table writing. The most popular practitioners of this skill seem to be those brethren whom it has been seen fit, to give a few moments notice that he has been cordially invited to reply to a toast. Having said that, the expertise is also practised by those whom while not having the ability to express a point phonetically, take to the pen and express their point diagrammatically.

Whatever their origins, my studies have found that the second most popular mark bears all the attributes of a financial nature, possible the evenings raffle takings, while diagrams of roads and streets, all with directional arrows, appear to take a close third place. Representations of Craft and Chapter fire take the fourth spot and are always found in the same area, that where the Initiate or newly Exalted Companion sits.

The fifth place goes to personal names. One lodge I know never posts a seating plan or produces named place cards at the table. Upon arrival at the meeting place and prior to the proper business of the evening, they head for the dining quarters or mess area and immediately proceed to select their seating point by writing their name at that place. When only one Brother arrives at a time, this custom can be carried out in a rather sober fashion. However, one can imagine the melee caused by several brethren seeking the best vantage point at the same time.

The final placing is reserved for building-related topics, such as: electrical circuits, plumbing diagrams and groundwork plans. One could almost assume at times that their respective Festive Boards are akin to the site meeting.

But, whatever the reasons for this new and rather unusual pastime, I salute my fellow brethren for the ingenuity they possess in recording such information. However, I pass on a salutary warning; the caterers and waiting staff are on to you, beware not to record anything offensive to them, lest your dinner may end up in your lap!

16th

If early Masonic history teaches us anything, I recently stumbled upon a way we can keep the cost of our Festive Board to a minimum. In 1752, two alleged Freemasons, named Thomas Phealon and John Macky, initiated many a man on the production of a joint of meat.

Known as the 'leg of mutton' Masons, they had their membership withdrawn, but in fact they were not Masons at all. However, in these days of spiralling costs, it might be worth giving the matter some consideration.

Of course, this type of profiteering in Freemasonry was not new and was somewhat similar to a poster seen in a London ale-house at the same time which read, 'Masons made here - 2/6d'. (12 ½p)

17th

The Royal Order of Scotland confers two Degrees:

The Heredom of Kilwinning

This Degree, so tradition tells us, originated during the reign of King David and it depicts Freemasonry in purely the Christian aspect. The Obligation is fascinating from the aspect that it is in rhyming verse, which apart from the serious nature of any Obligation, is rather quaint. Much of the other ritual is catechetical in style, based around the Craft lectures, but also alludes to certain elements in other Degrees. The Degree culminates in the Candidate being sent forth to seek the lost word.

Knighthood of the Rosy Cross

This Degree, we are told, was instituted by King Robert the Bruce just after his famous victory at Bannockburn, in 1314. It commemorates the Knights and Masons that had assisted him in the battle. The ceremony reaches its climax with the teachings of the secret doctrine of the life and death of the Saviour, Jesus Christ. It is believed that the ceremony is that once practised by the ancient Order of the Thistle.

18th According to Masonic historian Lionel Vibert:

> *The Grand Lodge that was brought into existence in 1717 did not find it necessary to possess a Constitution of its own for some years. Exactly what went on between 1717 and 1721 we do not know; almost our only authority being the account given by Anderson in 1738 which is unreliable in many particulars.*

According to Anderson's *Constitutions* of 1738, this is his version of how the events that lead to that date took place; written retrospectively, nineteen years after that date:

> *King George I, enter'd London most magnificently on 20 Sept. 1714 and after the Rebellion was over A.D. 1716. the few Lodges at London finding themselves neglected by Sir Christopher Wren, thought fit to cement under a Grand Master as the Centre of Union and Harmony, viz. the lodges that met,*
>
> *1. At the Goose and Gridiron Ale-house in St. Paul's Church-Yard.*
>
> *2. At the Crown Ale-house in Parker-Lane near Drury-Lane.*
>
> *3. At the Apple-Tree Tavern in Charles Street, Covent-Garden.*

4. At the Rummer and Grapes Tavern in Channel-Row, Westminster

They and some old Brothers met at the said Apple-Tree, and having put into the Chair the oldest Master Mason (now the Master of the Lodge) they constituted themselves a Grand Lodge pro Tempore in Due Form, and forthwith revived the Quarterly Communication of the Officers and Lodges (call'd Grand Lodge) resolv'd to hold the Annual Assembly and Feast, and then to chuse a Grand Master from among themselves, till they should have the honour of a Noble Brother at their Head.

Accordingly.

On St John Baptist's Day, in the 3^d^ Year of King George I A.D. 1717 the ASSEMBLY and Feast of the Free and accepted Masons was held at the foresaid Goose and Gridiron Ale-House.

Before Dinner, the oldest Master Mason (now Master of a Lodge) in the Chair, proposed a List of proper Candidates; and Brethren by a Majority of Hands elected Mr. Anthony Sayer Gentleman, Grand Master of Masons, Capt. Joseph Elliot, Mr. Jacob Lamball Carpenter, Grand Wardens, who being forthwith invested with Badges of Office and Power by the said oldest Master, and install'd, was duly congratulated by the Assembly who pay'd him Homage.

19th There are several types of columns and pillars referred to in Masonic teaching; this section deals with the 'Pillars of Enoch'.

In Masonic lore, the outer pillars of the Temple are often referred to as the Pillars of Enoch. Enoch, being aware that Adam predicted 'that the world was to be destroyed at one time by the force of fire, and at another time by the violence and quantity of water' (Flavius Josephus *Antiquities*, 1.2:3), feared the principles of the Liberal Arts and Sciences might be lost. His son Seth caused two pillars to be made, one of brick, the other of stone, (various other documents refer to other materials being used) and they inscribed their discoveries on them both, that in case the pillar of brick should be destroyed by the flood, the pillar of stone might remain, and exhibit those discoveries to mankind. The story of the Pillars became enshrined in Masonic teachings through the second earliest Masonic MS.

> *...knowing of that vengeance, that God would send, whether it should be by fire, or by water, the brethren had it not by a manner of a prophecy that God would send there, therefore they wrote their sciences on the two pillars of stone, and some men say that they wrote in the stones all the seven sciences, but as they had in their minds that a vengeance should come. And so it was that God sent vengeance so that there came such a flood that all the world was drowned, and all men were dead therein, save eight persons...and many years after this flood, as the chronicle telleth, these two* pillars were *found...'*
>
> The Matthew Cooke Manuscript c.1450 (Modern Translation)

20th In the explanation of the Second-Degree Tracing Board we are told the following:

Those Pillars were further adorned with two spherical balls on which were delineated maps of the celestial and terrestrial globes, pointing out Masonry Universal.

I have three problems with this statement:

In **I Kings 7:41 we read that:** 'The two pillars, and the two bowls of the chapiters that were on the top of the two pillars; and the two networks, to cover the two bowls of the chapiters which were upon the top of the pillars'. The Volume of Sacred Law explains that the 'spherical balls' were in fact 'bowls'.

The second issue is that there were maps of the celestial

and terrestrial globes delineated on those balls. Of course, there were no known such terrestrial maps when King Solomon's Temple was build.

The third point is that Masonry at that time was not universal and did not exist.

This all goes to show that our Traditional History is not historically accurate but written to highlight salient points of our discipline.

21st Bristol became the centre of a series of Degrees known as the Rite of Seven Degrees with Time Immemorial status, one of those being the Baldwyn Rite. With the earliest records dating from 1780, it was not until 1791, that the well-known Freemason Thomas Dunckerley, who was the Provincial Grand Master of Bristol and also the Grand Master of the Templars, issued a Warrant allowing brethren to hold a conclave at Bristol.

At the death of the Duke of Sussex, in 1843, the Grand Conclave of England, which oversaw the Knights Templar and the Degree of Rose Croix, of which the latter passed to the Supreme Council 33°, sought to bring the Degree under their supervision, but the brethren of Bristol declined. After some negotiation, in 1862, Bristol was established as the Provincial Commandery, known today as the Provincial Priory.

By 1884, a further Treaty of Union with the Supreme Council 33°, constituted Bristol with its own Inspector General and ritual. Today it is only practised in the Masonic Province of Bristol.

22nd The Degrees of the Rite of Baldwyn of Seven Degrees Time Immemorial are as follows:

I° the Three Craft Degrees: These form the first Degree.

II° the Supreme Order of the Holy Royal Arch: This forms the Second Degree, but must be received through a Bristol

Chapter which incorporates the ceremony of 'Passing the Veils'.

III° Knights of the Nine Elected Masters: The Degree being revived in 1934.

IV° Scots Knights Grand Architect and Scots Knights of Kilwinning: This Templar Degree was revived in 1921

V° Knight of the East and Sword of the Eagle: This Degree was revived in 1934, but it is believed that it was original introduced from France in 1813.

VI° Knights of St John of Jerusalem, Palestine, Rhodes and Malta, and Knights Templar: As can be gathered by the title, this Degree has a strong Templar influence.

VII° Knights of the Rose Croix of Mount Carmel: The most interesting and fascinating culmination of the Degrees.

23rd

The phrase 'darkness visible', as found in the Third Degree Charge, 'Let me now beg you to observe that the Light of a Master Mason is darkness visible…', first appeared in Milton's *Paradise Lost*:

A dungeon horrible on all sides round
As one great furnace flam'd, yet from those flames
No light, but rather darkness visible
Serv'd only to discover sights of woe.

Milton commenced his work in 1658, when he was already blind, and the somber gloom of these lines may well be contrasted with the many beautiful passages in which the poet was able to conjure up in his visions of light; words which seem to acquire a greater strength and majesty because of the perpetual darkness in which he lived.

The same phrase was used, far less effectively, by Alexander Pope, in *The Dunciad*, and Gilbert White, in his *Natural History of Selborne*. However, in 1952, the Rev. Walton Hannah chose the term as the title for his much publicised book, which was a Christian appraisal of Freemasonry.

24th Have you ever noticed that in some lodges, the Inner Guard gives the knocks of the Degree on his sleeve when the Candidate retires, and the lodge is opened in a higher Degree?

This is primarily to ensure that the Candidate is not privy to factors of a higher Degree or the Degree he is about to receive prior to his Obligation. Therefore, although the Inner Guard will give the knocks of the current Degree on his sleeve, the Tyler will give the knocks of the former Degree on the lodge door, indicating that a Candidate of that lower Degree seeks entry for further progress in the higher Degree.

However, where tradition dictates, a single knock is often used by the Tyler in all Degrees for the entry of a Candidate.

25th The York MS No.1, dated as 1600, like the Regius Poem and Matthew Cooke MS, contains the legendary history of the Craft and Charges for both Mason and fellows. Its provenance is claimed by an endorsement on the back of one of its pages which says, 'Found in Pontefract Castle at the demolishing and given to the York Lodge by Francis Drake in 1732'. Drake's father and grandfather were both vicars of Pontefract. His grandfather was also a Royalist, who was in the town when the castle surrendered and when it was demolished in 1649.

The handwriting confirms its date, and what certainly marks it out as an item for more than just working craftsmen is the distinctive introduction which reads:

An Anagraime upon the name of Masonrie
William Kay to his friend Robt Preston
upon his Artt of Masonrie as Followeth:'
There then follows a play on letters of the word MASONRIE.
M *uch might be said of the of noble artt*
A *Craft that's worth esteeming in each part*
S *undry Nations Noobles & their Kings also*
O *h how they fought its worth to know*
N *imrod & Solomon the wisest of all men*
R *eason saw to love this Science then*

I le say no more lest by my shallow verse I
E ndeavouring to praise should blemish Masonrie.

So who were William Kay and Robert Preston? Sadly, there are no records in existence from any lodge or group as to show who this document may have belonged, but the two persons mentioned at the introduction of the MS were definitely connected with York, as there are two Freemen with their names: William Kay was accepted as a Spurrier in 1569 and Robert Preston was accepted as a Fishmonger in 1571.

If, therefore, these contemporaries were the actual men linked with the anagram, then we have firm evidence that these persons, who were not operative masons, were associated with, and involved in, an organisation which concerned itself with 'Masonrie' and therefore become the first instance of the membership of non-operative members in England and Scotland.

26th What is Freemasonry? Freemasonry is not a charity, but it teaches men to be charitable and exhorts them to use their best endeavours to relieve the wants of the necessitous.

Freemasonry is not a religion, but it encourages men to honour their creator in the rites and practices of whatever Church he follows and that he should never be an irreligious libertine.

Freemasonry is not a service organisation, but it teaches its members that to be of service to one's fellow creature, is possibly the highest ideal to which we can aspire.

Freemasonry is not a political organisation, but it teaches us to be observant of the laws of the country, which from time to time provides us with a residence and a due respect for that land which gave us our infant nurture.

Freemasonry is not a publicity organisation; instead it teaches us that to seek clamorously after rewards will do little for us in the long run.

Freemasonry is not a social society, but its precepts will tend to equip

Freemasons with an ability to relate to and understand his fellow man to the benefit of all.

Freemasonry is a system or morality, veiled in allegory and illustrated by symbols.

Is that the Freemasonry you know, love and practice?

27th You are familiar with the question, 'Where were you first prepared to be made a Mason?' and you answered, 'In my heart'.

This is a perfectly reasonably response; for as we labour to meet the needs and desires of our heart, this is where each Mason should first feel the desire to join our fellowship. In a similar manner, as the heart is that life-giving organ, which we singularly pledge so carefully to our loved ones, so this pledge to Masonry is both sincere and true.

Therefore, it is our heart that we should open to prepare to receive the wonderful gift of brotherhood.

28th Pendent to the corners of the lodge room carpet, are four tassels, these are meant to remind us of the four cardinal virtues, namely: Temperance, Fortitude, Prudence, and Justice, the whole of which, tradition informs us, were constantly practiced by a great majority of our ancient brethren.

Here we examine Justice. In Latin, Justice is pronounced *Justina*, meaning to act righteous, equitable, even-handed and fair. In visual art it is often portrayed as a blindfolded female carrying a scale in one hand and a broken sword in the other.

The Emulation Lectures of the Three Degrees explain Justice thus:

> *Justice - Is that station or boundary of right, by which we are taught to render to every man his just due, and that without distinction. This virtue is not only consistent with the Divine and human Law, but is the standard and cement of civil society.*

Without the exercise of this Virtue, universal confusion would ensure, lawless force would overcome the principles of equity, and social intercourse no longer exist; and as justice in a great measure constitutes the really good man, so it ought to be the invariable practice of every Free and Accepted Mason never to deviate from the minutest principles thereof, ever having in mind the time he was placed at the North East part of the Lodge, feet formed in a square, body erect, when he received that excellent injunction from the Worshipful Master to be just and upright in all things; alluding to the Pedal.

First Lecture, Sixth Section Six

Justice is the cornerstone of Freemasonry, the standard on which it rests, the boundary in which it lives. It is a virtue consistent with Divine and human law and is the cement that supports civil society. It symbolises equality to the Freemason, who would treat others as he himself would be treated, that is without deception and he should undertake actions because he desires to, and not because he is forced to, thereby his actions are unselfish and self-sacrificing.

Therefore, each Freemason should govern his own actions by justice and be prepared to have his actions judged by the same standard of moral principles that have determined his own conduct.

29th The Noble Order of Corks is a universally known informal Degree, allied to Freemasonry with its principle aim being to raise funds mainly for children's charities. Nobody is too sure where the ritual originated but it has a distinct nautical feel based around Noah and the Flood. It has a satirical approach and is purposely humorous but honest it its endeavours. All Companions of the Holy Royal Arch, Past Masters, Masters and Wardens are eligible to join.

Candidates can be proposed and initiated on the same night and dress is informal, but includes a hat; the sillier the better. Meetings are considered boisterous affairs.

The presiding Officer is known as the Rather Worshipful Admiral supported by a range of Officers with names like, Hardly Worshipful Lookout, Barely Worshipful Cook and Mainly Worshipful Bosun to name but three.

Apparently, the meetings are characterised by the practice of ridiculous or humorous fines, levied against individuals or those present, all of which is donated to charity.

30th Examining the reasons why 18th century men would join Freemasonry, I found that at the time there was an interest in antiquity.

Sir William Dugdale believed that Freemasonry derived from a company of Italian masons in the time of Henry III and who had been commissioned by the Pope to travel across Europe building cathedrals and churches.

Elias Ashmole, whose third wife was the daughter of Dugdale, and is a name to which you are all familiar with, collected much historical material pertaining to the building of Windsor Castle.

While Randle Holme clearly states in his famous work *Accademie of Armory* (1688), 'I cannot but honor the Fellowship of the Masons because of its antiquity…'

31st Without a doubt, the early Craft ceremonies were of a definite Christian character and there were many references to God, Jesus, and the Trinity etc. When Anderson was instructed to prepare the 1723 *Constitutions*, it was evidently decided that if the Craft had anything to offer mankind, it should be available to all who 'Believed in the Glorious Architect of Heaven and Earth' and should not be restricted to Christians alone.

The first Charge, therefore, concerning God and religion, reads:

> *A Mason is oblig'd, by his Tenure, to obey the moral Law; and if he rightly understands the Art, he will never be a stupid Atheist,*

> *nor an irreligious Libertine. But though in ancient Times Masons were charg'd in every Country to be of the Religion of that Country or Nation, whatever it was, yet 'tis now thought more expedient only to oblige them to that Religion in which all Men agree, leaving their particular Opinions to themselves; that is, to be good Men and true, or Men of Honour and Honesty, by whatever Denominations or Persuasions they may be distinguished; whereby Masonry becomes the Center of Union, and the Means of conciliating true Friendship among Persons that must have remain'd at a perpetual Distance.*

One will never know why certain Christian elements escaped this revision.

June

1st Lecture Two, Section Five gives us a wonderful explanation of the moral advantages of Geometry.

Geometry, the first and noblest of sciences, is the basis on which the superstructure of Masonry is erected. By Geometry we may curiously trace nature through her various windings to her most concealed recesses.

By it we may discover the power, wisdom, and goodness of the Grand Geometrician of the Universe, and view with amazing delight the beautiful proportions which connect and grace this vast machine.

By it we may discover how the planets move in their different orbits, and mathematically demonstrate their various revolutions.

By it we may rationally account for the return of seasons, and the mixed variety of scenes which each season produces to the discerning eye. Numberless worlds are around us, all formed by the same Divine artist, which roll through the vast expanse, and are conducted by the same, unerring law of nature.

While such objects engage our attention, how must we improve, and with what grand ideas must such knowledge fill our minds! It was a survey of nature, and an observation of her beautiful proportions, which first induced men to imitate the Divine plan, and study symmetry and order. This gave rise to society, and birth to every useful art.

The architect began to design and the plans which he laid down having been improved by time and experience, have produced some of those excellent works which have been the admiration every age.

2nd One of the regular questions asked by the lodge interviewing committee to the prospective Candidate is what reasons he has for wanting joining Freemasonry?

It is here at the interview stage that one can really ascertain the interviewee's motives and it is absolutely crucial that the Candidate understands from the beginning that Freemasonry is an organisation that you bring something to, rather than take something from.

Freemasonry is not meant to benefit you, your family or your business, financially, or in any other way; nor is it intended to give you an advantage over others. Freemasonry is about serving others in the lodge and the community in general, it all of its many forms.

The Candidate's response to this question must reflect that understanding or the committee is quite at liberty to suggest the Candidate's entry be deferred to a later date or until he understands the ethos of the Craft.

3rd I notice that occasionally, our newer members get a little confused as to the process for, or reasoning behind, the Notice of Motion. Firstly, a Notice of Motion, in respect of Freemasonry, is when a Brother gives formal notice, to all members and in open lodge, that he will propose a certain action at the next scheduled meeting.

The Notice of Motion is printed on the Agenda and minuted so that all subscribing members are made aware that a formal Motion will be presented at the next meeting.

Some simple rules of etiquette are:

1) No discussion takes place, at this stage with regard to the Notice of Motion.
2) A Notice of Motion does not need a Seconder, or a vote by those subscribing members present.
3) It is not necessary for the Brother giving the Notice of Motion to give anything more than the bear minimum, as time will be allowed to discuss the Motion fully at the next meeting.

4) At the next meeting, the Motion can be debated and will need a Seconder. It will be accepted or declined by the Members present in the usual manner accepted among Freemasons.

On a final note, any Notice of Motion should be discussed, agreed and accepted by the Worshipful Master, through the Lodge Secretary, prior to any Notice being given. This will ensure the prudence of the Motion and maintain the harmony of the lodge.

4th

The origins of the Masonic and Military Order of the Red Cross of Constantine and the Orders of the Holy Sepulchre and of St John the Evangelist, often simply referred to as Red Cross of Constantine, are quite obscure. In Masonic terms, 'Red Cross', was mentioned as early as 1813, but it would be fair to say there were many groups using the same title with differing legends and rituals.

An exposure published in 1825, bears a close resemblance to the ritual used today, however, it was not until the late 19th century that the Order really began to take root thanks to the work of R. W. Little, W. H. White and W. J. Hughan. Today it has over three hundred conclaves on the roll of the Grand Imperial Conclave.

The legend is based around the Roman Emperor, Constantine, who after the death of his father was hailed by the Legions in York as Augustus and became the Governor of Britain and Gaul.

After several successful battles in Europe, he established himself as the Emperor of both the East and West Roman Empires transferring the capital of the empire from Rome to Byzantium, later to be named after him. He also openly encouraged Christianity and his conversion happened after he saw a sign from heaven, as the rays of the setting sun formed a shaft of light in the form of a cross.

After his conversion, he made a standard bearing a Cross and ordered it to be carried before him in the wars. His success on the battlefield continued and with the help of his chief Bishop, Eusebius, who formed a

Conclave of the Knights of the Order who became the bodyguard of their Sovereign.

One must be a Master Mason and Companion of the Holy Royal Arch to qualify for membership.

5th Mackey's *Encyclopaedia of Masonry* states that Napoleon Bonaparte was initiated in Malta in 1798. However, other historians claim that his movements indicate that it was unlikely that he was in Malta at that time.

In his book entitled, *Notes to serve as a history of Freemasonry at Nancy up to 1805*, Bro. Bernadin, a Past Master of a lodge in Nancy, records the following which was taken from an older work entitled, *Collection des sceaux de Lorraine* by M. Noel, which dates the following visit as 3 December 1797.

> *We remember having had in hand the engraved plate which proves that General Bonaparte, passing through Nancy after having signed the treaty of Campo Formio, visited the Lodge and, although but a Master Mason, was received with all honours possible…*

Bro. Bernadin also writes:

> *I cannot doubt the assertion of the celebrated historian of Lorraine, as he himself a Freemason, and a member of St John of Jerusalem Lodge, and could very well have had in his hands the plate to which he alludes, and have received an account of the visit from the mouths of those who assisted at it.*

Historians can confirm that Napoleon was indeed, at Nancy on that given date.

6th In the old MSS, exposures and lodge minutes, the role of the Entered Apprentices, Fellow Craftsman and Masters are not quite what we know today. For example, the degree of the Entered Apprentice and I will use modern day terminology to ensure we understand, was conferred upon all joining or accepted members, as was the degree of a Fellowcraft.

However, confusion arises because in the early days the terms Master and Master Mason were the same and were conferred only upon those who were to be Master of the lodge and then this was only done at Grand Lodge. It is at this point we can get confused with the language; a Brother was passed a Master as was an Entered Apprentice passed a Fellowcraft.

Hence, we read in the Haughfoot Minutes (1704), John Hoppringle should continue as Master till St John's Day next, which obviously means he should stay in the Chair until then. However, at York in 1725 at least three brethren were referred to in their minutes simply as Masters. At Dumbarton in 1726, Gabriel Porterfield, a Fellowcraft was unanimously admitted and received a Master of the Fraternity.

We do not read the word 'raising' before 1737, but what we do read is 'making' 'admitting', 'receiving' and even 'passing' masons. This confuses us in terms of 'past' and 'passed'. To complete the picture or even rather confusion, in the 2nd Edition of *Preston's Illustrations of Masonry* (1775), the author talks about the Initiation of a Master Mason.

Is it any wonder that Masonic historians can make no hard or fast statements about the origins of our tri-gradal-system of ritual?

7th It is believed that the three words, 'hele,' 'conceal' and 'reveal,' used in our ritual were meant to rhyme and two old recordings of the word by Chaucer, are used as an illustration.

A felowe that can wel concele,
And Kepe thy counsel and wel hele
(*Romaunt of the Rose*, c. 1360s)

But that tale is nat worth a rake-stele [a rake handle],
Pardee we wommen conne no thing hele
(*Wife of Bath's Tale*, 1380)

The late Bro. Bernard E. Jones suggested that if the original intent is to be maintained, they should be pronounced to rhyme, whether with 'heel' or 'hail'. But, if they are to be intelligible, then the old pronunciation 'hail' is quite out of the question. 'Hale, consale and never revale' would either be meaningless, or would invite a smile at a point in the ceremony where least desired.

Bro. E. H. Cartwright believes it should be pronounced 'heel' and that if a Master likes to affect the archaic form of the word, 'he should at least be consistent and say, 'hale, consale and never revale' thus preserving the jingle that with little doubt had its attraction for our predecessors of two hundred years ago.

Bro. Harry Carr is also inclined to support the pronunciation 'heel' given in the *Oxford English Dictionary*. He says we use an archaic word, out of sentiment perhaps, and explains he sees no reason for maintaining the archaic pronunciation.

The word 'hele' may be sounded 'heel' or 'hail', but if we are to preserve the original sentiment, then 'hele,' 'conceal' and 'reveal' should rhyme with 'heel' and not 'hail'.

8th The form of the lodge, which is a regular *parallelepipedon*, in length from East to West in breadth between North and South, in depth from the surface of the earth to the centre, and even as high as the heavens. The reason that a Freemason's lodge is described of this vast extent is to show the universality in the science; likewise, a Mason's charity should know no bounds save those of prudence.

In geometry, a parallelepiped is a three-dimensional figure formed by six parallelograms (the term rhomboid is also sometimes used with this meaning).

9th There are three distinguishing characteristics found in the breast of every good Freemason, these are Virtue, Honour and Mercy. With regard to Mercy, we are taught:

Mercy is a refined virtue, and when possessed by the monarch, adds lustre to every gem that adorns his crown; if by the warrior, it gives an unceasing freshness to the wreath that shades his brow. It is the companion of true honour, and the ameliorator of justice, on whose bench, when enthroned, it interposes a shield of defence on behalf of the victim, impenetrable to the sword. And as the vernal showers descend on the earth, to refresh and invigorate the whole vegetable creation, so mercy, acting on the heart, when the vital fluids are condensed by rancour and revenge, by its exhilarating warmth returns nature to its source in purer streams. It is the peculiar attribute of the Deity, on which the best and wisest of us must rest our hopes and dependence; for at the final day of retribution, when arraigned at His bar, and the actions of this mortal life are unveiled to view, though His justice may demand the fiat, we hope and trust His Mercy will avert the doom.

10th Many non-Freemasons often ask the question: 'Is Freemasonry a Religion?' From a statement adopted by Grand Lodge on 12 September 1962, and re-issued in the Extracts from the proceedings of the Quarterly Communications of Grand Lodge of 9 December 1981, we read the following:

> *It cannot be too strongly asserted that masonry is neither a religion nor a substitute for religion. Masonry seeks to inculcate in its members a standard of conduct and behaviour which it believes to be acceptable to all creeds, but studiously refrains from intervening in the field of dogma or theology. Masonry therefore, is not a competitor with religion though in the sphere of human conduct it may be hoped that its teachings will be complimentary to that of religion. On the other hand its basic requirement that every member of the Order shall believe in a Supreme Being and the stress laid upon his duty towards Him should be sufficient evidence to all but the wilfully prejudiced that masonry is an upholder of religion since it both requires a man to have some form of religious belief before he can be admitted as*

a Mason, and expects him when admitted to go on practising his religion.

11th Just like people, each lodge has its own personality and it is fair to say this is one of the reasons that make Freemasonry so fascinating. This individuality is often so apparent that one can be at a different meeting in the same lodge room where the whole ritual workings or Masonic paraphernalia used are entirely different. Unfortunately, it is tragic to think that unless each lodge has an archivist, which as we know there is no such office; nobody appears to know how these practices originated or unless recorded in the minutes, who donated the equipment. Very occasionally, an elderly Brother may recall a tale or two from his memory, but living memory soon fades and this precious information, if not committed to paper, is often lost forever.

I recall one evening when an elderly Brother delivered to a packed lodge room, a presentation of a Grand Lodge certificate. Every Brother there that night would have wished it was he that were receiving that certificate for the elderly Brother was articulate, informative and humorous and his words would have stayed with many of those present.

At a later point, I asked the Brother for a copy of his presentation whereupon he indicated that it was 'off the cuff'. I then suggested that I record the presentation on another night, for which I am sad to say he declined.

The point being made is that this presentation will only stay in the living memory of those present and when this Brother is called to the Grand Lodge above, all will be lost. How sad to think that there will be no record of this wonderful presentation other than a few words of thanks in the lodge minute book, which would hardly have done it justice.

Maybe the time has come for you to consider the prospect of detailing the origin of your lodge practices before they are lost in time.

12th The one major problem facing us when we study early ritual documents is quite simple, as the core principle of Freemasonry is, and always has been, secrecy and fidelity; we must ask ourselves why they were written in the first place?

Students quickly establish, with the help of modern-day commentaries, the difference between each document and are able to establish those, for example, that were written as an *aide memoir* like the Edinburgh Register House MS (1696) or the Chetwode Cawley MS (1710), and those that were written purely for monetary gain like *A Mason's Examination* (1723) and *Masonry Dissected* (1730), these were known as *exposures*.

There is a third category which are generally termed the 'Old Constitutions'. These have a distinct Operative theme and became embraced as part of Masonic folklore, however in general they are historic in content and moral in their teaching, but they contain no ritual.

Fortunately for us, the contents of the early ritual documents were latterly verified by the discovery of an original minute book, part of the ritual had been entered in the first pages as an aide-memoire and its similarity to the others verified their authenticity.

Surprisingly, even the exposures are quite accurate and have also proved to be an invaluable addition to the study of ritual development.

So, although there is scant evidence as to early Masonic practices, what we do have is enough to shed direct light on this fascinating subject, perhaps the saying, 'less is more' comes to mind, as there are many connections and cross-references we can make in the few documents we do have.

13th With regard to the duties of the Junior Deacon, first and foremost he is a messenger or attendant of the Senior Warden and his general position is in the south west corner of the lodge.

His one special duty is to act as a guide as it is his privilege alone to lead the blindfolded Candidate, with a firm but gentle manner, and instil confidence in the poor chap as he walks into the unknown while no doubt expecting the very worst of initiatory rites, and at any minute to be introduced to the goat.

Therefore, a firm workable knowledge of the correct perambulations and the answers to the questions that are put to the Candidate by the Worshipful Master, are crucial to the success of the ceremony of Initiation.

His other very important duties consist of assisting the Entered Apprentice when the Master invites him to prove his proficiency in that Degree, prior to being passed to the degree of a Fellowcraft.

Therefore, he must himself be knowledgeable of the answers to those questions so that he can gently guide the prospective Fellowcraft through his test with a gentle prompt if necessary, without fuss or bother, thus avoiding any embarrassment on the part of the nervous Candidate and ensuring the smooth running of the ceremony.

The Junior Deacon will also assist the Senior Deacon in the Raising ceremony, not by any verbal assistance, but by a general knowledge of the perambulations. Therefore, knowledge of the floor work of all the Degrees is an essential part of the duties of the Junior Deacon.

Finally, know your Candidate! Put him at ease by explaining that you will be his guide and that you will gently lead him in the darkness; you will prompt him when he needs to give answers and you will look after him. And for the aspiring Entered Apprentice as he prepares to take the next step, make sure you go through those questions with him before the meeting, be aware of any part the Brother may have difficulty with, be prepared, do not leave anything to chance.

14th

Were you ever told on the night of your Initiation to, 'Keep your back to the wall!', 'Make sure you are wearing clean underwear!' or 'Watch out for the goat!'?

Are we really warned about such things? Quite frankly, yes! However, putting this into prospective, we all know that it is no more than schoolboy pranks or rather, a gesture of brotherly affection.

Of course, there is absolutely no need to be pre-warned or concerned about anything, but initiatory rituals throughout the world have always been shrouded in mystery and invariably invoke within us great visions of personal pain or suffering.

Actually, it was the medieval Christian priests who began to equate the goat with the devil and all wickedness. Probably because of Matthew 25: 31-46 which explains what will happen when that Bright Morning Star (Revelations 22:16) rises. The sheep will be numbered among those on the right, a place reserved for those to inherit the Kingdom prepared for them from the foundation of the world. The left is a place which is reserved for those considered goats, who will be cursed into everlasting fire prepared for the devil and his angels.

Traditionally, it has been the enemies of Freemasonry who have tried to ridicule our practices and in particular our Initiation ceremony. However, the failure of such falsehoods can be judged by the way Freemasons themselves join in this raillery.

So, the next time somebody offers you some unconventional advice about our Craft, always remember that a true Freemason is obligated to '...never reveal any part or parts, point or points of the secrets or mysteries of or belonging to Free and Accepted Masons in Masonry...'

Therefore, if there is a goat, you can be sure you will be the last one to know about it.

15th In both England and Scotland, the term 'lodge' was often used to describe a group of masons working together on the same building operation. Thus, we find references to them at York in 1352, which refers to their by-laws and ordinances; Canterbury in 1429, which refers to its members as the 'masons of the Lodge'. Aberdeen in 1481, which refers to conditions of employment and Edinburgh in 1491, which refers to written statements of old established customs.

In effect, it is highly probable that the lodges or stone workers' organisations were in fact older than the respective dates shown here, which is only the earliest traceable evidence and not necessarily their start or formation dates.

16th The three Degrees of the Masonic and Military Order of the Red Cross of Constantine and the Orders of the Holy Sepulchre and of St John the Evangelist which are:

Knight of the Red Cross of Constantine
This Degree tells of the conversion to Christianity of Constantine the Great and the introduction of the special Standard that was carried into battle. The main part of the ritual relates to the secret doctrine connected to the banner and contains references to the Roman College of Architects.

Knight of the Holy Sepulchre
It has been said that this Degree, which concerns itself with the three days between the Crucifixion and the Resurrection was instituted at the behest of the mother of Constantine and in part, symbolises the vigil at the Holy Sepulchre. It also commends each Knight to perform the seven works of mercy.

Knight of St John the Evangelist
This degree concerns the discovery made in the ruins of the Temple at Jerusalem and how this led to the formation of the Knights of St John. Part of the ceremony is based on the explanation of the Christian nature of the Craft and Holy Royal Arch.

17th Here are the beautiful words to the 'Tyler's Ode', which I have oft head sung at the end of the Festive Board, prior to the Tyler's Toast.

Architect, for thy protection
Now we humbly pray,
Guard and comfort all our Brethren
Far away.

Grant that we in true remembrance

May not be remiss;
Let them know that in this hour 'tis
Them we miss.

May the bonds that bind them to us
Strengthen day by day,
Let them know our thoughts are with them
On their way.

If their absence be through wandering
Or through grief or pain,
Bless them, heal them, and bring them to us
Safe again.

18th Before you were Passed to the Degree of a Fellowcraft, you were asked the following test question, 'Where were you made a Mason?' You answered, 'In the body of a Lodge, Just, Perfect and Regular'. When therefore is a lodge considered to be 'Regular'?

A lodge is considered Regular, when the Charter or Warrant is on display. In the medieval period, a cathedral was deemed regular if it was part of a monastery. The clergy were monks who lived and conducted their lives by the strict monastic rule of whichever the Order they were part of. They took little notice of what was happening in the outside world and kept themselves entirely to themselves. History shows us that in many cases when masons arrived ready for work, houses were sometimes built for them and they tended to keep themselves in tight little communities and were probably looked upon by the locals as suspicious strangers.

In today's Craft, our work and business is kept strictly within the realms of our Regular lodges which are deemed so by the Warrant that each lodge holds. The warrant is representative of the monarch's authority issued in this form to working lodges or companies of Masons who were actively plying their trade and proof that they were bona fide tradesmen with permission from the Crown to work.

19th What is meant by the term, 'a willingness at all time to undergo an examination when properly called upon', when you were asked 'how do you know yourself to be a Mason?'

Being prepared to undergo an examination when properly called upon, is required particularly when visiting other lodges where we are not known. The Junior Warden of that lodge, as the ostensible Steward, may ask us to prove ourselves a Mason, at which point he will ask us for that sign, token and word.

After this trial or strict examination, he will grant his approbation thereby allowing us to enter a lodge of Entered Apprentices. It is not required or expected for an Entered Apprentice to visit any other lodge, unless specifically invited to do so by a well-known Brother of that lodge who can personally vouch for them.

Invitations such as this are only generally made on the night of another Initiation ceremony that we are at liberty to attend by virtue of the Degree that we hold, that we can more fully observe the ceremony.

The modes of recognition are reserved exclusively for use in the context of the lodge room only and you will never be expected, or never should you demonstrate them, outside of that situation, unless directed to by the ostensible Steward of the lodge you are attending.

20th In the 17th century, that turbulent era before the formation of Grand Lodge, the roots of Freemasonry was laid. What would a man, born in 1601, have witnessed and how would it shape Freemasonry?

For example, Elizabeth I would have died when he was two; while at age of four, the Gun Powder Plot was discovered. At ten, the ashes of the last martyr fire still smouldered at Smithfield, along with any poor woman who was considered a witch.

In the arts, the playwright William Shakespeare would have died when he was fifteen, Philosopher Francis Bacon when he was twenty-five and Ben Jonson, poet and dramatist when he was thirty-six.

When he was about thirty, he could have visited James I's great banqueting hall at Whitehall which had been designed by Inigo Jones and decorated by Rubens.

When he was fifty, Milton was writing *Paradise Lost*, while Pepys, a boy of sixteen had yet to start his diary. John Evelyn, Daniel Defoe and Jonathan Swift would also all have been born in his lifetime.

The execution of Mary, Queens of Scots and Drake's defeat of the Spanish Amada would be in the living memory of some of those still alive, while the Pilgrim Fathers left for New England when he was nineteen.

In his forties, he would have would have been witness to the English Civil War, the battle of Marston Moor, the rise of the New Model Army, the execution of Charles I and the rise of Cromwell.

While in his sixties he would have seen the restoration of the monarchy and the great plague, followed by the Great Fire of London.

I am sure you agree, a very turbulent century indeed, which pitted man against his neighbour and Protestant against Catholic and we will never know what of those events may have influenced the development of our fraternity.

21st

I have to say, I am not sure if we realise just how lucky we are when we meet in our lovely, well-appointed, warm and spacious lodge rooms, because according to the Old Charges, they certainly didn't seem to enjoy such privileges in olden days. If the Dumfries MS (1650) or the Sloane MS (1659), is anything to go by, their lodge was held, '...on the top of a mountain or in ye middle of a bog without the hearing of ye crowing of a cock or ye bark of a dog.'

The *Mason's Examination* (1723) and the *Grand Whimsey* (1730), suggest they held their lodges, 'in the Valley of Jehoshaphat behind a rush-bush.'

Whereas the Kevan MS (c. 1714), suggests their lodge was held, '...a day's Journey from a Borrows-Towne...'

Whilst another MS suggests their lodge was held, '...away from the turtle of a dove...'

No, I haven't heard a dove turtle either!

22nd Several researchers have suggested that our handshakes were originally believed to have been employed purely so that one Brother could recognise another Brother and that by using that handshake, one could readily identify his association with the fraternity showing he had the right to claim relief in times of distress.

Passwords it was believed, originated from the idea that as there were no written qualifications, a man could demonstrate his competence by using a word given to him at the point of achieving his apprentice standard, journeyman standard or master, and when applying for a job could show his level of training.

Signs, it was believed, were first based on a biblical legend that gives us the idea that man was not allowed to use the name of the Great Architect and therefore employed signs when referring to Him.

Later they were proved to have been taken from oaths used by mariners in the 15th century and were also part of the oaths taken by those being admitted to the bar in London, during the 16th century.

Still later, with the introduction of the story of the building of King Solomon's Temple and the murder of its chief architect by three ruffians, they became associated with the symbolic manner in which each ruffian was put to death.

Sadly, we cannot historically verify any of the above.

23th I find it really hard to sit through a Masonic ceremony without thinking 'I wonder where that originated?' or 'When did we first do that?' And that simple process has led me on many a research project which has given me a greater understanding of the Craft.

That brief introduction brings me to the point as to why we give the Sign of Fidelity three times at the closing of the lodge in time with the words 'Fidelity, Fidelity, Fidelity'.

There was only one reference I could find, which I attribute to the late Harry Mendoza. He explains that it is not meant to be a sign, as it comes at the end of the phrase: '…nothing now remains, but, according to ancient custom, to lock up our secrets in a safe repository, uniting in the act Fidelity, Fidelity, Fidelity.' It is therefore meant to be an affirmation or an acknowledgement that, that will be done, i.e. 'Quite truthfully, hand on heart, I will do that'.

24th A new Freemason was very keen to exercise the two great Masonic ornaments of beneficence and charity that had been recently introduced to him at his Initiation. As he walked home from work the following evening, a rather dishevelled man stopped him and asked him for food.

'I'll do better that that', he said, 'come into the pub and I'll buy you a drink.'

'Thank you for the kind offer', said the man, 'but I don't drink.'

'Then have a cigarette', offered the new Initiate.

'No, thank you, I don't smoke', said the beggar.

In his enthusiasm to help the man he carried on.

'I'll tell you what I will do, I have a dead cert tip for the 3.30 at Doncaster tomorrow, I'll place a bet for you and you can have the winnings and there'll be enough cash for food and some new clothes.'

'Please don't do that', said the down at heel man, 'I only need a little food.'

'Ok! That's no problem, come home with me and have dinner. I want you to meet my wife, so she can see for herself what happens to a man that doesn't drink, smoke or gamble.'

25th I must quote a tantalising eulogy that a colleague drew my attention to, which was found in the parish records of Much Wenlock, dated 26 May 1546; about one hundred years earlier that the Initiation of Elias Ashmole.

Of Sir William Corvehill it was said that: '...he was excellently and singularly expert in divers of the seven liberal sciences and especially in geometry, not by greatly speculation but by experience.'

As you can imagine, my first response was one of great excitement, for I thought this was the earliest evidence of Masonic activity in England. However, on closer examination we must accept that although phrases like 'the seven liberal sciences' and 'geometry' are used, we know such terms are found in the old MSS, we must therefore assume that this phraseology was common at that time or the recorder may have been acquainted with a copy. This may well have been because of the recorder's association with the masons that built the church.

It is generally accepted that the use of the word 'speculation' is probably coincidence, as 1757 is the first date that I can find that the term 'Speculative' was used to describe Gentleman or Accepted Masons.

26th Gould, tells us in his work, *The History of Freemasonry* (1883-1887): 'So it is more than evident that the first Grand Lodge of England was in truth, the Grand Lodge of London and Westminster.'

As late as 19 December 1727, according to Gould, there were still only nineteen lodges that attended the Quarterly Communications. This later assertion that the first Grand Lodge was to become the Premier Grand Lodge of England never sat well with Freemasons across England, particularly York.

This is evident in a speech delivered by Francis Drake, Grand Junior Warden, Grand Lodge of York, at the York Grand Lodge meeting, held at the Merchants Hall, York, 27 December 1726. When he said:

> *The Learned Author of the Antiquity of Masonry* [referring to Dr James Anderson], *annexed to which are our Constitution…that diligent Antiquary has traced out to us those many stupendous works of the Ancients, which were certainly, and without doubt, infinitely superior to the Moderns…the first Grand lodge ever held in England was in York.*

But York were not the only Freemasons upset by the stance of the self-styled Premier Grand Lodge of England and during the decade 1779-1789, there were no less than four Grand Lodges operating in England:

The premier Grand Lodge of England, 1717-1813
The York Grand Lodge of all England, 1725-1792
The Grand Lodge of England according to the Old Institutions, 1751-1813
The Grand Lodge of England South of the River Trent, 1779-1789

27th The term 'Cowan', which originated in Scotland and is used in Freemasonry in conjunction with the term 'intruder', generally refers to an eavesdropper or one who is unacquainted with the secrets of Freemasonry.

Over the years I have heard two other interesting theories of the origin on the word. The first is of French Gallic origin and pronounced *couanne*, meaning imbecile and refers to a term used by the Templars when protecting their encampments from eavesdroppers. The author of the theory connects the word with Scotland, by arguing that it was introduced when the Knights Templar took refuge there, after their dissolution. At this point I can find no correct translation of the word to determine the theory, nor has the theory been proved that the Templars fled to Scotland or were involved with the Operative building trade in Scotland.

The second theory is equally intriguing and suggests that it derives from the distinguished surname 'Cohen', which is a proud sign of an ancient Jewish culture. The surname Cohen is an occupational surname for a priest, and it comes from the Hebrew word *kohen*. The English medieval building trade, which predominately built cathedrals and castles for the Christian Church and Christian kings, would have been wary of 'Cohens' or 'Cowan's' who might just eavesdrop or intrude to learn their trade secrets. However, as interesting as this sounds, I feel this is no more than another attempt to explain a tradition that Freemasonry has inherited.

28th In the explanation of the Second-Degree Tracing Board we are told the following:

At the building of King Solomon's Temple an immense number of

Masons were employed. They consisted of Entered Apprentices and Fellow Crafts. The Entered Apprentices received a weekly allowance of corn, wine and oil; the Fellow Crafts were paid their wages in specie, which they went to receive in the middle chamber of the Temple. They got there by the porchway or entrance on the south side. After our ancient Brethren had entered the porch, they arrived at the foot of the winding staircase which led to the middle chamber.

Therefore, the Fellowcrafts were paid in the middle chamber of the Temple and that to access the middle chamber they had to ascend stairs.

We know that the building of King Solomon's Temple took 'seven years and upwards' to complete; so my question is, how long was it before the middle chamber was constructed and where did our ancient brethren go to receive their wages before then?

29th There are several types of columns and pillars, referred to in Masonic teaching, this section deals with the pillars found at the porch way or entrance to the Temple of King Solomon. In an article entitled, 'The History of the Two Pillars', W.L. Fawcette says:

The tradition of the Freemasons in regard to the two pillars, which are a prominent emblem of their Craft, is, that they represent the pillars Jachin and Boaz, which Hiram of Tyre made for Solomon, and set one on either side of the entrance to the Temple, to commemorate the pillar of cloud by day and of fire by night which guided the Israelites in their forty years wanderings in the wilderness.

Our ritual explains in respect of the two Pillars:

They were set up as a memorial to the children of Israel of that miraculous pillar of fire and cloud which had two wonderful effects. The fire gave light to the Israelites during their escape from their Egyptian bondage, and the cloud proved darkness to

Pharaoh and his followers when they attempted to overtake them. King Solomon ordered them to be placed at the entrance of the Temple, as the most proper and conspicuous situation for the children of Israel to have the happy deliverance of their forefathers continually before their eyes in going to and returning from Divine worship.

Whatever significance the Hebrews may have attached to these pillars, there is good reason for believing that they received the material emblem from the Tyrians at the time of the building of the Temple. The Scriptures give a detailed account of the dimensions and designs of the pillars, (2 Kings 7 and 2 Chronicles 3) but are silent as to their significance; and there is nothing in the whole Scriptural account of them to forbid the conclusion that the ideas symbolised by them were as much Tyrian as Jewish.

Tyre had been a rich and prosperous city for over two hundred years, when Solomon undertook the building of the Temple. The Tyrians had been skilled in architecture and other arts to a degree that implied a high state of mental culture, while the Hebrews were yet nomadic tribes living in tents. The tabernacle was only a tent, and in this first Hebrew endeavour to give it a more enduring structure of wood and stone, Solomon naturally appealed to the greater skill of the subjects of the friendly Hiram, King of Tyre.

When the Hebrews began to build the Temple, they ceased their wanderings, they became permanently established, and, as a memorial of this fact, they embodied in the architectural design of the Temple, a symbol which, by the Tyrians and many other nations descended from the ancient Aryan stock, was considered emblematic of a divine leadership that had conducted them to a new and permanent home; this was the true significance of the two pillars.

30th There are many words we use in our ritual that are not part of our everyday vocabulary or that we seldom, if ever use. The word 'inviolate' has always been one of those words that interest me.

If you recall, in some Degrees we agree to keep our Obligation or Oath, 'inviolate'; this quite simple means that we will keep that, which we have just repeated, unbroken, safe or intact.

A simple yet concise word that reminds us to keep the promises we make during our progress through Freemasonry.

July

1st Brother Richard Henry Sellers, better known to us as the inimitable and uniquely talented Peter Sellers, was born on 8 September 1925, at Southsea, Hampshire. In fact, he was almost born on stage as his mother, vaudeville artist Peggy Sellers, started her labour contractions in the middle of her act.

Peggy, who was a good all-round singer and dancer, was back on stage within two weeks, with Peter in her arms crying loudly to the applause of the audience. Just a year earlier, in 1924, his father, William Sellers, a pianist, was initiated into Chelsea Lodge No.3098, which no doubt was to ultimately influence Peter Sellers own reasons for joining.

Strangely enough, he was called Peter, after his elder brother who had died in infancy and which would no doubt be the reason why in later years, Sellers could be any character to anybody, but sadly he could never be himself.

This was no more evident than in 1958 during an interview on Canadian Television when he was asked. 'You have played so many very different characters in your career, who is the real Peter Sellers?' He paused, as tears visibly came into his eyes, as he slowly lowered and shook his head, 'I don't really know' he answered.

He was Initiated into Chelsea Lodge on 16 July 1948, Passed in January 1949 and Raised November 1951 and sadly, other than his Initiation, Passing and Raising, he never attended another Masonic meeting, although he continued to pay his subscriptions and was in good standing right up to the day he died.

2nd Did you know that St Thomas carries as his symbol, the square and sometimes a stone and some believe he has the greatest claim to be the Patron Saint of Masons.

St Thomas, so the legend goes, was sent by the Lord from Caesarea to Gondoforus, the King of the Indies, to build him a palace finer that that of the Emperor of Rome. On his arrival he found the King absent and instead of building the palace he shared the Kings wealth with the sick and the poor.

On his return, the King cast Thomas into prison to die, but the King receives a vision that Thomas was a servant of God and that in paradise, there was a wonderous pillar of gold, silver and precious stones, built by Thomas, that was awaiting him.

Thomas was released and told the King to use his riches to help him prepare the way to paradise.

3rd *The Letter G*
by Harry Carr

He entered the Lodge, and filled each Chair,
He was sent to the East, and presided there,
He could give the lectures of each degree
But, then he fell down on the Letter G.

Yes, he said each head must In honour bow,
But, out of the Lodge, he forgot, somehow
And from his careless and prayerless lip,
The name of Jehovah would often slip.

He recited the Lecture, with solemn tone,
When the Letter G to the Lodge was shown,
But, we knew at once why the world did scoff,
When it heard this man with his apron off.

The Fellowcraft too, when the Lodge was through,
Listened as you and I would do
And the work, though finely exemplified,

Was spoiled by the talk in the room outside.

For no one did as the Master said,
Not a humble bow from a single head
So the Fellowcraft thought, as he said goodnight,
I'll just talk as before, it will be all right.

If Masonry does what we claim for it,
We should guard our tongues, lest we forget
To use that Great High name with care,
While at work, at play, or engaged in prayer.

For the world is watching both you and me,
To see if we honour the Letter G
And our lives and teachings they compare.
To see if they're Plumb, and on the Square.

4th In 1724, the terms 'Guttural', 'Pedestal', 'Manual' and 'Pectoral' first appeared in the anonymous Masonic exposure, *The Grand Mystery of Free-Masons Discover'd.* They subsequently appeared again later in our catechetical lectures, Section Six, Lecture One. The exposure refers to them as 'signs', while the more modern lectures refer to them as 'original forms', but what exactly are they, what is their meaning or to what do they allude?

To be perfectly honest, I have yet to read a satisfactory explanation and the exposure gives no further detail on the so called 'signs', however, the Lectures do enlighten us a little more and explain they allude to the following:

Guttural refers to the symbolic penalty of the Degree, which implied that, as a man of honour, a Mason would rather have had his throat cut across than improperly disclose the secrets of Masonry.

Pectoral refers to the breast where those secrets are deposited safe and secure from the popular world, from those who are not Masons.

Manual refers to the hand placed on the Volume of Sacred Law as a token of one's ascent to the Obligation of a Mason.

Pedestal refers to the foot formed in a square at the North-East part of the lodge, denoting a just and upright Mason.

The lectures also go on to say that also allude to the four cardinal virtues.

Finally, a brief examination of the exposure reveals a small diagram next each of the four words, i.e. Pectoral = X and Guttural = >, and so on, they are brought together under the heading The Free-Mason's Signs, therefore they could well be an attempt to display details or directions of the how signs were given in those early days.

5th

Why is the Junior Warden also known as the ostensible Steward of the lodge?

One of the responsibilities of the Junior Warden is to ensure that all visitors are *bona fide* Masons before allowing them to enter the lodge. You will recall the words of the Worshipful Master when handing the Plumb Rule to the Junior Warden on the night he was appointed, he explains: '… particularly in the examination of Visitors, lest through your neglect any unqualified person should gain admission to our assemblies and the brethren be thereby innocently led to violate their Obligation…'

Under normal circumstances, you would not visit a lodge unless you had received an invitation and therefore your host would happily vouch for you.

In cases where you are not known, previous contact with the lodge Secretary by your own lodge Secretary is essential. First to ensure the lodge you intend to visit is 'Regular' and second, your Secretary will happily explain the reasons for your visit and vouch for your 'regularity', although you may still be expected to be tested.

6th

I read an interesting take on the origins of Freemasonry by R. J. Hollins, in an article entitled 'From whence we came':

The River Severn is the longest river in Great Britain. Its outfall to the sea is in the tidal reaches beyond the Clifton gorge, spanned by the famous suspension bridge, at Avonmouth the ocean port of Bristol.

Stand at the mouth of the river and none will dispute when you say, 'This is the Severn estuary'.

Nevertheless, no man can take up a cup of its water and say, 'This is the River Severn water, yonder is a drop or two of the Avon, beyond flows some of the Stour or the River Teme.'

We know the Severn itself rises near the Wye in Montgomeryshire and follows a semi-circular course to the Bristol Channel, joined by the Stour at Stourport and the Teme just south of Worcester, and the Avon at Tewkesbury.

Shakespeare's Avon rises from a spring in Naseby in Northamptonshire, touches Leicestershire, then traverses a large part of Warwickshire and Worcestershire and finally joins her mightier sister the River Severn in Gloucestershire.

Each of these rivers has dozens of tributaries, is formed of hundreds of springs, creeks, brooks and streams – all combined to flow into the Bristol Channel.

So where did the longest river in the British Isles really rise?

No one can really explain this question because the truth is so complex and has so many ramifications.

Only when we lump it all in to one phrase and say, 'The River Severn comes from many different counties', do we phrase the truth, and then, while truthful is not a proper answer.

Much the same is true of Freemasonry. From whence we came is unanswerable in a sentence, a paragraph, a page and certainly not in a short talk on the subject; hence the comparison with the query about the origin of the longest river in Great Britain.

7th The Grand Council of the Order of the Allied Masonic Degrees was formed in 1879 to bring together a rage of various Orders, which at that point were not regulated by any other body. Initially there were three named Degrees with a further three being attached in 1897. 1931 saw the release of the Order of Secret Monitor leaving five Degrees.

In 1972, the Order was changed to what it is today; The Grand Council of the Order of the Allied Masonic Degrees, with over one hundred and fifty Councils within its domain.

To qualify for membership of this Order, you must be a Master Mason, a Mark Master Mason and a Companion of the Holy Royal Arch.

8th The Halliwell Poem or Regius Manuscript is indexed as, No.17, A1 in the Bibl. Reg., British Museum. It is described in David Casley's Catalogue of the MSS of the Old Royal Library, 1734, as 'A Poem of Moral Duties: here entitled, Constitutiones Artis Gemetrie secundem Euclidem. 'Whoso wol bothe wel rede and loke'.'

The existence of this MS had been known for a long time, but its contents were mistaken until Mr. Halliwell-Phillips drew attention to it in a paper 'On the introduction of Freemasonry into England', which was read before the Society of Antiquaries in the 1838-9 session. He thereafter published two small editions of a work entitled 'The Early History of Freemasonry in England', giving a transcript of the poem.

Sims's *Handbook to Library of British Museum* (1854), tells us that:

> *In the year 1757, King George II, presented (the old Royal) Library to the nation. At that time it was deposited in the old Dormitory at Westminster, to which place it had been removed from Ashburnham House, at the time of the lamentable fire which broke out in that building on the 23rd October, 1731 from which it fortunately sustained but slight injury.*

It bears the Royal Arms stamped on both covers, and GR.II, with the date 1757. The lettering on the back has also been reproduced. The MS was bound in its present cover in or about the year 1838.

The age of the MS has been variously estimated. Mr. Halliwell and the late Rev. A.F.A. Woodford supposed it to have been written about 1390, or earlier.

The MS is accepted to be the oldest genuine record of the craft of Masonry known. Mr. Halliwell pointed out that the writer of the poem was evidently a priest, from the words, 'And when the gospel me rede schal', on line 629. He also drew attention to line 143, which intimates a still older MS must have existed when the poem was written, possible referring to the Polychronicon.

It is interesting that the MS is dated around the same time that the London masons were first becoming organised.

9th

When addressing ladies or non-Masons, I always clear up a couple of points first; this helps set the basis by which relevant and sensible discussions can take place.

First, I explain that we are not a secret society, neither are we a society with secrets. All our ritual, our pass words, our signs and grips can all be found on the internet and readily available in libraries. However, as a Freemason, I am obligated not to use them outside of the ceremony for which they were designed.

Second, I advise them that we are not a religion, neither do we replace religion. We do have a form of collective worship within our ceremonies by having an opening and closing ode or hymn, and an opening and closing prayer, this however is non-denominational and common to many institutions.

Third, I explain we are not political in any way, shape or form and as individuals are obligated to support the government of the day and uphold the laws of the land in which we reside.

Fourth, and this always raises a smile, I tell them we do not use any form of livestock by way of goats, lambs, chickens, nor as I've heard it suggested, virgins; nor do we make any sacrifices whatsoever.

Finally, I explain that in every lodge room throughout the world, nothing whatsoever is carried out that is distasteful, idolatrous and repugnant or in fact anything that might be considered offensive or contrary to the Volume of Sacred Law.

You will be surprised by how many queries that brief explanation immediately clears up.

10th The Immovable Jewels are the Tracing Board, the Rough and Perfect Ashlars.

The Tracing Board is for the Master to lay lines and draw designs upon; the Rough Ashlar for the Entered Apprentice to work, mark, and indent upon and the Perfect Ashlar for the experienced Craftsman to try, and adjust, his jewels upon. They are called Immovable Jewels, because they lie open and immovable in the lodge for the brethren to moralise upon.

As the Tracing Board is for the Master to lay lines and draw designs on, the better to enable the brethren to carry on the intended structure with regularity and propriety, so the Volume of the Sacred Law may justly be deemed to be the spiritual Tracing Board of the Great Architect of the Universe, in which are laid down such Divine Laws and Moral Plans, that were we are conversant therein, and adherent thereto, would bring us to an Ethereal Mansion not made with hands, eternal in the Heavens

The Rough Ashlar is a stone, rough and unhewn as taken from the quarry, until, by the industry and ingenuity of the workman, it is modelled, wrought into due form, and rendered fit for the intended structure; this represents man in his infant or primitive state, rough and unpolished as that stone, until, by the kind care and attention of his parents or guardians, in giving him a liberal and virtuous education, his mind becomes cultivated, and he is thereby rendered a fit member of civilised society

The Perfect Ashlar is a stone of a true die or square, fit only to be tried by the Square and Compasses; this represents man in the decline of years, after a regular, well-spent life in acts of piety and virtue, which cannot otherwise be tried and approved than by the Square of God's Word and the Compasses of his own self-convincing conscience.

11th I have always been led to believe that Grand Lodge has never sanctioned any specific form of ritual, but I have latterly discovered something new.

The ritual or system which was sanctioned and approved by Grand Lodge was the system as used by the Lodge of Reconciliation at the time of the Union. This was demonstrated at a special Grand Lodge Meeting on 20 May 1816.

The Emulation Lodge of Improvement was founded in 1823, therefore in one sense it cannot be said that Grand Lodge sanctioned Emulation ritual, however, the Emulation Lodge of Improvement claims to use the ritual taught by the Lodge of Reconciliation, without addition, alteration or variation of any kind.

If this is the case, then the ritual as practiced by the Emulation Lodge of Improvement is the only ritual that has received Grand Lodge approval.

12th What is meant by the term, 'By…repeated trials and approbations…' when we are asked how do we know ourselves to be a Mason?

At our Initiation, and after having taken that great and solemn Obligation of a Mason, we were given three especial things; a sign, a token and a word.

A sign, which was an allusion to a penalty, which a Mason would rather suffer than improperly disclose the secrets entrusted to him.

A grip or token, which when regularly given or received goes to distinguish a Brother by night as well as by day.

A word, which is so highly prized amongst Masons that too much caution cannot therefore be observed in its communication, it should never be given at length but always by letters of syllables.

It was immediately after receiving these that we underwent our first trial and approbation, in the south of the lodge, when the Junior Deacon presented us to the Junior Warden and then secondly, to the west of the lodge when the Junior Deacon presented us to the Senior Warden. On both these occasions we underwent a trial or test while receiving the approbation or approval of those two Principal Officers of the lodge, when we answered their respective question correctly.

Each subsequent meeting we attend, we are required to demonstrate we are a Mason. For example, in the opening of the First Degree we have the following exchange:

WM. The next care?
SW. To See that none but Masons are present.
WM. To order Brethren in the First Degree.

In the Second-Degree we have the same opening exchange, with the addition of the words from the Junior Warden who commands us on behalf of the Worshipful Master to, 'prove ourselves Craftsmen'. The Third-Degree is the same, for having been asked to prove yourself Craftsmen, this Degree demands that we prove ourselves Master Masons by signs.

Hence, repeated trials and approbations.

13th

Until it is pointed out, many of us fail to see the significance of somethings and in all honesty, carry out actions we are not actually familiar with.

Take for example the sign of Grief and Distress; as you recall the sign has three downward movements. But did you know the three movements correlate to the signs of the Three Degrees. The first drop is to the position we hold in the First Degree prior to discharging the sign. The second drop is to the position of the Second Degree prior to discharging the sign and so on in the Third Degree.

A simple explanation that will give us a greater understanding next time we use the sign of Grief and Distress.

14th

I have to recall a funny incident which happened to me many years ago. Early one afternoon, prior to my Regular Meeting, I was contacted by the lodge Secretary to be advised that our Tyler, a ninety-year-old, well loved and respected Brother, had been called to the Grand Lodge above.

Devastated by the news, I was asked to convey the information to all lodge members. I duly complied, only to be contacted an hour later again by the Secretary to be advised that the Tyler had not died.

Can you imagine the furore that this caused, and I was reminded of the quote by Mark Twain: 'The reports of my death have been greatly exaggerated.'

I eventually saw the funny side as the embarrassed Secretary offered his apologies to the lodge.

As for the dear old Tyler, I sat next to him that evening and I saw him struggle to eat his dessert.

'Are you alright?' I asked in a concerned manner.

'I'm fine', was his reply, 'it's just that my wife made me eat my dinner before I came out.'

No wonder he was struggling.

15th

The Allied Masonic System confers five Degrees:

St Lawrence the Martyr

This Degree is taken first and explains how Lawrence gave his life rather than betray his principles; responsibilities, integrity and fortitude are the lessons to be learned here. The ceremony was believed to have originated in Lancashire and be the remnants of an old operative ceremony which distinguished operative from speculative Masons.

Knight of Constantinople

This Degree examines the relationship between the Emperor Constantine and his subjects and teaches the lesson of equality and humility. Many suggest the ceremony is rather amusing, but the Candidate is left in no doubt as to importance of the virtue of humility.

Grand Tilers of Solomon
The Degree is set in the secret vault beneath the Temple and very dramatic. It relates the accidental intrusion of a craftsman into the secret vault and reflects on the danger of hasty judgment.

Red Cross of Babylon
The Degree covers the time between the Craft and Holy Royal Arch and tells of Zerubbabel gaining permission to rebuild the Temple. The lesson of this Degree reflects the supreme importance of truth.

Grand High Priest
In this Degree, the Candidate is anointed, consecrated and set apart to the service of God. It is founded on the blessing of Abraham and the consecration of Aaron

16th It used to be easy deciding which tie to wear for a lodge meeting, as a plain black tie was always the order of the day. However, with introduction of the more fashionable Provincial and Grand Lodge ties, things are now different. We have all asked the question, 'Why do or did we wear black ties?' And we always receive the same answer, '...it goes back to the 1914-18 War to commemorate those who fell in battle...' So, if that was the case, what did Freemasons wear before that date?

Ties were first worn in about the middle of the 19th century and tended to be large, floppy and of various colours; white being the normal colour for the lodge. In about 1860, formal evening dress was considered as black swallow-tail coat, black cut away waistcoat, black tie and black trousers, but by 1870, the colour of the tie and waistcoat changed to white, as it has been ever since. There does not seem to have been any suggestion in the 19th century that the tie, worn in lodge with formal morning dress or a lounge suit, should be black. That seems to be a 20th century custom, possibly connected with the black tie worn with the dinner jacket.

Surprisingly, there was no mention of dress, beyond regalia, i.e. aprons, jewels and collars, in any of the *Books of Constitution* from the Union to the present. The United Grand Lodge Proceedings from 1918-19 did not mention ties.

In 1917, the Board of General Purposes issued the following, '...during the war, gatherings of the Craft should be conducted with simplicity and the wearing of morning dress to Lodges is preferable to evening dress'.

In the Proceedings of 4 June 1919, the following statement was issued, '...lodges now may fittingly resort to their accustomed practice in the matter of dress'.

Therefore, it seems the black tie had simply become a tradition, because that was what was traditionally worn with dinner jackets in the early 20th century.

17th

Evidence of the origin of our Craft can easily be found in the ritual that we hear at every meeting.

In medieval times, the apprentice mason, like other trades, lived in the home of his Master. The household included the Master's wife, his children and, in many cases, his unmarried sister and even his parents. Placed in the situation of living in a house with the Master's extended family, the apprentice was given rules by which to conduct himself. This is evident in the Third-Degree Obligation when under Oath we repeat:

> *...that I will maintain a Master Mason's honour and carefully preserve it as my own: I will not injure him myself or knowingly suffer it to be done by others if in my power to prevent it but, on the contrary, will bodily repel the slanderer of his good name and most strictly respect the chastity of those nearest and dearest to him in the persons of his wife, his sister, and his child.*

This little piece of the Obligation sheds much light on what was expected of an Apprentice Mason in relation to his conduct while in his Master's home.

18th Lecture One, Section Seven, gives us a wonderful, yet simple explanation of two types of Freemasonry is:

Q. - How many sorts of Masons are there?

A - Two: Free and Accepted, and Operative.

Q - Which of those are you?

A - Free and Accepted.

Q - What do you learn by being a Free and Accepted Mason?

A - Secrecy, Morality, and Good Fellowship.

Q - What do Operative Masons learn?

A - The useful rules of Architecture; to hew, square, and mould stones into the formation required for the purposes of building; and unite them by means of joints-level, perpendicular, or otherwise; and by the aid of cement, iron, lead, or copper; which various operations require much practical dexterity and some skill in geometry and mechanics.

Q - And what by being both, and frequenting sundry lodges?

A - To act on the square, observe a proper deportment in the lodge, pay due and becoming respect to the Worshipful Master and his presiding officers, to abstain from all political or religious disputes which might breed dissension among the Brethren and in time entail a scandal on the Craft.

Applying to our conduct, the symbolic teachings of the Operative Mason and the practical teachings of the Free and Accepted Mason would go a long way to preventing anything that might affect the harmony and discord of our lodges.

19th Euclid was a mathematician who lived in Alexandria about 300 BC; he is famous for his writings on Geometry. Pythagoras was a Greek philosopher and also a mathematician, famous for his theorem, who lived during the 6th century BC. Neither were masons by trade, nor of course Speculative Masons since that did not start before the 17th century, yet their influence persists in Freemasonry.

The significance of their work is incorporated in the Past Master's jewel. The correct description of this jewel was given in the first *Book of Constitutions* following the Union of the two Grand Lodges in 1813. It reads: 'The square and the diagram of the 47th Proposition 1st Book of Euclid engraven on a silver plate pendant within it.'

The 47th Proposition had been used in Craft Masonry since 1723, when Anderson referred to it in the *Book of Constitutions*. However, there is no evidence of it being used as a jewel until about 1780. The pattern at that time was different and it was known as the 'gallows' type. The square was in the form of a right angle, long side down and a plate suspended downwards from to the short side showing the diagram, hence the term 'gallows'.

We cannot be certain why this was chosen at the Past Master jewel other than in the *Old Charges*, we are told, 'Geometry is now called masonry...'

20th Any good lodge interviewing committee will always ask a prospective Candidate if his work commitments will allow him to attend Masonic meetings.

The Candidate must always answer in the affirmative. Basically, if the Candidate has a job which precludes him from attending the meetings, then there is little point in him joining your lodge. It may be that another lodge that meets at a more suitable time may be more appropriate for the Candidate's working arrangements.

The Candidate must also always understand that great reliance, at times, will be placed upon his attendance and the commitment to Freemasonry, when accepting an office is not his choice, but his duty. Therefore, it would be wise at this point to ensure that the prospective Candidate is both willing and able to attend and serve the lodge.

Members of the Armed forces or the Emergency Services are generally excluded from this scenario.

21st The Candidate should be guided and prompted at all times by the Junior Deacon, with the exception of one occasion, that is when the Candidate is asked by the Worshipful Master: '…Are you therefore willing to take a Solemn obligation, founded on the principles I have stated, to keep inviolate the secrets and mysteries of the Order?'

Apart from his interview, where he was expected to answer all questions voluntary, this is the only part of the ceremony where the same applies, the Candidate is expected to give his assent voluntarily and of his own free will, as he is at liberty to refuse.

However, as the Candidate for Initiation would have been advised that he will be prompted and guided throughout the ceremony, and up until that point he had been physically manoeuvred during the perambulations and instructed how to answer, he may well be expecting a further prompt. Therefore, it is suggested that if there is some hesitancy in the Candidate answering, then the Junior Deacon would be expected to give guidance to the Candidate in the form of a whisper using the simple term 'Answer', but on no account, should the Junior Deacon audibly prompt him by saying 'I am'.

22nd According to Robert Plot, the famed English Naturalist and first keeper of the Ashmolean Museum, in 1686, Freemasonry was being practiced throughout the nation. In his work, *The Natural History of Staffordshire*, 1686, Plot says:

> *To these add the Customs relating to the County, whereof they have one, of admitting Men into the Society of Free-masons, that in the moorelands of this County seems to be of greater request, than any where else, though I find the Custom spread more of less all over the Nation.*

This is exactly thirty-one years before Dr Anderson recorded the fact that Grand Lodge was formed in London.

23rd During my own research, I have identified seven tranches of documents, which aid the student in understanding the development of our ritual, usages and traditions, these are:

1) Statues and Ordinances, 1248-1370
2) Gothic Constitutions 1390-1690
3) Scottish Statutes and Charters 1475-1628
4) Early Catechisms, 1696-1730.
5) French Exposures 1737-1751
6) English Exposures 1760-1769
7) Literary and printed references to Freemasonry 1638-1736

Having had the opportunity over the years to amass copies, and to study in detail, all the seven sets of documents, I would encourage all budding Masonic students to make this their first point of study.

24th John Boswell, 3rd Laird of Auchinleck, was a Scottish gentleman and generally considered the first recorded non-operative Freemason in Scotland. Boswell's signature and mark are found on the records of a meeting of the Lodge of Edinburgh held at Holyrood on 8 June, 1600. According to many Masonic historians, this was the earliest authentic record of a non-operative Mason attending a Masonic lodge. However, there are others who disagree. It is not clear in what capacity Boswell was in attendance at this meeting. It was not an ordinary meeting of the lodge, but a trial of its Warden 'Jhone Broune'.

While it is possible that he was there as a member (or an honorary member) of the lodge, it is also possible that he was there only as counsel for prosecution or defence and was not a member of the lodge at all. There is no evidence of his Initiation in the lodge on that occasion or any other occasion, and the meeting of 8 June 1600 was the only occasion to which Boswell's connection with this or any other lodge can be traced.

25th Students of our ritual will agree that the Masonic Exposures of the 18th century are some of the only means by which we can monitor the introduction and development of our practices. As no Brother ever committed any ritual to paper, had it not been for certain unscrupulous people publishing our secrets for gain, it probably would have been of great determent to Masonic scholars.

To Grand Lodge, in 1730, the publishing of *Masonry Dissected* by Samuel Pritchard caused absolute uproar. The effect was that there began to appear irregular Masons trying to gain admission to bona fide lodges. To combat this practice, Grand Lodge began a programme of reversing the signs and tokens of the First and Second Degree. They hoped that irregular Masons would be detected. Of course, these changes to our Ancient Landmarks were disastrous and ultimately led to the formation of another Grand Lodge

In 1751, thirty-four years after the Premier Grand Lodge was founded, a rival body was established in London and became known as 'The Grand Lodge of England according to the Old Institutions'. This new body accused the first or Premier Grand Lodge of England of having introduced innovations and claimed that they alone preserved the ancient customs and practices of Masonry. They dubbed the older body as the 'Moderns' and assumed the title of 'Ancients'. They were also known as 'Atholl' Masons because the 3rd Duke of Atholl became their Grand Master.

One such innovation is described by Laurence Dermott, who in 1752 was elected Grand Secretary of the new Grand Lodge of the Old Institutions. In his work, *Ahiman Rezon*, he says of the 'Moderns':

> *There was another old custom that gave umbrage to the young architects, i.e., the wearing of aprons, which made the gentleman look like mechanics, therefore it was proposed that no brother should wear an apron. This proposal was rejected by the oldest Members, who declared that the aprons were all the signs of Masonry, and for that reason they would keep and wear them.*
>
> *It was then proposed, that as they were resolved to wear*

aprons they should be turned upside down, in order to avoid appearing mechanical. This proposal took place, and answered the design, for that which was formerly the lower part, was now fastened round the abdomen, and the bib and strings hung downwards, dangling in such manner as might convince spectators that there was not a working mason amongst them.

Agreeable as this alteration might seem to the gentlemen, nevertheless it was attended with an ugly circumstance: for, in traversing the lodge, the brethren were subject to tread upon the strings, which often caused them to fall with great violence, so it was thought necessary to invent several methods of walking, in order to avoid treading upon the strings.

After many years' observation on these ingenious methods of walking, I conceive that the first was invented by a man grievously afflicted with the sciatica. The second by a sailor, much accustomed to the rolling of a ship. And the third by a man who, for recreation or through excess of strong liquor, was wont to dance the drunken peasant.

Fortunately, I am pleased to note, that these days, our aprons cause us no such embarrassment, nor encumbrance.

26th At the time of the Norman Conquest, the French were more architecturally advanced than the English, and it was the Norman influence that led to the development of stone building, which in the aftermath of the invasion of 1066, saw the commencement of the building of abbeys, priories, cathedrals and castles and the substitution of wood and clay, for stone.

Up until that point, Saxons mainly built in timber and merely carved stone, but by virtue of the earlier importation of masons from France, there is little doubt that the art of building and carving was eventually acquired by native artisans. However, the likelihood that early building work was performed by masons, as their own specialist occupation, is not actually true; as in this country, stone working carried out by natives or locals, during the first millennium, was a by-occupation of farming.

27th Have you noticed that on Installation nights, the Worshipful Master gives two knocks when summoning the Tyler to come into the lodge room to be invested? He also gives two knocks at the end of the Festive Board when signaling the Tyler to give the Tyler's Toast. Why does he do this?

In his book *Commentary on the Freemasonic Ritual,* Dr. E. H. Cartwright wrote:

> *...the curious custom, of the Master giving a resounding double knock (which is not repeated by the Wardens) when the presence of the Tyler is required in the Lodge, for instance when he is about to be invested on Installation night. The custom is, strictly speaking, irregular. In the first place, it is a knock that has no Freemasonic significance. Secondly, the fact that the Wardens do not repeat it contravenes the old established rule that every knock given by the Master should be 'answered' by the Wardens. Further, while the obvious reason for the knock being given so loudly as is invariably the case is that the Tyler may hear it and take it as a summons to enter, that Officer cannot possibly act on it until the Inner Guard opens the door to admit him. Although, in view of the wide prevalence that the practice has now obtained, the writer is not prepared incontinently to condemn it, it does appear to him that it is an unnecessary innovation and that it would be more seemly for the Master, instead of knocking, simply to request the Inner Guard to call in the Tyler.*

Harry Carr says:

> *The variations in the different knocks used in the degrees, and in the Openings and Closings, were undoubtedly introduced to mark distinctions between degrees, or between different parts of a ceremony. The variations however, have no symbolical significance*

and this applies, like wise, to the double-knock. It is now so widely accepted as being the customary knock for the Tyler, that there is not the least danger of its being misunderstood. It serves its purpose perfectly.

28th I never realised how naïve I was when I joined Freemasonry, until I cast my thoughts back to the night of my Initiation. I am not sure what I actually expected on the night, but after receiving the token and word, I was quite disappointed, as I think I was expecting to receive some life-changing information. I remember waiting for something else but nothing else was forthcoming. I really was, without a doubt, that rough ashlar, that unpolished stone, desperate for the touch of the master.

If only I had considered at the time that my Initiation was merely the start of the journey, the beginning of my enlightenment, but in truth, gems of wisdom given me that night went straight over my head.

The deprivation of light actually made me more conscious of sounds, but not words, and when light was restored, the surroundings overtook the restored senses so much so that I became oblivious to the ceremony. I am sure I am no different to many others who felt the same on our special night

Fortunately, Freemasonry is very kind to us and it allows us to witness the same ceremony time and time again, not, I hasten to add so we can learn it verbatim, although it does help, but to ensure we hear, learn and understand the wisdom repeated.

29th Surprisingly, there is much confusion at times concerning that distinguishing badge of a Mason, the apron. The most common question I hear asked regards the flap of the Entered Apprentices apron, should it be worn with the flap lifted or lowered?

Quite simply, it depends on the system being worked, for example, in Emulation the flap is always worn down, whereas the tradition is different with other workings.

The second question asked, is whether or not, when investing a Fellowcraft or Master Mason with their apron, should the new apron be placed over the lower degree apron first? The simple answer is no! The lower degree apron is always removed first.

The third question is should the Senior Warden leave his seat when investing the Candidate with the apron? Once again the answer is no. The Deacon should always ensure the Candidate is at a convenient distance so that the Senior Warden need not leave his seat.

The last question relates to the apron being worn inside or outside the jacket. Under the English Constitution, the apron is always worn outside with respect of dinner jackets, morning dress and lounge suits. Other systems dictate other traditions.

Never be dismayed or unsure of the traditions of the lodge you are attending, as a discreet word in the ear of the Director of Ceremonies will ensure appropriate lodge traditions are explained. As a rule of thumb, when visiting a lodge, I always ask the host for details of any traditions I may need to observe. A little forethought often saves a lot of embarrassment.

30th Did you know there is no specific direction the Volume of Sacred Law should face during open lodge, and it would appear that different systems suggest different positions, for different reasons.

Having said that, as the Candidate always takes his Obligation on the V of SL it is incumbent upon the lodge to insure they provide the appropriate V of SL suitable to the faith of the Candidate.

Therefore, the V of SL should face him during his Obligation so at the very least he can recognise it as being that tome approved for study by his faith and religion.

31st It was not until I visited a lodge in the North that was I acquainted with the term 'the dark corner'. I was seated quite comfortably at the Festive Board when the usual questions were asked of the Wardens, i.e. 'How do you report your respective corners?' and with that came the usual replies: 'All charged in the West' and 'All charged in the South', but then the brethren responded, 'All charged in the dark corners'.

I cannot say that I understood the practice, with the exception of the fact that the Master illuminated the East, leaving the North in darkness, or the dark corner.

It was explained to me later that the concept was practised in churchyards and the north side, being the darker side was reserved for the less fortunate members of the parish.

Yet another interesting and rather unusual practice, which seems to evade all questions of origin.

August

1st With regard to the Annual Prestonian Lecture, here is an extract from the Grand Lodge Proceedings for 5 December 1923:

> *In the year 1818, Bro. William Preston, a very active Freemason at the end of the 18th and beginning of the 19th centuries, bequeathed £300, @ 3 per cent. Consolidated Bank Annuities, the interest of which was to be applied 'to some well-informed Mason to deliver annually a Lecture on the First, Second, or Third Degree of the Order of Masonry according to the system practised in the Lodge of Antiquity' during his Mastership. For a number of years the terms of this bequest were acted upon, but for a long period no such Lecture has been delivered, and the Fund has gradually accumulated, and is now vested in the M.W. the Pro. Grand Master, the Rt. Hon. Lord Ampthill, and W. Bro. Sir Kynaston Studd, P.G.D., as trustees. The Board has had under consideration for some period the desirability of framing a scheme which would enable the Fund to be used to the best advantage; and, in consultation with the Trustees who have given their assent, has now adopted such a scheme, which is given in full in Appendix A [See below], and will be put into operation when the sanction of Grand Lodge has been received.*

The Grand Lodge sanction was duly given and after a lapse of some sixty years, the Prestonian Lectures were revived, in their new form, and, with the exception of the War period (1940-1946), a Prestonian Lecturer has been appointed by the Grand Lodge regularly each year.

2nd A chance discovery of a scrap of paper found with certain documents provided some interesting information. Randall Holme, a contemporary of Elias Ashmole and the author of a 1688 publication, in which he stated the following: 'I cannot but honour the fellowship of the Masons because of its antiquity, and the more as being myself a member of that society of Freemasons.'

Randal Holme III, who died in 1700, left a paper containing the names of twenty-six brethren, all members of the Old Lodge at Chester, in about the year 1650. Research has shown that of those twenty-six members, at least sixteen were non-operative masons as six were identified as Mayors or Aldermen, eight were identified as Freeman of the Town, one was identified as a Churchwarden and one was identified as the son of an MP.

This scrap of paper, known as the Harliean fragment and dated by the British Museum at about 1650, is the first known allusion to Masonic words and signs and says the following:

> *There is several words and signs of a free mason to be revealed to you which as you will answer before God at the great and terrible day of judgement you keep secret and not to reveal the same to any in the ears of any person but to the masters and fellows of the said Society of Free Masons so help me God.*

3rd The Grand Council of Royal and Select Masters is better known to us as Royal and Select Master or the Cryptic Degrees.

Formed in 1873, by four Councils originally chartered by the Grand Council of New York, they organised themselves into a sovereign body. The first Grand Master of the Order was the Reverend Canon G. R. Portal who had previously been Grand Master of Mark Master Masons. Over the years, the Order has been subject to some variations and changes but today, prospers in this country and with overseas Councils.

I have been unable to discover why the Order is termed 'Cryptic Degrees'. Keith B. Jackson, in his excellent book, *Beyond the Craft*, disagrees with those that suggest it is because two of the Degrees refer to the crypt beneath the Temple of King Solomon, but offers no further explanation.

All applicants are required to be Mark Master Masons and a Companion of the Holy Royal Arch.

4th I came across this beautiful poem entitled 'The Temple', several years ago; unfortunately I have been unable to discover the author.

Through Solomon's' Temple, they tell us of old
Excelled in its marbles, its cedars and gold,
Its Altars on incense, its tables of bread,
Its Ark, where the sight of the Presence was shed,
A far nobler Temple each Mason may raise,
In Wisdom and Strength to endure through the days;
Of which Israel's proud pile was the type and the plan,
And this Temple so stately, so perfect - is MAN.

How more precious than gold, are honour and truth,
With these let him build in the days of his youth,
Its sight of the Presence - sweet peace may be there,
Its Altar of incense - humility's prayer,
Its Table of Shewbread - his gifts to the poor,
A Temple thus built, through all time shall endure,
And to perfect the shrine, though no gems form a part
The bright Holy of Holies be found in his heart.

5th In Masonic terms 'Lewis', as defined by the Board of General Purposes, Point of Procedure, is the uninitiated son of a Freemason and first used in the Wilkinson MS (1727) where we read:

Q. What's a Mason's Sons Name?
A. Lewis.

Some would argue that the son has to be born after the father becomes a Freemason, but UGLE has stipulated that a Lewis is the uninitiated son of a Freemason, regardless of date of birth. The term however, has been in general use since about 1738, possible earlier.

Lecture One, Section Seven, gives us a good all-round explanation of the term.

Q - If you wished to give your son a Masonic name, what would you call him?

A - Lewis.

Q - What does Lewis denote?

A - Strength.

Q. - How is it depicted in our Lodges?

A - By certain pieces of metal dovetailed into a stone, forming a cramp; and when in combination with some of the mechanical powers, such as a system of pulleys, it enables the Operative Mason to raise great weights to certain heights with little encumbrance, and to fix them on their proper bases.

Q - Lewis being the son of a Mason, what is his duty, to his aged parents?

A - To bear the heat and burden of the day, which they by reason of their age, ought to be exempt from; to assist them in time of need, and thereby render the close of their days happy and comfortable.

Q - His privilege for so doing?

A -That of being made a Mason before any other person, however dignified.

6th The Senior Deacon is a messenger or attendant of the Master and there is, you will note, a subtle change in words in the ritual, for the responsibilities of the Junior and Senior Deacons. That is: the Junior Deacon carries all messages of the Worshipful Master, meaning that they have been given him from the Senior Deacon. The Senior Deacon bears all messages from the Worshipful

Master meaning he has received them direct from the Master himself.

His position in the lodge is generally the north-east corner and he is a guide to all those that seek promotion to a higher degree.

It is the privilege of the Senior Deacon to act as guide to every Entered Apprentice seeking promotion. Therefore, it is his duty to have a workable knowledge of the correct perambulations and the answers to the questions that are put to the Candidate by the Worshipful Master; this is crucial for the success of the ceremony of Passing and Raising.

His other very important duties consist of assisting the Fellowcraft when the Master invites him to prove his proficiency in that Degree, prior to being passed to the degree of a Master Mason. Therefore, once again he must himself be knowledgeable of the answers to those questions so that he can gently guide the Fellowcraft through his test with a gentle prompt if necessary, without fuss or bother, again avoiding any embarrassment on the part of the nervous Candidate and ensuring the smooth running of the ceremony. Knowledge of all the floor work in the Degrees is an essential part of the duties of the Senior Deacon.

Finally, the same applies to the aspiring Fellowcraft, as he prepares to take the next step, make sure you go through those questions before the meeting, be aware of any part the Brother may have difficulty with, be prepared, and do not leave anything to chance.

7th

We know that the moral teachings of Masonry have been in existence for many centuries, no more so than in Ireland and that was evident during the excavation of Baal's Bridge, Limerick in 1830. Unearthed in the eastern corner of the northern land pier, was a brass square, with the following inscription:

Upon the level and by the square
I will strive to live with love & care 1507

Each arm measuring four inches each, it shows the early Irish system of morality that was connected with Masonry.

In Ireland, we can in fact, go back even further in time to one of the traditional heroes of Celtic mythology, *Goban Soar*, the stone mason. I am told that in Old Irish, the word 'Soar' denotes both 'Free' and 'A mason'. Legend tells us that it was the Goban, that built Ireland's famous round towers, but that's another story.

8th The motto of the Craft is, *Audi, Vidi, Tace*, meaning, 'hear, see and be silent'. Quite simply, it reminds us of certain things we see and hear within the confines of our lodges, which we do not speak about outside of that setting.

In my own view, the only things we do not speak about, are the modes of recognition, the signs, tokens and words, which are purely designed to be used within the ceremonies inside the lodge and nowhere else.

Discussing the ritual, the Initiation and any other such usages, practices and traditions are allowed with (my own) this proviso, before you embark on a discussion regarding the finer points of Freemasonry, please try not to enter areas that you do not have sufficient information about, especially if you are speaking with non-members.

Quite frankly, if you do not know the answer to a genuine enquiry, then please do not try to answer. Far better that you explain that you will find the answer and get back to the person, then to give a wrong answer, which will, more often than not, lead you deeper into the unknown subject you are already trying to answer.

It is a simple but successful tool I use when talking with people and I always consider a genuine question deserves a proper response; particularly as you are the representative of Freemasonry that this person has approached.

9th Pendent to the corners of the lodge room carpet, are four tassels, these are meant to remind us of the four cardinal virtues, namely: Temperance, Fortitude, Prudence, and Justice, the whole of which, tradition informs us, were constantly practiced by a great majority of our ancient brethren.

Here we examine Temperance. In Latin, Temperance is pronounced *Temperantia* meaning self-moderation or self-restraint. In visual art it is often shown as two vessels or goblets.

The Emulation Lectures of the Three Degrees explain Temperance thus:

> *Temperance - Is that due restraint of the passion and affections, which renders the body tame and governable, and relieves the mind from the allurements of vice. This virtue ought to be the constant practice of every Mason as he is thereby taught to avoid excess, or the contracting of any vicious or licentious habits, whereby he might, unwarily, be led to betray his trust, and subject himself the penalty contained in his Obligation; alluding to the Guttural.*
>
> First Lecture, Sixth Section Six

Temperance therefore gives us control, and to the Freemason that properly appreciates the secrets which he has solemnly promised never to reveal, will not, by yielding to the unrestrained call of appetite, permit reason and judgment to lose their seats and subject himself, by the indulgence in habits of excess, to discover that which should be concealed, and thus merit and receive the scorn and detestation of his brethren.

And lest any Brother should forget the danger to which he is exposed in the unguarded hours of dissipation, the virtue of temperance is wisely impressed upon his memory, the practice of which is inculcated in the First Degree.

In the Masonic setting, this has led to resolutions being sought in Grand Lodges which declare the use of stimulating liquors in any quantity a Masonic offence. However, the law of Freemasonry authorises no such regulation and leaves to every man the indulgence of his own tastes within due limits, and demands not abstinence, but only moderation and temperance, in all things.

A Freemason will therefore avoid all excesses, and learn to exercise caution in his action, speech, thought, feeling, judgment, and life.

10th What is the situation of the lodge? Our lodges stand on holy ground, because the first lodge was consecrated on account of three grand offerings thereon made, which met with Divine approbation.

First, the ready compliance of Abraham with the will of God in not refusing to offer up his son Isaac as a burnt sacrifice, when it pleased the Almighty to substitute a more agreeable victim in his stead.

Secondly, the many pious prayers and ejaculations of King David, which actually appeased the wrath of God, and stayed a pestilence which then raged among his people, owing to his inadvertently, having had them numbered.

Thirdly, the many thanksgivings, oblations, burnt sacrifices and costly offerings which Solomon, King of Israel, made at the completion, dedication and consecration of the Temple at Jerusalem to God's service.

Our lodges are situated due East and West, because all places of Divine worship, as well as Freemasons regular, well-formed and constituted lodges are, or ought to be, so situated; for which we assign three Masonic reasons:

First, the sun, the Glory of the Lord, rises in the East and sets in the West.

Second, learning originated in the East, and thence spread its benign influence to the West. Third, the last and grand reason refers to the situation of the Tabernacle in the wilderness.

11th There are four Degrees within the Order of Royal and Select Masters which are:

Select Master

This builds on the legend of the Mark Degree and explains the background to the secret vault beneath the Temple where the secrets were deposited. It tells the story of how Adoniram that well-known character celebrated in the Mark Degree, was employed by King Solomon and accidently intrudes upon the Three Grand Masters and the outcome of that intrusion.

Royal Master
Set at a time prior to the dedication of the Temple, this takes place within the Holy of Holies where Hiram Abif inadvertently explains to one of those Select Masters, Adoniram, why the Masters Word will never be lost. Said to be a most enthralling and interesting piece of ritual.

Most Excellent Master
Dealing with the final stages of the construction of the Temple and the installation of the Ark of the Covenant, King Solomon rewards those skilful workmen that have assisted him.

Super-Excellent Master
This degree brings the timeline down to the invasion of Jerusalem and the eventual destruction of the Temple. The Jews are taken into bondage and remain in captivity until their return to rebuild the Second Temple as described in the Holy Royal Arch.

12th We have all heard the expression used when the Master asks the assembled brethren to confirm the minutes of the last meeting '…in the usual manner observed among Masons', but have you ever asked yourself, what actually is the usual manner observed among Masons?

First and foremost, the raising of a hand is the collective ratification of the lodge members present and your personal assertion that the minutes are a true and accurate record of the previous meeting. However, there is a general custom that the hand is held outstretched rather than raised.

Historians have conceded that there is little or no historical reference to this action, other than it is similar to the position we employ during the Obligation, although one scholar suggested if that was the case then maybe the thumb should also be extended thus forming a square.

Early 18th century catechisms indicate that 'squares' and similar unobtrusive modes of recognitions were commonly used by Masons in everyday life and the custom of the outstretched hand may extend from that period. Such is its popularity, I have attended many lodges, and all follow a similar pattern with no exception.

On 6 April 1736, Grand Lodge advised that the mode of voting should be the 'holding up of one hand' and those same words apply today in our *Book of Constitutions*. Therefore, we must assume that holding out the out-stretched hand is not the usual manner observed among Masons, although it must be admitted that even the vast majority of Grand Lodge Officers hold out the hand when confirming their minutes of Grand Lodge.

13th Did you know, the use of aprons, hoodwinks and cable tows, for example, are widespread throughout primitive cultures; while customs such as the symbolic Raising ceremony are not only commonly used, but representative of resurrection, reincarnation, re-birth and eternal life.

In India, the caste marks of Vishnu are characteristically that of the Junior Warden and are emphasised by the upright lines of the plumb-rule, likewise the caste marks of Shiva are parallel like the level of the Senior Warden.

Also in India and in parts of ancient Egypt, we find the Preserver in early mythology always depicted as trampling or stepping on the serpent of evil with his left foot.

Conclusion? There is nothing new under the sun and our usages of certain traditions, practices, signs and symbols etc., have merely been borrowed from various cultures that have been in existence long before Freemasonry, or long since ceased. They are used to illustrate salient points of our discipline, not necessarily related to the same, as practiced in earlier cultures, but given a new definition to suit our science.

14th There is some confusion as to the manner or sequence regarding the salutation given to the Worshipful Master, in the Second-Degree, during the Installation ceremony.

Personally, I have read of three methods, 1) heart, hand, badge, 2) heart, apron, glove, 3) Heart, Breast, Badge; the latter two being practiced in Yorkshire and Bristol respectively, although I am told there are as many as six variations.

I guess the definitive answer to the question lies in the outcome of the Board of Installed Masters, set up in 1827 by the H.R.H. the Duke of Sussex, to standardise the Installation ceremony. Abbreviated minutes from the meeting of 24 February 1927, found in the Grand Lodge Library, read thus:

Sal: Br: ha: Ba:
Hence, Breast, Hand, Badge.

Needless to say, as each Lodge practices its own customs, conformity to the local traditions are far more important and unless one is breaking any of the Landmarks of the Order, there is no right or wrong.

15th Little explanation or detail is given about the 'Point with a Circle'; that phrase we are familiar with in the opening of the Third Degree.

WM. What is a Centre?
JW: A point within a circle, from which every part of the circumference is equidistant.
WM: Why with the Centre?
SW: That being a point from which a Master Mason cannot err.

Consider this, if we think of the centre as being the Volume of Sacred Law, adherence to which we have been commanded to do by our own beliefs, our conscience and the Charge. Now take the skirrit, that working tool which acts on a centre pin and place that centre pin on the point within the circle. We can now control the length we release to ensure we stay within the centre.

Symbolically, the circle is God's word and by staying within its bounds we cannot err, particularly if we restrict the length of our thoughts and actions to ensure we stay within that circle.

And nothing less is expected of a Master Mason.

16th I was questioned a while back for the reason why the signs associated with the Five Points of Fellowship are given in the dark; implying that that was the reason why many Master Masons employ and discharge the signs associated with the Degree incorrectly.

Truthfully speaking, nothing in the lodge is done in total darkness, as the Master's light is never extinguished and is sufficient for the Candidate to follow what is happening; although I would agree the lights are dimmed to an ambient level to suit the salient message contained in the Third Degree.

Any confusion with regard to the signs, are generally the fault of the Lodge of Instruction which has failed to allow time to teach the correct method of signage in each degree to new Candidates.

17th The ballot for a Candidate or joining member should generally take a form, similar to the following.

At the announcement of the ballot, if it is for a joining member who is present, the Director of Ceremonies will collect and lead the Brother out of the lodge room, during the ballot and after the appropriate saluting protocol.

The Director of Ceremonies will, according to lodge tradition, collect the ballot box and display the 'nay or no' draw to the assembled brethren to show that it is empty, while being joined by the Senior and Junior Deacons at a pre-arranged moment.

It is customary for the Junior Deacon to distribute the voting tokens and the Senior Deacon to follow with the ballot box and collect the tokens. Tokens are issued to subscribing members only. Depending on the lodge custom, the Worshipful Master will be the first to cast his vote or the last and if so, will generally be responsible for displaying the 'nay or no' draw.

After a circuit of the lodge has been completed, the Deacons will return to the Director of Ceremonies who will allow them to take their vote and then relieve the Deacons of the ballot box and tokens.

The Director of Ceremonies will then present the ballot box to the Worshipful Master for him to declare the result, which under normal conditions he will do by raising the empty 'nay or no' draw before the assembled brethren to show there has been no negative votes and at the same time making a verbal declaration.

The Worshipful Master will them authorise the Initiation to go ahead, if the Candidate is present, defer the Initiation to an appropriate later date, or invite the Director of Ceremonies to fetch the joining member.

All subscribing members of the lodge should be aware of their own responsibility of ensuring the suitability of any prospective Candidate or joining member; therefore, there should never be an instance where a blackball is used.

18th Can you imagine the uproar that was caused one evening at a lodge meeting I was attending, when the Secretary, who was known for his wit and humour, announced the news to all those present that a well-known Past Master had changed his name and, as far as he knew, may be considered for gender-reassignment.

Apparently, after sending out the lodge agenda and usual pre-meeting information, the said Past Master had urgently contacted him to say that his name had been misspelt.

It took members several minutes to realise the humour of the Secretary and the fact that the Past Master's name had in fact been, misspelt on the agenda and had not been changed to 'Miss Spelt'.

19th There has always been some controversy over the character of Dr Anderson. Herbert Inman, *Masonic Problems and Queries* claims:

> *Dr. James Anderson is said to have been appointed Chaplain of St. Paul's Operative Lodge in London in 1710* (It has been suggested that this was the Lodge that met at the Goose and Gridiron Ale-house in St. Paul's ChurchYard), *and it has been alleged that he was expelled from the Society in 1715* (for some unknown misdemeanour) *and that he never became a Master Mason...*

According to Douglas Knoop and G.P. Jones', *The Genesis of Freemasonry*, Anderson was the Master of Lodge No.17, which has never been identified, but Robert Freke Gould, claims in *The History of Freemasonry*, that of the nineteen lodges that attended the Quarterly Communications in 1727, No.17 was the 'Mag: Pye, against Bishopsgate Church', although there appears to be no uniformity regarding lodge numbers, so this may not be the case.

Anderson's character and credibility, with regard to the enthusiasm shown in editing the 1723 and 1738 *Constitutions* can also be questioned further, as Knoop & Jones explain:

> *Although Anderson was only the editor of the Book of Constitutions, and although it was issued with the approval of Grand Lodge, it was nevertheless his 'sole property', out of the sale of which he doubtless hoped to make a profit. In other words, Anderson owned the copyright. In February1735, when the first edition of the Constitutions was exhausted, he sought the approval of Grand Lodge for the preparation of a new revised edition.*
>
> *In February 1735, when seeking approval for a second edition, Anderson represented a Grand Lodge that a certain William Smith (in A Pocket Companion for Freemasons) had pirated a considerable part of his Constitutions, (to the prejudice of the said Dr. Anderson, it being his sole property'; Grand Lodge*

resolved that the master and Wardens of the Lodges should discourage their members from buying Smith's books.

There was also the suggestion that Anderson lost heavily in the South Sea Bubble and that owning the copyright of the *Constitutions* helped his financial status.

20th For reasons not known to us today, but most probably because the employers of stone masons in those days were the church, the State or local boroughs or Corporations, the trade of masons, unlike most other trades of the day, were not regulated in the same way that trades that produced and sold goods were, but in 1356 we learn that:

> *Twelve Master Masons came before the Lord Mayor and the Aldermen at the Guildhall, London, to seek permission to draw up a simple code for trade regulation. The documents say that these men had come together because their trade had never been regulated. They ruled: 'That every man of the trade may work at any work touching the trade if he be perfectly skilled in knowing the same.' This prevented untrained men from stealing the work of a trained man.*

You might recall in the sixties and seventies we would have called that a demarcation dispute, when unions would ensure non-skilled men would not be allowed to do the work of a skilled man. In Scotland, they used the term Cowan to describe an unskilled mason doing a skilled mason's work. However, it was not until about 1376, that we find the first specific reference to a permanent organisation of Masons in London, when four masons were elected to the Common Council to represent the fellowship or mystery and the probability is that an organisation for masons was established sometime between 1356 and 1376.

So in essence, we now have an organised fellowship of masons. However, in reality, the building of the Tower of London, Westminster

Abbey and London Bridge would seem to indicate that there were hundreds of stone masons working in London for the Church, the State and the Corporations from about 1080 onwards, but as can be seen, it took over three hundred years for their trade to become regulated.

21st What was meant by the term 'By the regularity of my Initiation', when I was asked how do I know myself to be a Mason?

You will recall that the term 'regular', when applied to Freemasonry, refers to the manner in which the lodge has been constituted. All lodges issued with warrants under the United Grand Lodge of England are therefore deemed 'regular'. Members of 'regular' lodges are not permitted to attend any lodge that has not been duly constituted in this manner or those considered by definition to be irregular. Advice should be sought from your own lodge secretary before visits to lodges in other parts of the world be considered.

So the regularity of your Initiation quite simply means you were initiated into a regular, constituted lodge.

22nd Over the years, many Masonic historians have claimed that our ritual came through the Ancient mysteries of Isis and Osiris of Egypt, Mithras of Persia, Adonis of Syria, Dionysus, Bacchus, Eleusis and the dreams of the Grecian mythologists, but there is no evidence to prove these claims.

Others have suggested we evolved from the Roman Collegia, the Comacine Masters of Italy, the Steinmetzens of Germany, the French Compagnonnage, the Ancient Mysteries, the Trade Guilds, the Knights Templars, or the monks from the dissolved monasteries.

But it could be fair to say that many of these may have had some influence on today's Speculative Freemasonry, but there is not one definite shred of evidence to prove the exact origin of Freemasonry

We are I have no doubt, mere imitators of past ceremonies, rites, signs and symbols; those of which over the past 3,000 or so years have been freely or partially adapted by man and man alone to suit the Speculative and allegorical needs of our Craft.

I think you would therefore agree that this is why so many aspects of Freemasonry can be found throughout the world's peoples, practices and religions.

23rd

Something for us all to consider: I attended a meeting by invitation on one occasion and I was pleasantly surprised how well the evening went. The Worshipful Master was a word-perfect ritualist and unusually presented all the evenings work.

Greatly impressed by what I had heard, I remarked to my host what a wonderful evening I had enjoyed, especially the excellent demonstration in ritual presentation. To my surprise he retorted, '...he may well be proficient in the ceremonial and his duties, but I fear his brightness often fails to include an awareness of the principles the Order has been founded upon, namely, Brotherly Love, Relief and Truth.'

I held my council, but considered the deeper implications of what he had said and resolved to ensure I lived by the words I frequently repeated.

24th

Freemasonry is *a peculiar system of morality, veiled in allegory and illustrated by symbols*.

Morality or decency, I really do not need to dilate here other than to say we all know the levels of behaviour and conduct that makes man unique. That is to say that in all the animal kingdom, man alone can knowingly raise his standards to those expected by that Great Architect of the Universe to whom we acknowledge as our Creator and Overseer.

Since the dawn of time allegory, or allegorical story-telling by way of parables, analogies or tales have been employed to teach, train and help man to understand an important or salient point. Man could communicate by mouth, long before he could read and many of the world's most ancient histories were related in this form before any other means.

The power of symbols or images teaches man in an even-handed manner, for each sees the same. I believe it was Thomas Aquinas, that Dominican Friar, of the 13th century who said, '...man cannot understand without images...' In a similar fashion, Richard Taylor, author of *How to read a Church* believes that there are three characteristics of an image or symbol:

i) They can express concepts that language cannot.
ii) They can bridge gaps where language can be too difficult.
iii) They can touch us at a depth that wordy exposition does not.

Thus, like allegory, symbols have been employed since the dawn of time to educate man.

25th Here is a simple part of our ritual that has never changed, but is an illustration of the early lodge lay-out.

Like me, I am sure you would have wondered why, as the Initiate, you had to lean awkwardly across to the pedestal to tap the Wardens on the shoulder when being presented by the Junior Deacon.

Back in the 18th century, the Candidate was led around the outside of the brethren who were seated at one large table and this is reminiscent of the practice of approaching the Wardens from behind and a part of the ceremonial that has never been adapted.

26th My wife recently surprised me by asking an interesting question about the teams that qualify for entrance into the World Cup. I explained that only those countries that were affiliated to FIFA, the football world governing body, would be allowed to enter the competition.

This question brought to mind the situation of the UGLE and those Grand Lodges that are not affiliated to it; particularly that old chestnut relating to the recognition of lodges consisting of lady Freemasons and those of Co-Masonry.

I must say, over the years I have heard some pretty silly arguments both for and against recognition and amalgamation, and it reminded me of the older schisms of the past, when at one time there was in fact four Grand Lodges vying for supremacy in England.

This question of recognition in therefore not new to Freemasonry, but it is nevertheless one of great importance. We must all realise that it is not just a case of 'giving the nod' to groups that may well be Masonic in their practices, but may not necessarily meet other Masonic criteria. We cannot dilute our own traditions for the sake of increased membership, but neither can we dismiss a chance of a policy review or even constitutional reform, out of hand.

We must not denigrate UGLE for their current stance, but rather let us question our own attitudes and motives. Let us look long and hard at the trend and be sure that such a move would benefit us. A wrong decision, as we are all aware, would be absolutely disastrous for all Freemasonry.

27th No Freemason has the right to enter any lodge for which he is not a member. Visiting lodges by invitation is a congenital part of Freemasonry and on those occasions the host would be called upon or expected to vouch for the guest or if he is not known to any member, after due examination.

It is within the power of the Worshipful Master to refuse entry to any person for whom he considers cannot prove himself, or who he may have reason to believe may disturb the harmony of the lodge or if the visitor is of previous bad character.

28th I have been asked many times why Candidates wear a hoodwink. Here is my response.

The hoodwink placed upon us, represents the darkness of ignorance and has its place in many age-old rituals. It enables us to reflect more upon the new life we are about to enter, i.e. from darkness to light. It also ensures that our heart may conceive before our eyes shall discover. We may also consider that if we have had a change of mind, it serves as a shield and prevents us seeing the formation of the lodge room before having taken the Obligation, whereupon we can be led out of the room. It should also remind us to keep the entire world from our mysteries.

Lastly, it acts as the test of the faith we had previously acknowledged at our interview, in the Great Architect, ever knowing that where His name is invoked no harm will befall us.

29th Looking closer at the origins and early practices that are common place to us, the Edinburgh Register House MS (1696), asks the question regarding Signs, Tokens and Perfect Points of Entrance.

> *Q. What is the first Point?*
>
> *A. Tell me the first point ile tell you the second, The first is to heill and conceall, second, under no less pain, which is then cutting of your throat, For you most* [must] *make that sign, when you say that.*

Other *MS* of the same date, but not of the same family, answer in a similar manner. For example the *Sloan MS* c. 1700, says:

> *Q. Which is the first signe or token shew me the first and I will shew you the second?*
>
> *A. The first is heal and Conceal or Conceal and keep secrett by no less paine than cutting my tongue from my throat.*

The *Masons Examination*, 1723 says:

> *Q. What is the first Point of your Entrance?*
>
> *A. Hear and conceal, on Pain of having my Throat cut, or Tongue pull'd out.*

The *Grand Mystery of Free-Masons Discover'D*, 1724 says:

> *Q. Which is the Point of your Entry?*

A. I Hear and Conceal, under the Penalty of having my Throat cut, or my Tongue pull'd out of my Head.

Clearly a demonstration of the symbolic penalty of the Degree, first recorded in 1696, probably introduced many decades previously, and certainly carried over into the next three centuries.

30th One of the most amusing afternoons I have ever spent, was at the farm of a friend of mine who was hosting a Masonic picnic. As usual, I was knee-deep in non-Masons who were firing all manner of questions at me. As is my want, apart from the modes of recognition, I am always happy to discuss any Masonic topic.

The question and answer session was going well, but unbeknownst to me there was a newspaper reporter in the crowd and as I finished answering one question, he called out from the back of the crowd, '... and how far do you roll your trouser leg up!'

The crowd went silent, but without any hesitation whatsoever I answered, 'Just above the knee so you don't restrict the blood flow as you kneel to take your obligation.'

I feared the reporter had scuppered what had up until that point been an excellent half-an-hour of free Masonic publicity. I was so wrong, in fact he actually skulked away and the crowd turned their attention immediately back to me and continued to ask sensible questions about the Obligation.

31st In my opinion, Bernard E. Jones (1880-1865) became one of Freemasonry's 20th century heroes.

At a time when there was an obvious deficiency in good honest Masonic literature, Bro. Jones published two evergreen books, suitable for reading and reference for any Masonic student at any level.

The Freemasons' Guide and Compendium (1950) and *The Freemasons' Book of the Royal Arch*, (1957) are essential reading and give well-researched answers to as many questions you might have. They are a must for your library.

Bro. Jones became the Prestonian Lecturer for 1952 before being invited to full membership of Quatuor Coronati Lodge in 1953, and becoming Master in 1960.

September

1st During my tenure as Worshipful Master, I was once asked to adjourn a lodge meeting to allow brethren to leave because of unexpected severe weather conditions; it was argued that for the safety of the brethren we adjourn the meeting till another occasion.

Unfortunately, under the English Constitution, a lodge meeting cannot be adjourned or deferred to a later date. The lodge can be called-off, for a brief adjournment and called-on again, but not adjourned for another day. The date of all Regular and Installation meetings, of all private lodges, are fixed. They are part of the lodge by-laws which are approved by both Provincial and Grand Lodge and cannot be adjourned, deferred or changed without the authority of the Province within which the lodge meets, which acts of behalf of Grand Lodge.

On that occasion, as the safety of the brethren was paramount, we simply excused brethren that had a distance to travel, opened the lodge, read and approved the minutes, gave notice of motion that was needed to be given in open lodge and closed the lodge. The rest of the brethren then disassembled and returned safely to their homes.

2nd The first record we have of some sort of trade organisation in Scotland is found in 1474; over one hundred years after the English masons were first properly regulated.

The Seal of Cause was granted by the Edinburgh authorities when the Masons and Wrights combined to form an 'incorporation', or a single association for both trades. The document gives the rules by which each trade was to be governed. Each of the trades appointed two of the best and worthiest of their craft that were sworn to search and see that the craftsmen work was lawfully done. Apprentices at the end of their terms of training were examined by four men to ensure that they were qualified to become fellow craft, if found worthy, they had to pay the required fee to achieve this new status. The Seal of Cause does not mention a lodge and there is no evidence of a lodge in Edinburgh at this period.

What this document actually shows is that there was a clear and distinct development of the mason's trade in Scotland and Scotland now had trade organisations called 'incorporations' rather than the fraternities or mysteries that existed in England, prior to this date.

3rd Prior to the Union in 1813, Freemasons enjoyed the customs of adorning their white aprons with any number of symbols or devices associated with Freemasonry. These include pillars, crescent moons, globes or chapiters, radiant suns, triangles, squares, compasses, levels, bibles and various working tools, etc., many of them very elaborate indeed. The *Constitutions* of 1815 provided the first direction for uniformity and the practice of self-decoration ceased.

The earliest mention of the colour blue, in connection with Masonic clothing, is found in the Minutes of 17 March 1731, where Grand Lodge agreed the following:

> *...that all those who have served in the Grand Offices shall wear their white leather aprons lined with blue silk. That those brethren who have served as Stewards shall wear their aprons lined with red silk, and the Master and Wardens of Lodges shall wear their aprons lined with white silk.*

We do not get any indication of the shade of blue until 1734, when on the authority of the Deputy Grand Master an order was given for Masonic clothing. This was described as:

> *Two Grand Master's aprons lined with Garter blue silk and turned over two inches, with white strings; two deputy Grand Master aprons turned over one inch and a half, ditto.*

Here we arrive at a definite shade of blue, the Garter blue, and there is no possibility of doubt about the appearance on the fronts of the aprons, which from the modest turnover, binding the edges, has developed into the borders on the aprons which we now have.

In 1745, George II altered the shade of Garter blue to the darker colour which we are now accustomed. This was in order to distinguish his Garter Knights from those supporters of James II and his heirs who had been created Knights of the Garter by the exiled family, and were not recognised by the Hanoverians.

When this alteration to the darker shade of blue for the Garter took place, the aprons of the Grand Officers followed suit and so still remain Garter blue. The light blue was left available for the Craft in general and in time was adopted at the Union in 1813.

4th The first recorded Initiation on English soil was that of Sir Robert Moray. Moray, was Quartermaster-General to the Scottish army, which were at the time, occupying Newcastle upon Tyne.

On 20 May 1641, several Freemasons who were members of the St Mary's Chapel Lodge of Edinburgh initiated Moray on English soil giving him the distinction of holding the record of the first recorded non-operative initiated. He was also a founding member of The Royal Society and was influential in gaining its Royal Charter and formulating its statutes and regulations.

Six years later, Elias Ashmole, also a Fellow of the Royal Society, was the second recorded Initiation into Freemasonry at Warrington. It would be interesting to consider if the two men discussed Freemasonry.

Although these are the first two recorded ceremonies of Initiation on English soil, there is evidence of Masonic activity involving non-operatives in Scotland from about 1600, but recorded retrospectively and in England, recorded a year of two earlier.

5th The earliest of the exposures of Freemasonry, entitled, *A Mason's Examination* appeared in the *Flying Post* or *Post Master*, No. 4712, from Thursday, 11 April, to Saturday, 13 April, 1723.

This exposure professes to have been compiled from the papers of a deceased Mason, obviously to give it some dramatic authenticity. Interestingly, it alludes to the Second Degree, the Mark of a Master Mason and to the Pattern of an Arch, which interestingly is the first mention of the word 'Arch' in connection with Freemasonry.

Like all exposures, they were published for gain and not in support of Freemasonry; therefore they must be viewed with a jaundiced eye. Having said that, we are fortunate to have at our disposal, a number of authenticated ritual documents, which can at times verify some of the statements and practices made in such exposures, but one must always proceed with caution and never take unverified statements and practices as being bona fide Masonic customs of the day.

6th I was fascinated to come across a piece of allegorical ritual used in the Red Cross of Constantine Degree, it does not have any historical accuracy and is merely part of the story of the Degree. Nevertheless, I found it very colourful and interesting as it appears to expound the theory of the origin of Freemasonry that has been lately disproved.

> *It is now my duty to explain to you the legendary origin of Masonic rites as now practised. It is said that the Crusaders, finding themselves unable to expel the Saracens from the Holy Land, agreed with Godfrey de Bouillon to veil the mysteries of religion under emblems, by which they would be enabled to maintain their devotions in secret, and secure themselves against the intrusion of traitors or pretended friends.*
>
> *In this respect they followed examples laid down in the sacred scriptures, the style of which is figurative. The model which they selected was Solomon's Temple, which emblematically represents the Christian Church. Hence it follows that the mysteries of the craft are in reality the mysteries of religion. The Knights were, however, carefully not to entrust this important secret to any whose fidelity and discretion had not been fully proved. They*

therefore invented different degrees to test their Candidates, and gave them only symbolical secrets without explanation, to prevent treachery and solely to enable them to make themselves known to each other. For this purpose it was resolved to use different signs, words and tokens in each degree, by which they would be secured against the Saracens, Cowan's and intruders.

It was, however, only in the Master Mason's Degree that our knightly brethren began to unfold the true mystery by narrating the assassination of Hiram Abiff at the hands of false brethren. The symbolic mystery of Hiram's death represents to us that of the Messiah. For instance, the three attacks that were made on the master builder at the three gates of the Temple allude to the three points of condemnation against Christ at the tribunals of Caiaphas the High Priest, Herod the King and Pilate the Roman Governor. It was from the last tribunal that our Lord was led to a violent and shameful death.

The three blows that were given with the plumb rule, level and the heavy setting maul are also symbolic of the buffet on the cheek, the flagellation and the cruel crown of thorns.

The brethren assembled around the tomb of Hiram represent the disciples lamenting the death of Christ on the Cross. The master's words, which is said to be lost since the death of Hiram Abiff, is the same that the Messiah pronounced on the Cross, and which the Jews did not comprehend: 'Eloi, Eloi, Lama Sabachthani.' Instead of these words, our ancient brethren substituted the word of our Master Mason's Degree, which signifies 'the son of the widow is slain.'

This was done to guard the real secrets from traitors, warned by the example of Judas, who betrayed his Master. The sprig of acacia is the figure of the Cross, which was made of wood from an acacia tree.

The Royal Arch, referring to the captivity of the Jews, shows us the persecution of the Christians under the Roman Emperors, and their liberty under Constantine the Great.

The Red Cross Order is the first degree in which the ultimate objects of freemasonry were revealed. In the ceremony of Knights of the Holy Sepulchre the allegory was further explained. The Knights of St. John the Evangelist, however, alone received the true words; and it was only after warfare with enemies of the faith that they obtained this privilege, and were granted full communion with the holy brotherhood.

7th The Operatives, officially named The Worshipful Society of Free Masons, Rough Masons, Wallers, Slaters, Paviours, Plaisterer's and Bricklayers, was founded in 1913. The ritual they use is like practical instruction rather than what we know and expect in the Craft. The Order claims to be a Masonic Society which exists to perpetuate a memorial of the practices of Operative Free Masons existing prior to modern speculative Freemasonry. Membership of the Society is restricted to those who are Master Masons, Mark Master Masons and Holy Royal Arch Companions in good standing.

The Order has seven Degrees which are as follows:

I° Indentured Apprentice
II° Fellow of the Craft
III° Super-Fellow, Fitter and Marker
IV° Super-Fellow, Setter Erector
V° Intendent, Overseer, Superintendent and Warden
VI° Passed Master
VII° Passed Grand Master Mason

8th One of the duties of the Tyler, prior to any postage system, was to deliver the lodge Summons.

In 1736, the records of the Lodge of Antiquity, No.2, which met at the Queens Arms, St Pauls Churchyard, showed that the Landlord (the Landlord was often used as the Guard or Tyler) was:

'Allowed 12d each Lodge night for carreing ye Letters to each member'

On 3 July 1744, this was changed to: 'Ordered that the Tyler for the future do deliver out the Summons for the meeting of this Lodge, and be paid for the same one shilling exclusively of his money for the Tyling.'

The fee was raised to two shillings the following year.

However, earlier in a minute of the *Lodge of Felicity*, No.58, dated 12th July 1738, they took another view:

> *This night the Lodge took into consideration the Great Expence of the Tyler and came up with the following Resolution nem. Con:* (with no one dissenting; unanimously) *The House* (by which was meant the Gun Tavern, Jermyn Street) *shall send the Summons to each Member one day before the Lodge night and that the Tyler shall have one schilling only for Tyling the Lodge.*

9th Keeping your feet on the ground is something I have always advised new Freemasons to do. Why? Because so many Freemasons seem to forget that whatever lofty rank they achieve, whatever noble order they might join, whatever grand title they are given, once they leave the lodge room, the convocation or the encampment etc., they return to the more pressing and important duties of their life which are, your wife, your family and your employment.

Titles like Most Wise Sovereign, Most Puissant Sovereign, Excellent Companion, Worshipful Master, Thrice Illustrious Master, Eminent Preceptor, High Priest, Most Potent Commander, etc., are of no value in the real world, for when the meeting is over you return to being Mr. Jones or Mr. Smith.

But there are even greater rewards and titles awaiting you at home, and these are those of husband, father, uncle, brother and grandfather and it is those, non-Masonic titles that you must honour as they are enduring.

So remember keep your feet well grounded; Freemasonry is your hobby or pleasant pastime, and it holds absolutely little or no significance in other circles of your lives.

10th A Toast to all Guests and Visitors – Unknown

Tonight I have the pleasure, to all I must confess,
So please all be upstanding, here's health to our Visitors and Guests.
The fellowship you bring tonight is something that can't compare,
You know we like to see you and glad you're always here.
The Harmony and chat we have with our old and new-found friends
We wish it could last for many hours, but it always has to end.
But as all good things must come to pass and we go our separate way,
We hope you enjoyed yourself and will return again someday.
And now I ask the members here to raise a glass in cheer,
A toast to all our visitors and guests who have supported us this year.

11th The English Exposures of 1760–1769 consist of nine ritual documents:

- *A Master Key to Freemasonry*
- *Three Distinct Knocks*
- *Jachin and Boaz*
- *Hiram*
- *Mystery of Free Masonry Explained*
- *Shibboleth*
- *Mahhabone*
- *Solomon in All His Glory*
- *The Free-Mason Stripped Naked*

Six of the nine have been found to be copies or similar to the other three. These are:

Three Distinct Knocks (1760), purported to be the ritual used by the Antients.

Jarchin and Boaz (1762), said to cater for both Modern and Antients.

Shibboleth (1765), used by the lodges of the Moderns.

I am fortunate to have copies of these documents as part of my library.

12th When you were Passed to the Degree of a Fellowcraft, you were asked the following, 'Where were you made a Mason?' and you answered, 'In the body of a lodge, Just, Perfect and Regular'. When therefore is a lodge considered to be 'Perfect'?

A lodge is considered 'Perfect' when seven members are present. The seven that make a lodge 'Perfect' are '...the Master and his two Wardens...two Fellowcrafts...two Entered Apprentices...'

Seven or more make a perfect lodge, because King Solomon was seven years and upwards in building, completing, and dedicating the Temple at Jerusalem. They have likewise a further allusion to the seven liberal arts and sciences.

Seven appears repeatedly throughout the Bible and is considered to be a powerful and mystical number.

- God rested on the seventh day after completing the work of the creation.
- Jacob bowed seven times before his brother Esau to show perfect submission.
- God ordered the lamp stand or (Menorah) should have seven branches.
- The feasts of the Lord lasted seven Sabbaths.
- The land was divided into seven lots.
- There were seven loaves that filled seven baskets.

These are just a few of the numerous references to the number seven found in the Bible.

13th The Edinburgh Register House MS (1696) was discovered early in 1930, in the Old Register House, Edinburgh by Bro. Charles T. McInnes. It was among a number of old documents transferred there in 1808 from the Court of Session, Edinburgh, to the Historical Department of the Register House. Apparently it is in no way related to any of the records among which it was found. Apart from this the early history of the catechism is unknown.

It consists of a double sheet of folio paper folded once to form four pages about 17.7cm x 29.2cm, (approx. 7 inches by 11½ inches) and shows some considerable signs of use.

The catechism is written on pages 1, 2 and 3; the document was then folded again. Across the top of the outside is endorsed: 'Some Questions Anent the mason word 1696'.

It starts with the following:

> 'Some questions that Masons use to put to those who have ye word before they will acknowledge them.'

There follows a series of question culminating in the heading:

> 'The forme of giving the Masonic word.'

The document was authenticated as genuine after similarities were found with part of the ceremony recorded on the first page of the minute book of the Lodge of Haughfoot, which was the first wholly non-operative Scottish lodge, founded in 1702.

14th

The splendour of our ritual and the parallels it often uses to accentuate salient points never fails to excite me and these gems of English that was in use at the time the ritual was written, go to beautify our work.

I am reminded of that phrase from the First Degree Working tools which says:

> '...yet ought no eminence of situation make us forget that we are Brothers, for he who is placed on the lowest spoke of fortune's wheel is equally entitled to our regard...'

Apart from reminding us of the respect we should show our fellows, regardless of their status, it uses as an analogy, 'fortune's wheel'. In medieval and ancient philosophy, the Wheel of Fortune, or *Rota Fortunae*, is a symbol of the capricious nature of Fate. The wheel belongs to the Goddess Fortuna, who spins it at random, changing the positions of those on the wheel, some suffer great misfortune, and others gain windfalls. Regardless of our place on Rota Fortunae, we are obliged by our tenure, to meter out the same, courtesies, respect and judgement to all, irrespective of their situation or status.

15th It was the Apostle Paul who said in the 13th chapter of his first epistle to the Corinthians that, 'Charity never faileth'.

Over a millennia later in Christian theology, Thomas Aquinas understands charity as 'the friendship of man for God' and holds it as 'the most excellent of the virtues' and that 'the habit of charity extends not only to the love of God, but also to the love of our neighbour'.

Whilst two centuries later in 1360, we find the last three words of the earliest document recognised by Masonic historians relating to the Craft stating, 'Say we so all per charyté'.

By 1724, this understanding of love and charity become enshrined in Masonic lore when we read from a catechism:

Q. How many particular Points pertain to a Free-Mason?
A. Three; Fraternity, Fidelity, and Tacity.
Q. What do they represent?
A. Brotherly Love, Relief, and the Truth…

And to bring the subject right up to the 21st century we read from another catechism:

Q. Name the grand principles on which the Order is founded?
A. Brotherly Love, relief and truth.

Therefore, in the Masonic setting, the terms 'charity' and 'love' are, like that Volume of Sacred Law states, synonymous and as I have said on previous occasions, 'should adorn our noble science like the flowers in a well-kept garden. It should lie at the very heart of our organisation'.

16th In all regular, well-formed, constituted lodges, there is a point within a circle round which the brethren cannot err; this circle is bounded between north and south by two grand parallel lines, one representing Moses, and the other King Solomon. On the upper part of this circle rests the Volume of the Sacred Law, supporting Jacob's ladder, the top of which reaches to the heavens; and were we as conversant in that Holy Book, and as adherent to the doctrines therein contained as those parallels were, it would bring us to Him who would not deceive us, neither will He suffer deception.

In going around this circle, we must necessarily touch on both those parallel lines, likewise on the Sacred Volume; and while a Mason keeps himself thus circumscribed, he cannot err.

17th In Freemasonry, we have heard references to Jacob's Ladder; here therefore is the story of how it received its name.

Rebecca, the beloved wife of Isaac, knowing by Divine inspiration that a peculiar blessing was vested in the soul of her husband, was desirous to obtain it for her favourite son Jacob, though by birth right it belonged to Esau her first-born. Jacob had no sooner fraudulently obtained his father's blessing, than he was obliged to flee from the wrath of his brother, who in a moment of rage and disappointment had threatened to kill him.

Arid as he journeyed towards Padan-aram, in the land of Mesopotamia (where by his parents' strict command he was enjoined to go), being weary and benighted on a desert plain, he lay down to rest, taking the Earth for his bed, a stone for his pillow, and the Canopy of Heaven for a covering. He there in a vision saw a ladder, the top of which reached to the Heavens, and the angels of the Lord ascending and descending thereon.

It was then the Almighty entered into a solemn covenant with Jacob, that if he would abide by His laws, and keep His commandments, He would not only bring him again to his father's house in peace and prosperity, but would make of his seed a great and mighty people.

This was amply verified, for after a lapse of twenty years Jacob returned to his native country, was kindly received by his brother Esau, and was afterwards, by Pharaoh's appointment, made second man in Egypt, and the children of Israel, highly favoured by the Lord, became, in process of time, one of the greatest and most mighty nations on the face of the earth.

18th

The Movable Jewels of the lodge are the Square, Level and Plumb Rule.

Among operative masons, the Square is to try, and adjust, rectangular corners of buildings, and assist in bringing rude matter into due form: The Level to lay levels and prove horizontals and the Plumb Rule to try, and adjust, uprights, while fixing them on their proper bases.

Among Free and Accepted Masons, the Square teaches morality, the Level equality, and the Plumb Rule justness and uprightness of life and actions.

They are called Movable Jewels, because they are worn by the Master and his Wardens and transferable to their successors on nights of Installation. The Master is distinguished by the Square, the Senior Warden by the Level, and the Junior Warden by the Plumb Rule.

19th

By far one of the most enduring misunderstandings in Freemasonry relates to the 'snake' clasp which affixes the apron around the body.

Let me make it clear, the snake or serpent has no association with Freemasonry or our symbolism. However, opponents of Freemasonry have repeatedly made every effort to use this as evidence that Freemasons worship the snake/serpent, which is representative of Satan.

The snake clasp was commonly used for uniforms, including that of the Police and Navy and was quite simply adopted by the apron manufacturers as the simplest pattern or belt fastening that had previously been successful with other uniforms. It is also fair to say that most boys had an elasticated belt with the same snake clasp.

20th It is incumbent on every Proposer and Seconder to discuss with every prospective Candidate the questions he most likely will be expected to answer, if he decides to make an application to become a Freemason.

This is absolutely crucial and will help to avoid any unnecessary embarrassment or misunderstanding of the commitment or expectation of the Candidate during the interview. The Proposer and Seconder will also have a reasonable intimate knowledge of the Candidate and would have gauged his reliability as a person and his suitability as a prospective member of their lodge. This would include ensuring that he is not at variance with any existing member.

Not every Candidate will suit every lodge, and it will benefit those proposing new members to ensure entry to the lodge, for the Candidate, is clear and that there will be no complications.

You would have heard this old adage on many occasions, but it's always worth repeating: 'If in doubt…leave it out'.

21st The condition of being slipshod that the Candidate finds himself in is possibly associated to two Jewish customs. We are all familiar with the first of these in which we find Moses '…at the mountain of God, even to Horeb' and the miraculous appearance of the burning bush, which '…burned with fire, and the bush was not consumed', culminating in the appearance of Jehovah to Moses and the instruction to remove his shoes. We read in Exodus 3:5: 'And he said, draw not nigh hither: put off thy shoes from off thy feet, for the place where on thou standest is holy ground.'

Compare with Joshua 5:15: 'And the captain of the Lord's host said unto Joshua, loose thy shoe from off thy foot; for the place whereon thou standest is holy. And Joshua did so.'

Acts 7:33: 'Then said the Lord to him, Put off thy shoes from thy feet: for the place where thou standest is holy ground.'

The second reference we find to the removing of a shoe is in the book of Ruth 4:7

> *Now this was the manner in former time in Israel concerning redeeming and concerning changing, for to confirm all things; a man plucked off his shoe, and gave it to his neighbour: and this was a testimony in Israel. (The manner referred to in the former time in Israel can be found in Deuteronomy 25:7-9.)*

In relation to this second reference, Bernard Jones takes up the commentary:

> *The second of the Jewish traditions is to be found in Ruth 4:7 where we learn that to unloose the shoe and give it to another person was a gesture of sincerity, of honest intention, a confirmation of a contract that had been made between the two parties. The inference to be drawn from this is that the Candidate's slipshod condition is in itself a token of fealty or fidelity.*
>
> *A catch question in an 18th-century irregular print runs:*
>
> *Q. What did you pay for freemasonry?*
>
> *A. An old shoe, an old shoe of my mother's.*
>
> *From this we may conclude that the Initiate probably wore a slipper belonging to the lodge, just as he does to-day.* Bernard E. Jones, *Freemasons Guide and Compendium*, p.269.

The reference to 'mother' is part of a secret code of words some Freemasons have used to determine the number of the lodge to which you belong, when non-Masons are present, by asking, e.g. 'How old is your mother?'

22nd

The Order has been founded on three grand principles namely Brotherly Love, Relief and Truth. Here we look at Relief.

The term relief encompasses our attitudes towards the whole of mankind, for no Freemason should ever turn his back on any poor soul in need of assistance where it was in his capacity to help.

The Emulation Lectures of the Three Degrees explain Relief thus:

> *To relieve the distressed is a duty incumbent on all men, particularly Masons who are linked together in one indissoluble chain of sincere affection; hence, to soothe the unhappy, sympathise in their misfortunes compassionate their miseries, and restore peace to their troubled minds, is the grand aim we have in view; on this basis we establish our friendships and form our connections.*
>
> First Lecture, Sixth Section Six

On the night of our Initiation we learn one of the most dramatic lessons: the importance of helping others. That moment of symbolic destitution is not intended to teach us merely how it feels to be poor, but we are also made to feel embarrassed by our inability to contribute. To relieve the distress of the victims of misfortune, whatever their predicament, for it is not our role to judge, is a duty expected of all men, but it is particularly incumbent on Freemasons because they believe that an unbreakable chain of sincere affection binds them close together. That lesson, impressed so strongly on our heart also reminds us that such relief is not restricted to Freemasons, but to all mankind.

23rd Why is it said that in our lodges, Jacob's Ladder rests on the Volume of the Sacred Law?

It is because the doctrines contained in that Holy Book we are taught to believe in the dispensations of Divine Providence; which belief strengthens our Faith, and enables us to ascend the first step. This Faith naturally creates in us a Hope of becoming partakers of the blessed promises therein recorded; which Hope enables us to ascend the second step. But the third and last, being Charity, comprehends the whole; and the Mason who is possessed of this virtue in its most ample sense, may justly be deemed to have attained the summit of his profession; figuratively speaking, an ethereal mansion, veiled from mortal eyes by the starry firmament, emblematically depicted in our lodges by seven Stars, which have an allusion to as many regularly made Masons; without which number, no lodge is perfect, neither can any Candidate be legally initiated into the Order.

24th There are several types of columns and pillars, referred to in Masonic teaching, this section deals with the symbol of the 'broken column'.

We learn that under the Hebrews, columns or pillars were used metaphorically to signify Princes or Nobles, as if they were the pillars of a state. In Psalm 6:3 we read, 'If the foundations be destroyed what can the righteous do?' meaning in the original, 'when the columns are overthrown, that is, when the firm supporters of what is right and good have perished.'

Isaiah 14:10 reads '…her (Egypt's) columns are broken down, that is, the nobles of her state.'

Thus, in Freemasonry, the broken column, which is not commonly used in the English Masonic system, is the emblem of the fall of one of the chief supporters of the Craft. The use of the column or pillars as a monument erected over a tomb was a very ancient custom, and was a very significant symbol of the character and spirit of the person interred.

25th The funniest story I ever heard was that of a young Freemason who was marrying his childhood sweetheart. The ceremony was held in a very large church, which was full of family and guests of both the Bride and the Groom.

I am not sure if the groom was overcome by the solemn occasion or just nervous, but the Minister pressed on and asked the groom, 'John will you take Jane to be your wife? Will you love her, comfort her, honour and protect her, and, forsaking all others, be faithful to her as long as you both shall live?'

Looking to John for the affirmative response, John replied, 'So mote it be'.

The men in both families and the Minister were all Freemasons and saw the funny side; as did the Bride…eventually.

By the way, the names have been changed to protect the innocent.

26th The Dumfries MS (1710), gives us the earliest insight into the manner in which an Entered Apprentice was received. The catechetical exchange states:

Q. Hou [How] were you brought in?
A. Shamfully w^t [with] a rope about my neck.
Q. What pouster [posture] were you in when you Receved?
A. Neither sitting nor standing
nor running nor going but on my left knee.
Q. Whay a rope about your neck?
A. To hang me If I should betry may trust.
Q. Why upon your left Knee?
A. Because I would be in too humble a pouster to ye receiving o[f] ye Royall secret.
Q. What Obligation are you under?
A. [A] great oath.
Q. What punishment is inflicted on these y^t [that] reveals y^e [the] secret?
A. Y^r [Your] heart is to be taken out alive y^r [your]head to be cut off & y^r [your] bodys to be buried in y^e [the] sea mark & not in any place Qr [where] christians are buried.

I have added the bracketed words to help with the understanding, but the method of reception and modern current workings shines through in these words.

27th Martin Clare was a distinguished and celebrated Freemason, who it was believed was initiated at the Old King's Arms Lodge. He later became Master of the lodge that met at the Shakespeare's Head, St James, which was constituted in 1721 and appointed a Grand Steward in 1734, Junior Grand Warden in 1735 and Deputy Grand Master in 1741. Although his birth is not known, he was a London schoolmaster of some renown who was elected a Fellow of the Royal Society in 1735.

It is believed that he was the author of *A Defence of Masonry* which was written in repose to Pritchard's *Masonry Dissected* which was reproduced in the 1738 edition of the *Constitutions*. His Masonic fame rests on an oration he gave before the Grand Lodge in 1735, which was subsequently translated into several foreign languages.

The Freemason, dated June 6, 1925, says:

> *The second name in the roster of Old King's Arms Lodge, No.28, London, is that of Sir Cecil Wray's Senior Warden in 1730—Martin Clare; one of the greatest worthies the Craft in England has known, who represented the Lodge on the Board of Grand Stewards in 1734, became Junior Grand Warden in the following year, and in 1741 was appointed Deputy Grand Master to the Earl of Morton. There seems little doubt that he was initiated in the Lodge, and, although he never sat in the Master's Chair, the Minute Books contain many references which testify to his love for it and to the great services he rendered to it. When Sir Cecil Wray was invited to become the Master, he accepted on condition that Martin Clare would undertake the duties of Senior Warden. Many of the Lodge Minutes are in his handwriting, and those Minutes are certainly a model, both in penmanship and composition, of what such chronicles should be. He frequently lectured at the Old King's Arms Lodge. It was the custom for many years for his Oration to be read in the Lodge annually.*

He was also asked by the Grand Master to prepare a system of Lectures for use in lodge and those are which we are familiar with today.

He died in 1751.

28th Piecing together our early ritual is difficult, but with the aid of early exposures we can get a taster. The *Mason's Examination* (1723), tells us:

> *When a Free-Mason is enter'd…having given to all present of the Fraternity a pair of Man and Women's Gloves and Leathern Apron, he is to hear the history belonging to the Society read to him by the Master of the Lodge. Then a Warden leads him to the Master and Fellows; to each of whom he is to say - I fain would a Fellow-Mason be, As all your Worships may plainly see.*

The *Grand Whimsy* (1730) offers a little more detail:

> *...two Wardens took me under each arm, and conducted me from Darkness into Light...to the upper End of ye Room...whence I touched ye Master...on the Shoulder, to which he replied 'Who have we here' To which I answered 'A Gentleman who desires to be admitted a Member of the Society' He asked me, if I came there of my own Desire, or at ye request or desire of another, I said, My own. He then told me, if I would become a Brother of their Society, I must take the Oath…*

The *Scottish Masons Confession*, 1727, tells us that the Candidate was:

> *...made to kneel on the bare right knee...and the open compasses pointing to his breast, and his bare elbow on the Bible with his hand...*

After the Oath, *the Harlian Fragment* (c.1690) says that:

> *There is several words and signs of a free mason to be revealed to you which you will answer before God at the Great and terrible day of Judgement unless you keep secret to any but to the Masters and fellows of the said Society of free masons so help me God.*

Just an example of the importance of these early exposures.

29th I have often found it to be a complete paradox as to the way we take every opportunity, when we bring somebody into the Craft, to extol the virtues of Freemasonry by detailing the fact that, a single belief in a Supreme Being is enough 'religion' for one to satisfy that enquiry.

We take great pains to express the deist nature of our Craft, and indeed, even go so far as to forbid the discussion of one's personal religious beliefs. However once they are members, they then become aware that unless their religion is one that is based upon Christianity and in some cases, its tenets are that of a Trinitarian form, they cannot progress into certain side Orders.

Therefore, if an adherent of Christianity, Judaism, Islam and Sikhism were friends, and all were initiated on the same night, only one could progress to certain Degrees.

Surely, this therefore makes the original Charges founded in our first *Book of Constitutions* and still used today, somewhat outdated. As the last paragraph of section, one states: 'Thus masonry is the centre of union between good men and true, and the happy means of conciliating friendship amongst those who must otherwise have remained at a perpetual distance.'

Do we not bring all religions together under the Craft and then divide the same with certain additional or side degrees?

Just a thought to ponder.

30th Here is an interesting point of protocol. Traditionally, when the Entered Apprentice is presented to the Worshipful Master by the Senior Warden, the Senior Warden is instructed to invest the Entered Apprentice with the distinguishing badge of a Mason. At the conclusion of the presentation the Senior Warden states: 'I strongly exhort you ever to wear and consider it as such; and further inform you that if you never disgrace that badge…it will never disgrace you.'

During the brief halt in his comments, the Senior Warden strikes the Initiate's badge with his right hand and the brethren present should strike their own badge simultaneously, rather than clap their hands.

October

1st I love to hear the closing of the Second degree when the Junior Warden exclaims:

Happy have we met,
Happy may we part,
And happy meet again.

George Claret's version of 1835, is similar:

As happily we have met,
So happily may we part,
And happily meet again.

An old Exeter version of 1732 is also similar:

Happily have we met,
Happily may we part,
And happily meet again.

All three versions, although slightly different, express the same sentiment. However, I really had to chuckle at this version I once heard at one lodge I visited:

Merry have we met, merry have we been.
Merry may we part and merry meet again.
With our merry sing-song happy gay and free,
And a merry ding-dong, happy let us be.

2nd As part of the Management Committee for my local Masonic Centre, we often had cause to use contractors for various repairs and always followed the usual procedure when obtaining more than one quote.

At times, the centre was also blessed with volunteers to carry out works, other times there was a definite shortage of willing helpers.

By far the funniest incident I remember was when a Brother generously offered to re-paint a large room free of labour charges, but not materials. His invoice to the committee included the words:

15 Litres of Vinyl Silk Brilliant White Emulation!

I was told later that the ritual he practised was Emulsion!

3rd There are several phrases found in our ritual that have allusions specifically to Christianity. This is somewhat surprising when we consider that the Craft was an actively de-Christianised before its move towards Deism and religious tolerance.

One paragraph that has caused much attention is found in the Third Degree Charge which states: '…and lift your eyes to that Bright Morning Star, whose rising brings peace and salvation to the faithful and obedient of the human race.'

Revelation 22:16, King James Version of the Bible explains who the Bright Morning Star is: 'I Jesus have sent mine angel to testify unto you these things in the churches. I am the root and the offspring of David, *and* the bright and morning star.'

Some students of Freemasonry believe the Morning Star is Venus, when it appears before sunrise; however Venus is also known as the Evening star. Sirius and Mercury also appear before sunrise on certain days of the year, but none of these stars 'brings peace and salvation to the faithful and obedient of the human race'.

Confirmation of the allusion to Jesus comes from the fact that lodges made up mainly of Jewish brethren, have changed the wording to avoid any embarrassment: '…and lift our eyes to Him, whose Divine Word brings Peace and Salvation to the faithful…'

A most suitable amendment to ensure inclusion.

4th Did you know at the preparation for our Initiation, our right arm was made bare to show we were ready for labour and our left breast was made bare to show that we carry no concealed weapon.

Of course, it is of paramount importance that nothing offensive or defensive is brought into the lodge to disturb its harmony and here was the opportunity for the Tyler to ensure that you, the Candidate, are not an intruder or Cowan. Many also consider it confirms the gender of the Candidate, although I do not necessarily subscribe to that theory. Finally, it shows that we are prepared to discover the secrets and mysteries with an open heart.

We have our left knee made bare, for it is upon that knee we kneel to take the Great and Solemn Obligation. The left was once considered the sacred side of the body, which coincides with the teaching of the Matriarchal Age, for the left is supposed to be feminine and the right masculine. Jason, the leader of the Argonauts, in the quest for the Golden Fleece, came before Pelias without a shoe on his left foot. Vervain, used by the Druids in casting lots, was dug up with the left hand. The Caduceus, the magical wand, was carried by Hermes in his left hand.

5th Freemasonry really does have a lighter side and over the years I have seen and heard so many things that have made me chuckle.

I recall one evening when we had a rather overzealous Initiate, who was anxious to please and keen to learn. As one would expect, his Proposer, the Junior Deacon and even the DC, had taken great pains to explain that he will be guided throughout the ceremony and will only be required to speak when directly asked a question, at which time the Junior Deacon will be there to give him the answer necessary or to prompt him.

The ceremony went very well and the Candidate was exemplary; well, that was until the Worshipful Master invited him to leave the lodge to restore himself to his personal comforts.

The Junior Deacon took the Candidate by the right-hand, moved him off to the west, turned him to face the Worshipful Master and said, 'Salute the Worshipful Master as a Mason'.

Before the Junior Deacon could instruct the Candidate, he clicked his heels together, threw his right hand up and offered the Worshipful Master a full military salute.

6th When addressing and saluting the Worshipful Master, many brethren rise, salute and maintain the sign during their speaking, regardless of the length of time they may take.

The correct procedure is for the Brother to stand to order and salute the Worshipful Master, in that particular degree before speaking, discharge the sign as he commences, and salute again when finished speaking and before resuming their seat.

7th There is a distinct difference between Permanent, Permissive, Regular and Elected Officers of the lodge.

Permanent

In truth, there are no permanent Officers of the lodge as each Officer is appointed or elected annually. Having said that, in many cases, the Treasurer, Secretary, Director of Ceremonies and Organist, for example, hold office for long periods, but are not considered permanent.

Permissive

These are the Officers of the lodge who may be appointed by the Worshipful Master if he so desires, as distinct from those that the *Book of Constitutions* says he must appoint, they are the Chaplain, Director of Ceremonies, Assistant Director of ceremonies, Almoner, Organist, Assistant Secretary and Steward.

Regular

The Regular Officers of the lodge are those that according to the *Book of*

Constitutions, the Worshipful Master must appoint. They are the Wardens, Treasurer, Secretary, Deacons, Inner Guard, and Tyler.

Elected
The Treasurer and the Tyler are elected annually by the members and invested, rather than appointed, by the Master.

8th What are the 'perfect points of my entrance'?

There are three distinct possibilities that one could consider that the phrase 'perfect points of my entrance' refers to:

One's Entrance as a Candidate
One's Entrance into Freemasonry,
One's Entrance into a lodge at work.

The First Lecture, First Section, seems to point to all three for we have this exchange:

W.M. Will you give me the points of entrance?
CAN. If you give me the first I will give you the second.
W.M. I hele.
CAN. I Conceal.
W.M. What is it that you wish to conceal?
CAN. All secrets and mysteries of or belonging to, Free and accepted Masons in Masonry.
W.M. This being open Lodge, what at other times you wish to conceal may now safely reveal?
CAN. Of, at, and on.
W.M. Of, at, and on what?
CAN. Of my own free will and accord. At the door of the Lodge. On the point of a sharp implement presented to my naked left breast.

Of my own free will and accord – indicating his entrance into Masonry.
At the door of the lodge – indicating his entrance into a lodge at work.

On the point of a sharp implement presented to my naked left breast – indicating his willingness to undergo such trials and approbations to prove his membership or entrance into Freemasonry.

The perfect points of one's entrance then being, *Of*, *At* and *On*.

9th We have heard how Jacob's Ladder rests firmly on the Volume of Sacred Law in our lodges and reaches to the Heavens, and the angels of the Lord ascend and descend thereon.

The staves of the ladder we are told are many and they point out the several moral virtues, but have specific reference to the three principle virtues which are Faith, Hope and Charity. This is because we should have Faith in the Great Architect of the Universe; Hope in Salvation; and to show Charity to all men. Here we look at Charity.

Lovely in itself, it is the brightest ornament which can adorn our Masonic profession. It is the best test and surest proof of the sincerity of our religion. Benevolence, rendered by Heaven-born Charity, is an honour to the nation whence it springs, is nourished, and cherished. Happy is the man who has, sown in his breast, the seeds of benevolence; he envies not his neighbour; he believes not a tale reported to his prejudice, he forgives the injuries of men, and endeavours to blot them from his recollection. Then, brethren, let us remember, that we are Free and Accepted Masons, ever ready to listen to him who craves our assistance and from him who is in want, let us not withhold a liberal hand. So shall a heartfelt satisfaction reward our labours, and the produce of love and Charity will most assuredly follow.

10th The Scottish operative term for an untrained mason or a dry stone dyker, was 'Cowan' and was initially used in first of William Schaw's Statutes of 1598.

> *Item, that na maister or farow of craft ressaue ony cowan is to wirk in his societie or cumpanye, nor send nane of his servands to wirk w'cowanis, under the pane of twentie punds sa oft as ony*

persone offendis heirintill.
(Item, No master or fellow of craft shall accept any Cowan to work in his society or company, nor send any of his servants to work with Cowan's, under the penalty of twenty pounds as often as any person offends in this matter.)

The term next appears in a non-operative form in a ritual document in England, known as *A Mason's Confession* (1727), which originated in Scotland.

N.B: One is taught, that the cowan's siege is built up of whin stones, that it may soon tumble down again; and it stands half out half in the lodge, that his neck may be under the drop in rainy weather, to come in at his shoulder, and run out at his shoes.

The next exclusive English use of the term is found in *Masonry Dissected* (1730), when the Master asks the position and duty of the *Junior Enter'd 'Prentis*.

Q. What is his Business?
A. To keep off all Cowans and Eves-droppers.
Q. If a Cowan (or Listner) is catch'd how is he to be punished?
A. To be plac'd under the Eves of the Houses (in rainy Weather) till the Water runs in at his Shoulders and out at his Shoos.

According to Harry Carr, the phrase 'Cowans and intruders' does not fully appear in our ritual till the late 18th century (*The Freemason at Work*, 1976).

11th Surprisingly, records exist in Ireland of the Degree of the Holy Royal Arch Templar Priest dating back to the late 18th century, but there appears to be no governing body and it seems Knights Templars from various Craft lodges would join together to confer the Degree.

The 19th century saw the expansion of the Order followed by a sharp decline as by the 1890s interest in the Order was failing. The Grand Council of Allied Masonic Degrees took the Degree under its jurisdiction.

But it was Henry Hotham, who in 1894 was the last remaining Knight Priest, admitted nine Knights into the Order thus injecting fresh impetus. Conscious of the jurisdiction of the Grand Council of Allied Masonic Degrees, negotiations took place and by mutual consent the separation took place.

By 1923, the Grand College was formed, and the Order has subsequently grown. Sadly, the Order is no longer practised in its country of origin, Ireland.

To be considered for membership you must be a subscribing member of a Craft lodge, a Royal Arch Chapter, a Knight Templar Preceptory and the Trinitarian Christian faith.

12th Here is an amusing story which coincides with the first official mention of the term 'Tyler'.

According to the minutes of Grand Lodge, dated 8 June 1732, a complaint was received from several Grand Stewards concerning a Bro. Lewis, who they had engaged as an attended for the Grand feast.

Apparently, Bro. Lewis had been entrusted to lock up thirty dishes of meat that had been prepared for the said banquet. Grand Lodge were told that due to his carelessness, the dishes of meat had been taken away by those who had no manner of right to do so.

When challenged about the same, Bro. Lewis became insolent and was immediately called to Grand Lodge where he made only a frivolous and trifling defence of the accusation. He would have received an official censure had it not been noted that he was 'Tyler' to several lodges and '...if the Grand Lodge should Strictly pursue their Resentment it might deprive him of the best part of his subsistence...'

The matter was resolved when Bro. Lewis asked publicly, the pardon of the Grand Stewards, faithfully promising to take better care and 'behave decently', in the future.

13th Did you know there is no formal practice for toasting Absent Brethren and it has simply become a custom? Formal toasts are taken after Grace has been said or sung and any such wine-takings prior to Grace are merely considered that: 'taking wine with'. As you cannot actually take wine with a Brother that is not present, the suggestion that one should toast Absent Brethren sounds a little absurd.

Some lodges refer to Absent Brethren when they consider the clock is on the square. This, more often than not, is considered nine o'clock. However, probably like me, you have seen some Directors of Ceremony abuse this and suggest any combination of the clocks hands can be construed, with a little imagination, as being on the square.

But whatever tradition your lodge follows when thinking of Absent Brethren, the most important thing you can do is to couple your toast with the name or names of your good friends who are not present; that way you are truly considering those absent and acknowledging that they are truly missed.

14th What is significant of the East? Facing the East probably predates any Christian significance, as facing the sunrise during worship is a universal custom.

With regard to the Gothic cathedral or the early churches, these were always built in the same fashion, and their position depended to whom or to which saint the building was to be dedicated.

As you know, our lodges also lie on that East to West axis with the Master always seated in the East.

15th An absurdity we often hear, when being called upon to drink a toast, is the demand to be 'upstanding' for the toast to be proposed. Now technically, this is a slightly illogical request as etiquette demands that all toasts should be taken standing up; unless on board ship where Navy toasts are traditionally taken seated. This is most probably due to the height restrictions on the lower deck or the inability to stand firm in rough weather.

However, the word 'upstanding' is not the opposite of 'sitting down'; it is in fact an obsolete word which in past times referred to one character and not any specific posture.

16th Euclid, the Greek mathematician, who according to the Second Section, Second Lecture, presided over a lodge in Alexandria, Egypt, and digested, arranged and brought geometry into a Regular system for the benefit of the Egyptians who, because of Euclid, were able to measure land and put an end to their quarrels.

The Matthew Cooke MS (*c.*1450), states that Euclid was a student of Abraham from whom he learnt the art and science of geometry. Euclid also taught geometry, so the MS tells us, to the sons of the lords of the country, charging them to call each other 'Fellow and no other'.

However, according to Biblical chronology, Abraham lived about *c.*1900 BC while Euclid *c.*350 BC.

17th *A Master Key to Freemasonry*, or to give it its full title – *A Master Key to Freemasonry. By which all the Secrets of the Society are laid open & their Pretended Mysteries exposed to the Public with an accurate Account of the Examination of the Apprentice, Fellow Craft, & the Master,* was an exposure of 1760, *and* the first full ritual exposure to be published after *Masonry Dissected* in 1730.

Included on the title page were the words: 'The public may depend upon this being a genuine Account of their whole Secrets, by which a Person may gain Admittance to a Lodge.'

The exposure itself was copied from an exposure published in France some fifteen years earlier, entitled *L'Ordre des Frances-Macons Trahi*. It contained many obvious mistakes; the main being its reference to the pillars as I & B. It did not reflect English ceremonies of the day and was quickly overshadowed by the more complete and correct

Three Distinct Knocks which was published a month or so later.

It was however, the forerunner of a series of exposures which were published in the 1760s.

18th Have you heard of the expression 'the Furniture of the lodge'? Well, what actually constitutes the 'Furniture of the lodge'?

The Furniture of the lodge is the Volume of the Sacred Law, the Compasses and Square.

The Charge recommends to our most serious contemplation the Volume of the Sacred Law, charging us to consider it as the unerring standard of truth and justice and to regulate your actions by the divine precepts it contains. Therein we are taught the important duties you owe to God, to your neighbour, and to yourself.

a) To God, by never mentioning His name but with that awe and reverence which are due from the creature to his Creator, by imploring His aid in all your lawful undertakings, and by looking up to Him in every emergency for comfort and support.

b) To your neighbour, by acting with him on the square, by rendering him every kind office which justice or mercy may require, by relieving his necessities and soothing his afflictions, and by doing to him as in similar cases you would wish he would do to you.

c) And to yourself, by such a prudent and well-regulated course of discipline as may best conduce to the preservation of your corporeal and mental faculties in their fullest energy, thereby enabling you to exert those talents wherewith God has blessed you, as well to His glory as the welfare of your fellow creatures.

With regard to the other two items, the Square and Compasses, when united, is a guide to regulate our lives and actions. Therefore, the Sacred Volume is derived from God to man in general; the Compasses belong to the Grand Master in particular, and the Square to the whole Craft.

19th Have you heard of the seven works of mercy? They are alluded to in the ceremony of the Knight of the Holy Sepulchre, one of the Degrees of the Red Cross of Constantine.

They are worthy of mention here as they truly befit the lives of every Freemason.

1) Bury the dead
2) Visit the imprisoned
3) Feed the hungry
4) Shelter the homeless
5) Clothe the naked
6) Visit the sick
7) Refresh the thirsty

The seven acts of mercy are depicted in a famous oil painting by the artist Caravaggio, c. 1607. It shows the traditional Catholic beliefs, which are a set of compassionate acts concerning the material needs of others. The original painting is housed in the church of *Pio Monte della Misericordia*, in Naples, Italy.

20th In Scotland in 1702, the lodge at Haughfoot became what was the first wholly non-operative Scottish lodge. Crucially, a member of that lodge, probably the first secretary, wrote in the first several pages of the first minute book, the complete admission procedure of that period.

Sometime later, a well-meaning Brother tore out the pages so as not to reveal to any unauthorised person the details of the ritual or ceremony.

However, the last twenty-nine words of the ceremony were left at the top of the page with the heading underneath 'The same day' with the start of the minutes of the lodge. The twenty-nine words were authentic ritual and verified three other important documents which up until the discovery of the minute book of the lodge could not be verified as authentic.

The documents are, the Edinburgh Register House MS (1696), the

Chetwode Crawley MS (*c*.1700), the Kevan MS (*c*.1714).

The fragment provided the all-important link to a ritual that was believed to have been practiced for the previous fifty to one hundred years.

What were the words?

> *'...of entrie as the apprentice did Leaving out (The Common Judge) Then they whisper the word as before – and the Master Mason grips his hand after the ordinary way.'*

21st In the early days of Speculative or non-Operative Freemasonry, lodges met in the upstairs or back rooms of inns or ale-houses. It was at these early Regular meetings that Freemasons continued to drink, smoke and feast throughout the evening.

Because of the demand for a steady flow of refreshment during the meeting, the inn keeper, a non-member, was often sworn-in as a serving Brother so that he could wait on the brethren in the lodge when required. The inn keeper's wife was also sworn-in and known as the Mason's Dame, and was also allowed to assist in the serving of brethren during the open lodge.

22nd During the 19th century, much of the focus of the origins of Freemasonry concentrated on the supposed links with the Ancient Mysteries. These were the Mysteries of Osiris (Egypt) Mithras (Persia) Adonis (Syria) Dionysus, Bacchic and Eleusis (Greece) and Druids (Gaul and Britain).

Many Masonic students of the day felt that the description given by Plato, when he declared that: 'the mysteries were established by men of great genius to teach purity, to ameliorate the cruelty of the human race, to refine its morals and manners and to restrain society by the obligation of fraternity', not only aligned itself with Freemasonry, but was the very foundation of the Craft.

The problem was compounded further by the practice, first identified in the medieval period in England, where a man's art, skill, cunning or profession, was known as his 'mystery'. The word 'mystery' is derived from the Latin word *ministerium* meaning professional skill and as one can imagine, all craftsmen maintained a code of secrecy to maintain the status of their skill. In fact, the fraternal trade companies of this period were often termed as the 'Mystery', the terms gild, or guild, being more associated with merchants than tradesmen.

Therefore, the association of the word used within the medieval London Companies, leant itself to the 19th century Masonic students who confused the meaning of the word 'mystery' with the term 'mysteries' and associated it with ancient traditions. The early Operative writings we inherited, known to us as the Regius Poem and the Cooke MS, to name but two, both written in the 14th and 15th centuries, only went to underpin the belief that Freemasonry was, time immemorial; as did Andersons *Constitutions* of 1723 and 1738, where he foolishly traces Freemasonry to the days of Adam.

23rd In the *Constitutions* of 1723 it was stated that no man should be made a Mason under the age of twenty-five years unless by dispensation from the Grand Master. In the *Constitutions* of 1784 it was changed to twenty-one years. However, it was the practice of lodges constituted under the Grand Lodge of the Antients, to reserve the mature age as being that of twenty-five years. This however was finally resolved at the Union in 1813 when the minimum age became twenty-one.

24th Lodge customs and tradition being what they are, here is a lovely song I have only ever heard sang once at a London lodge I visited.

Brethren from the East and West,
Who have stood the Tyler's test.
You will find a welcome here.
Bright, fraternal and sincere.

Chorus: Warm Masonic hearts to meet you,
hands of fellowship to greet you,
may our welcome here today,
cheer each brother on his way.

We salute the man of worth,
Whether high or low his birth,
Whatsoever be his lot.
Rich or poor it matters not.

Chorus

And when we have said 'Adieu',
May our love remain with you.
And may we renew that love
in a Grander Lodge above.

Chorus

25th Who was the man Naymus Graecus mentioned in the Grand Lodge MS, No.1, (1583)? Here is a modern transcription of the relevant passage:

> *Curious Craftsmen walked widely about into other countries, some to learn more craft, and some to teach others that had little skill and cunning. And it happened that there was one curious Mason named Naymus Grecus that had been at the building of Solomon's Temple; he came into France and there he taught the Science of Masonry to men of that land. And there was one of the royal line of France called Charles Martell, and he was a man that loved well such a Craft, and came to this Naymus Graecus, and learned from him the Craft, and took upon himself the Charges and manners.*

Taking the story literally, means that Naymus Graecus, who associated with King Solomon, who reigned c.970–931 BC and Charles (the Hammer) Martell, who lived *c*.686–741, would have been some sixteen hundred years old.

The story of this curious craftsman is repeated many times in the *Old Charges* with an equal amount of name variation; however, lest we forget, allegory is repeatedly used in Freemasonry to highlight salient points and this is no exception.

26th The Grand College which oversees the Holy Royal Arch Knight Templar Priests has jurisdiction over some thirty Degrees, mainly conferred upon by name only.

With the most exotic sounding Degrees like Master of the Veils, Jacob's Wrestle, Knight of Rahab and Knight of Eleusis, we concern ourselves here with the Knight Templar Priest.

The ceremony consists of biblical readings as the Candidate is conducted to seven pillars placed in a triangle. At each pillar, the Officers read from the V of SL and impart a word referring to Jesus, the Lamb of God. The secrets and taken from a series of biblical quotes and many of the signs are a combination of those from the qualifying Degrees.

27th If Freemasonry has one specific flaw which devalues man's basic obligation to serve his fellow man, it is this: it rewards its members with appointments, promotions and honorifics for their acts of kindness.

This means that a Freemason can be rewarded, not necessarily for any great act of self-sacrifice or act of kindness to their fellow man, but the way they use their wealth, and we have all watched it happen.

It has disappointed us, yet we have said nothing; yet we all know of those unfair promotions, appointments or honorifics given to brethren of whom it would appear have managed to develop their Masonic career, merely on the basis of who they know and how much they have given, rather than what they have done.

I once heard the story of how a wealthy Brother arranged, at his own expense, to have aids and adaptations made to each Masonic Hall in his Province, for the benefit of those brethren suffering with audio and ambulatory problems.

A noble and philanthropic gesture indeed, until the following year when the Brother was appointed Assistant Provincial Grand Master in a somewhat *Quid pro quo* gesture; thus bringing our society somewhat closer to the prickly question of *cash for honours*, not dissimilar to the 2006/7 Lord Levy scandal concerning the connection between political donations and the award of life peerages.

Subsequently, and in the eyes of many, this promotion devalued that act of generosity by rewarding the beneficiary and underpinned the belief that one can buy their way to promotion.

Therefore, in an organisation which honours and rewards its members openly for their works of charity; that laudable ethos of service to others is occasionally squandered on those who become motivated by less than honourable sentiments when carrying out acts of kindness.

28th

The visit of Balkis, the Queen of Sheba, to Solomon, King of Israel as recorded in Kings 10:1-13 has touched Masonic legend and is related, in some Masonic systems, in the ceremony of Installation.

The kingdom of the Queen of Sheba is shrouded in antiquity, but possibly, as modern excavations have suggested, the south westerly part of Arabia where the Yemen is now located was most probably the area.

The biblical record found in Kings 10:1-13 records the visit thus:

> *1) And when the queen of Sheba heard of the fame of Solomon concerning the name of the LORD, she came to prove him with hard questions.*
>
> *2) And she came to Jerusalem with a very great train, with camels that bare spices, and very much gold, and precious stones: and*

when she was come to Solomon, she communed with him of all that was in her heart.

3) *And Solomon told her all her questions: there was not any thing hid from the king, which he told her not.*

4) *And when the queen of Sheba had seen all Solomon's wisdom, and the house that he had built,*

5) *And the meat of his table, and the sitting of his servants, and the attendance of his ministers, and their apparel, and his cupbearers, and his ascent by which he went up unto the house of the LORD; there was no more spirit in her.*

6) *And she said to the king, It was a true report that I heard in mine own land of thy acts and of thy wisdom.*

7) *Howbeit I believed not the words, until I came, and mine eyes had seen it: and, behold, the half was not told me: thy wisdom and prosperity exceedeth the fame which I heard.*

8) *Happy are thy men, happy are these thy servants, which stand continually before thee, and that hear thy wisdom.*

9) *Blessed be the LORD thy God, which delighted in thee, to set thee on the throne of Israel: because the LORD loved Israel for ever, therefore made he thee king, to do judgment and justice.*

10) *And she gave the king an hundred and twenty talents of gold, and of spices very great store, and precious stones: there came no more such abundance of spices as these which the queen of Sheba gave to king Solomon.*

11) *And the navy also of Hiram, that brought gold from Ophir, brought in from Ophir great plenty of almug trees, and precious stones.*

12) *And the king made of the almug trees pillars for the house of the LORD, and for the king's house, harps also and psalteries for singers: there came no such almug trees, nor were seen unto this day.*

13) *And King Solomon gave unto the queen of Sheba all her desire, whatsoever she asked, beside that which Solomon gave*

> *her of his royal bounty. So she turned and went to her own country, she and her servants.*

Students have suggested the four reasons for the visit were:

1) She wanted to see the wonderful Temple recently completed at Jerusalem.
2) She desired to ensure good trading relations between Sheba and Israel.
3) She wished to consult the wise king on the well-ruling of her country.
4) She desired to ensure a successor to her throne by a child sired by him.

29th There is always much confusion over the terms the 'Antients' and the 'Moderns' and I will endeavour to explain it simply.

In London in 1751, a group of Irishmen, temporarily resident in London and who had not been made welcome in English Masonic circles, formed a rival Grand Lodge called the Grand Lodge of England according to the Old Institutions. The new Grand Lodge accused the first or Premier Grand Lodge of having introduced many innovations and claimed that they alone preserved the ancient customs and practices of Masonry. They dubbed the older body the 'Moderns' and assumed the title of the 'Antients'.

Some of the so-called innovations made by the first Grand Lodge included reversing the passwords and signs of the First and Second degrees so as to confuse irregular Masons that tried to gain access to Regular lodges. Their other main innovation was to turn their aprons upside down so as the gentlemen would not look like mechanics.

The brethren that formed this rival lodge were looked upon, for many years as traitors, schematics and men that had not only set out to destroy the Premier Grand Lodge, but were in violation of their Masonic Obligation. However it was later proved by Henry Sadler, in his book *Masonic Facts and Fictions*, that the new Grand Lodge was established by humble men, whose only wish was to practice the Pure and Antient Freemasonry in the form they had known in their native country of Ireland, under their own Grand Lodge to whom they owed their allegiance.

Therefore the Antients were the new Grand Lodge formed in 1751 and the Moderns were the old Grand Lodge formed in 1717.

30th

What is a cable tow and why is it placed about our neck?

This small length of cable is used for towing, hauling or safeguarding against too much speed on a strong current. It was customary among the ancient Semitic races for captives, bondmen and other menials to wear a halter as a token of submission. The Candidate can therefore demonstrate the act of perfect acquiescence.

It was also used by the Druids, Brahmins, and Greeks in their religious ceremonies; in our setting, it acts as a restraint, rendering any attempt by the Candidate to rush forward, fatal, although we must remember it is symbolic and would not be used to injure, or restrain, any man.

31st

How is the sun at its meridian during our Initiation if our meetings are held in the evening?

Quite simply, the sun being that great luminary, which guides man's path by day and reaches its meridian at high noon; at this time during the day, the activities of the Operative lodge would have been in full swing, thus indicating by this answer that the lodge was open and at labour. In reality, this question purely goes to point out that Masonry is universal, and technically speaking at any given time around the world, there would be at least one speculative lodge at labour.

It is also evidence of our long lost association with our Operative cousins and reminds us that our lodge room is symbolically a mason's workshop.

November

1st The lodge known in earlier times as, *logium fabrica* (workshop, place of production) or *tabulatum domicialem* (residence, i.e. place of work) or as one old record described it in 1200, as the shed in front of the Abbey Church, St Albans, was in real terms where the masons carried out their work and there are many early records relating to the lodge.

In 1321, 2/6d (12 ½ pence) was paid for straw to cover the masons' lodgings at Carnarvon.

In 1330, at St Stephen Chapel, Westminster, a man was instructed to clean out the lodge.

In 1337, the City of London records show stone being removed from a lodge in the Garden.

In 1395, at Westminster Abbey, a dauber was paid 15/6d (77 ½ pence) for work on the lodge for masons.

In 1399 at York, we find a list of the stores in the lodge in the cemetery.

In 1421, the masons at Catterick were provided with a lodge of four rooms.

Finding evidence of the existence of lodges is by no means difficult; the difficulty stems from the question why did masons moralise on their work, their tools and their trade and what was the reason non-masons became fascinated with the same.

2nd There is a specific issue with the setting up of the first Grand Lodge and Anderson's account that need to be examined closer. Douglas Knoop and G.P. Jones take up the story with regard to concerns about the jurisdiction of the first Grand Lodge;

> *The events of 1716 and 1717 which led to the formation of Grand Lodge have been referred to as 'a resuscitation of English*

Masonry' and as 'the Revival'. These descriptions are somewhat misleading; the events of 1716 and 1717 related not to English masonry in general, but masonry in London and Westminster in particular. There is nothing in the surviving accounts to suggest that the members of the Four Old Lodges had anything more in mind than a gathering or organisation of local lodges. Even six years later, in Anderson's Constitutions of 1723 (but not, it should be noted, in those of 1738) *the Charges were stated to be 'for the use of the Lodges in London', and the General Regulations 'for the use of the Lodges in and about London and Westminster'. According to the MS. List of Lodges which was begun 25 November 1723, and entered on the first pages of the original minute book of Grand Lodge, the 'regular constituted lodges' further afield were at Edgworth (Edgware), Acton and Richmond. The fact that Grand Lodge in 1723 and 1724 passed various resolutions concerning lodges 'in or near London', 'within the Bills of Mortality' and 'within ten mile of London', indicates the restricted jurisdiction of Grand Lodge in those years.*

Douglas Knoop and G.P.Jones, *The Genesis of Freemasonry*, published by Q.C. Correspondence Circle Ltd., 1978 edition, p.186-187

3rd Early medieval buildings in Britain consisted mainly of wood and clay and therefore the artisans engaged in these buildings were carpenters and daubers, not masons. In fact, both Britons and Scots were unfamiliar with stone building, which involved the use of squared stone and mortar and we must never confuse this with the flat stone, mortar-less buildings, which have existed in these lands since earliest time civilisation.

It was probably the Church that introduced the art of the squared stone building and it was evident from early in our history that craftsmen from abroad had to be brought to England to do any form of squared stone work. For example, in 674, Benedict Biscop brought craftsmen from Gaul to help build a stone church, in the Roman style, at Wearmouth Abbey. In 709, St Wilfred, according to a 12th century chronicler, brought masons from Rome to build his church. Further records by Bede in the 7th century; make references to Norman stone churches in Lastingham and Lincoln.

4th There is a general misunderstanding that a 'Lewis' or, the uninitiated son of a Freemason is afforded special privileges. Other than his right, to be the first to be Initiated on the night of becoming a Freemason, should there be more than one Candidate, he has no other privileges.

He cannot claim precedence over Candidates proposed previous to him and must take his place along with other applicants, in the normal rota for joining members.

The significance of the term 'Lewis' seemed to take off after an additional stanza was added to the 'Deputy Grand Master's Song', said to have been written for Frederick Lewis, Prince of Wales, and included in the 1738 *Book of Constitutions*. The prince was Initiated, Passed and Raised on 5 November 1737 and the stanza was written during the princess' pregnancy. The additional verse says:

Again let it pass to the Royal love'd Name,
Whose glorious Admission has crown'd all our Fame:
May a Lewis be born, whom the World shall admire,
Serene as his Mother, August as his Sire.

It was said that the author, a Brother Gofton, used the term 'Lewis' as a pun with the Prince of Wales' anglicised surname.

5th On the night of my Passing, I was fascinated by the term 'bark' as referred to in the long version of the Second Degree Working Tools: 'To steer the bark of this life over the seas of passion without quitting the helm of rectitude is the highest perfection to which human nature can attain'.

However, much later it made more sense to me when I learnt that a barque, barc or bark is a sailing vessel with three or more masts, having the fore and main masts rigged square and only the mizzen (the aft most mast) rigged fore and aft. So, when I read it again, I was reminded of the sheer poetry of the ritual.

6th The quasi-Masonic Order, the Ancient and Primitive Rite, was established at Montauban, France in about 1814 and teaches the immortality of the human soul with a Sovereign Sanctuary, being established in Britain in 1872.

Originally having some ninety-seven Degrees, it was considerably reduced by John Yarker, who trimmed the Degrees to thirty-three by eliminating repetitive and duplicate parts of the ceremony. Known in America as the Rite of Memphis, it claimed a history of Napoleon Bonaparte's armies in Egypt.

Yarker claimed that:

> *Its Rituals embrace all Masonry, and are based on those of the Craft universal; they explain its symbols, develop its mystic philosophy, exemplify its morality, examine its legends, tracing them to their primitive source, and dealing fairly and truthfully with the historical features of Symbolical Masonry. They contain nothing in their teaching but what Mahommedan, Christian, Jew, Buddhist, Brahmin, or Parsee may alike acknowledge.*

The head of the Order was known as the Grand Hierophant of the Supreme Council of Sublime Masters of Light. The Rite is not part of the English Masonic system and not recognised by the United Grand Lodge of England.

7th We have all heard the 'Master's Song' sung on so many occasions but here are the beautiful words:

This world is so hard and so stony,
That if a man is to get through,
He need have the courage of Nelson,
And plenty of Job's patience too.
But a man who is kind to another
And cheerfully helps him along,
We'll claim as a man and a brother,
And here's to his health in a song.

Chorus: And here's to his health, here's to his health
And here's to his health in a song.

This life is as cheerless as winter
To those who are cold in the heart,
but a man who is warm in his nature
Bids winter for ever depart
The ground that he treads on will blossom,
Till beauty around him shall throng;
God Bless such a man and a brother,
And here's to his health in a song.

Chorus

As clouds that in sunshine are open,
And silver'd by light passing through,
So men who are generous in spirit,
Are bless'd by the good deeds they do;
There's nothing like helping another
For getting one's own self along;
Who does this is truly a brother.
And here's to his health in a song.

Chorus

There's something in other men's sorrows
That strengthens a man who is true,
They melt him at first, and then mould him,
The manliest actions do.
There's lots of both sorrow and trouble,
Our poor fellow-creatures among;
But God makes the blessings all double
To those who help others along.

All, standing, sing Chorus

8th In 1802, an application was received by Grand Lodge, from four lodges in Portugal seeking the authority to work under the banner of the English Constitution. The petitioning lodges sent Hippolyto Joseph Da Costa to England to represent them. Da Costa, who was born in a Portuguese settlement in Uruguay, made a Mason if Philadelphia and had settled in Lisbon some years earlier, signed the Treaty with Grand Lodge to recognise the Grand Lodge of Portugal.

On his return to Lisbon, he was immediately arrested by the Inquisition and condemned to six months solitary confinement. After three years of captivity he finally escaped; possibly with the help of English Freemasons. On his return to England he joined Lodge of Antiquity in 1808.

In 1811, he published an account of his sufferings and privations at the hands of the Inquisition but never revealed any details of those brethren that assisted him with his escape.

In 1813, and probably as a reward for his service as Masonic Secretary to the Grand Master, the Duke of Sussex, Da Costa was appointed Provincial Grand Master of Rutlandshire; a somewhat curious appointment as there were no recorded Masonic lodges in that county at that time.

He died in 1823.

9th

You have heard the names of the two great pillars that stood at the porch way or entrance of King Solomon's Temple.

2 Chronicles 3:17 'And he reared up the pillars before the temple, one on the right hand, and the other on the left; and called the name of that on the right hand Jachin, and the name of that on the left Boaz.'

I Kings 7:21 'And he set up the pillars in the porch of the temple: and he set up the right pillar, and called the name thereof Jachin: and he set up the left pillar, and called the name thereof Boaz.'

In Masonic teaching, we learn we learn that the import of both names being 'In Strength' and 'To Establish' respectively. This conforms to the writings of Flavius Josephus who wrote in the 1st century A.D. that Boaz means 'In Him Strength or In It Strength' and Jachin means 'He Will establish or It will establish' (Antiquities of the Jews). Masonic teaching also advises us that when conjoined, the words mean 'Stability', for God said, 'In strength I will establish this mine house to stand firm for ever.' However, nowhere in any version of the bible do we read God using these words. The nearest we can get to the phrase is found in I Chronicles, 17:12 which says: 'He shall build me an house, and I will stablish his throne for ever.'

10th

The term 'Degree' as used in the Masonic setting is to differentiate the progress one has made, i.e. First, Second and Third. The term was first used in Prichard's *Masonry Dissected* (1730) and hence adopted to mark one's progress. In Operative masonry, the term 'Grade' was used to differentiate classes of workman; while other forms of Freemasonry are known as Higher, Additional or Appendant Degrees.

In the English Masonic system, the Holy Royal Arch is the completion of the Third Degree and not considered the Fourth Degree. The Mark Master Mason ceremony does not complete the Second Degree, but is an individual and separate system, although one must be a Master Mason to join.

Likewise, higher, additional or appendant Degrees available to Master Masons in England, other than the Holy Royal Arch, although recognised by Grand Lodge, are not necessarily part of the English Masonic system as they are all independent of the United Grand Lodge. They are not considered higher, but in many cases, they do continue similar themes which complement the traditional histories of the Craft. However, they are not essential to, nor do they give any greater understanding of, the English Masonic system.

11th We have heard how Jacob's Ladder rests firmly on the Volume of Sacred Law in our lodges and reaches to the Heavens, and the angels of the Lord ascend and descend thereon.

The staves of the ladder we are told are many and they point out the several moral virtues, but have specific reference to the three principle virtues which are Faith, Hope and Charity. This is because we should have Faith in the Great Architect of the Universe; Hope in Salvation; and to show Charity to all men. Here we look at Hope.

Hope is an anchor of the soul, both sure and steadfast, and enters into that within the veil. Then let a firm reliance on the Almighty's faithfulness animate our endeavours, and teach us to fix our desires within the limits of His most blessed promises; so shall success attend us. If we believe a thing impossible, our despondency may render it so, but he who perseveres in a just cause will ultimately overcome all difficulties.

12th I do not think I have ever felt so sorry for a Candidate as I did on the night of his Initiation when the Tyler omitted to remove the metal buckled belt, which was holding up his trousers.

As he stood, in a state of darkness, at the Worshipful Master's pedestal, in between the Deacons, and ready to take his obligation, the DC noticed the buckle and desperately tried to motion to the Master to stop the ceremony.

The Master, who had not seen the buckle, continued with the ceremony, whereupon the DC crawled on his hands and knees to the Candidate and proceeded to remove his belt.

Now, we all approached our Initiation with some trepidation, having received the usual jibes from friends advising us to, beware of the goat, etc., but can you imagine how you would have felt, standing there hoodwinked, between two men, when you suddenly feel somebody trying to undo your belt?

I guess he will look back and see the funny side of the evening; particularly the extra explanation given him in respect of being divested of all metal substances.

13th The Order has been founded on three grand principles namely Brotherly Love, Relief and Truth. Here we look at Truth.

Truth stands for honesty, integrity, loyalty and fidelity; those attributes that should be about us in all of our daily undertakings. These should be the characteristics that set us apart from the world, so that when people judge Freemasonry, and they will, they will look upon it favourably.

The Emulation Lectures of the Three Degrees explain Truth thus:

> *Truth is a Divine attribute and the foundation of every Masonic virtue; to be good men and true is a lesson we are taught at our Initiation; on this grand theme we contemplate, and by its unerring dictates, endeavour to regulate our lives and actions. Hence, hypocrisy and deceit are, or ought to be, unknown to us, sincerity and plain dealing are our distinguishing characteristics, whilst the heart and tongue join in promoting each other's welfare, and rejoicing in the prosperity of the Craft.*
>
> First Lecture, Sixth Section Six

Truth is the last of the three principal tenets and means much more than the search for truth in the intellectual sense. It is the cornerstone of society, a vital requirement for civil law and a necessity to establish justice.

Therefore, all Freemasons should strive to be truthful in character, honest in their habits, honourable in their dealings and thus dependable as men.

14th I was recently reading an article by W. Bro. Don Falconer, which explained that the 'Point within a Circle' was an ancient and sacred device or hieroglyph that has become a symbol of great importance in Craft Freemasonry. However, the usual explanation that is given in modern rituals differs significantly from the original symbolism

This does not imply that it is a recent invention, but rather like that of many other Masonic symbols, they have evolved over a period of time and have taken on various interpretations to accentuate salient points of our discipline. As the ancient interpretation of this sacred hieroglyph is a fundamental tenet of the philosophical system that forms the basis of Craft Freemasonry, so it is important to examine the origins of the symbol.

In its decorative form on Egyptian monuments, two erect parallel serpents represent power and wisdom of the Divine Creator; the parallels support the point within a circle. Sometimes a serpent with its tail in its mouth represented the circle, which was called the *Ananta* from the Sanskrit word meaning eternity, i.e. no beginning and no end. At the centre of the circle, on either side of the point, the Egyptian equivalents of the Alpha and Omega were often inscribed to represent the omnipotence of God, symbolically surrounded by His whole creation, which was considered to have no limits within the scope of His boundless power and wisdom. Therefore, in this form, the circle is also expressive of the protection of the collective people of the world by those two great and parallel attributes of the Divine Creator, His boundless power and wisdom. The two grand parallel lines referred to in modern rituals of Craft Freemasonry, are believed to have derived from this ancient symbolism.

15th Boaz was a biblical figure appearing in the Book of Ruth in the Old Testament and in the genealogies of Jesus Christ in the New Testament. It is also the name of the left hand pillar at the porch way or entrance to King Solomon's Temple. The word is found 24 times in the Scriptures.

Boaz was the son of Rahab and Salmon, and was a wealthy landowner of Bethlehem in Judea. He was a kinsman of Elimelech, Naomi's late husband. He noticed Ruth, the widowed Moabite daughter-in-law of Naomi, a relative of his, gleaning grain in his fields. He soon learned of the difficult circumstances her family was in, and Ruth's loyalty to Naomi. In response, Boaz invites her to eat with him and his workers, as well as deliberately leaving grain for her to claim while keeping a protective eye on her.

Ruth approaches Boaz and asks him to exercise his right of kinship and marry her. Boaz accepts, if another with a superior claim, declines. Since the first son of Ruth and a kinsman of her late husband would be deemed the legal offspring of the decedent and heir to Elimelech, the other kinsman defer to Boaz. In marrying Ruth, Boaz revives Elimelech's lineage, and the patrimony is secured to Naomi's family. Their son was Obed, father of Jesse, and grandfather of David.

16th The story of the four crowned martyrs, from which Quatuor Coronati the world-famous research lodge takes its name, is fascinating.

There are several versions of the story but in a nutshell, in 302 AD, four stone workers or carvers, plus their apprentice were ordered by the Emperor Diocletian to carve a statue of Aesculapius. The sculptors were secretly Christians and either refused or avoided the instruction. For their refusal, the five were put to death on 8 November. The names of the five were: Claudius, Castorius, Symphorian, Nicostratus, and Simplicius.

Two years later, the Emperor ordered all Roman soldiers to burn incense at the foot of the same god, Aesculapius. Four refused to do so, on the basis that they too, were Christians. They were subsequently beaten to death on the same date, 8 November. The names of the four were: Severus, Severian, Carpophorus and Victorinus.

Learning of the stories, Pope Melchiades, (310-314 AD) ordained that the memory of both sets of martyrs would be celebrated each year on 8 November under the name Quatuor Coronati. At a later point, Pope Gregory confirmed the date and later still, Pope Honorius built a church in their honour.

Their involvement with Freemasonry stems from their mention in the Regius MS, Freemasonry's oldest recognised document and an Ordinance of London Masons, 1481, which stated: '...every freeman of the Craft shall attend at Christ-Church on the Feast of the Quatuor Coronati, to hear Mass, under penalty of 12 pence.'

17th We often here the term 'Landmarks of the Order' being used, yet there does not appear to be a definitive list, for example:

Mackey lists twenty-five, Oliver lists forty, Newton lists one, Pound lists six, the Commission on Information for Recognition of the Conference of Grand Masters of Masons in North America lists three, the Grand Lodge of West Virginia lists seven, the Grand Lodge of New Jersey lists ten, the Grand Lodge of Nevada lists thirty-nine, the Grand Lodge of Kentucky lists fifty-four and John Hamill, Director for Special Projects for the United Grand Lodge of England lists six.

What, therefore, actually constitutes a 'Landmark'?

Firstly, a Landmark must have notional immemorial antiquity, meaning that it has existed in the past, but that it was so long ago that people have no knowledge or memory of it.

Secondly, a Landmark must be absolutely irrevocable, meaning that it is an element or form of such importance that the society would not be that society if it were removed.

Here, Harry Carr gives us a reliable list of five landmarks:

1) That a Mason professes a belief in God (the Supreme Being).
2) That the V.S.L. is an essential and indispensable part of the lodge to open in full view when the Brethren are at Labour.
3) That a Mason must be male, free-born, and of mature age.
4) That a Mason, by his tenure, owes his allegiance to the Sovereign and to the Craft.
5) That a Mason believes in the immortality of the soul.

18th The First Regular Step in Freemasonry, as with the Second and Third, are designed to represent a device found replicated three times on an Installed Master's apron, namely the Tau or Tau Cross.

The Tau Cross, named after the 19th Greek letter it resembles, is also called, St Anthony's cross, Anticipatory Cross, Cross Commissee, Croce Taumata etc. The device was known in ancient times as an emblem of Life and a hieroglyphical representation of Deity; therefore the regular steps may be said to be symbolic of Life.

But it is not until the Master Mason enters or progresses to the Order of the Royal Arch, that being the completion of the Third Degree, will he discover the three devices replicated together to form the mysterious Triple Tau, emblematical of the Triune Essence of God.

Thomas Dunckerley described it as a 'T' over 'H', *Templum Hierosolyma or* the Temple of Jerusalem, which some Masonic students have argued became altered with the downward stroke of the 'T' resting on the crossbar of the 'H' resulting in a device that that represented the three Tau's of the Installed Master's Apron and acquiring a significance explained in the lectures of that Order.

In early Masonic times, only Installed Masters whose aprons displayed the three devices could join the Holy Royal Arch.

19th On many lodge carpets we find an indented border around the edge of the mosaic or tessellated pavement. In older Masonry, it is said that the border was made of threads twining in and out, but now it is a machined border in a sort of dog-tooth arrangement. Two older exposures use the term 'Danty Tassley' (Sloane MS *c.*1700) and 'Indented Tarsel' (*Masonry Dissected*, 1730) but it is clearly referred to in the First Degree Tracing Board Lecture, which says:

> *The Ornaments of the Lodge are the Mosaic pavement, the Blazing Star, and the Indented or Tessellated Border...The Indented or Tessellated Border refers us to the Planets, which in their various revolutions form a beautiful border or skirtwork*

round that grand luminary, the Sun, as the other does round that of a Freemasons' Lodge.

In the early 18th century, before the innovation of the Tracing Boards, the symbols of the Order were marked out in chalk upon the floor, and this diagram was then encircled with a wavy cord, ornamented with tassels, and was therefore called 'the indented tassel', later corrupted into the 'tessellated or indented border'.

The reasons for the patterned carpet border or the term are quite incomplete and no real explanation, other than what tradition dictates is available.

20th Over the years, I have attended lodges that sing 'Lead Kindly Light' as the Candidate enters for Initiation and 'Kyrie Eleison' when he completes his Obligation.

Surprisingly, the words of either song do not have any relevance to the ritual or part of the ceremony; however, it is perfectly permissible for lodges that are lucky enough to have an Organist, to play the tunes at those times.

Similarly, I have also witnessed Organists, who on Installation night plays humorous and relevant pieces of music, during the appointment of certain Officers.

Whereas I do not think it adds to the occasion, sometimes the relief of a humorous tune can brighten up a difficult evening.

21st Do you wear a Masonic ring? Which way round do you wear it? Here are two pieces of advice I took from the web:

1) The ring should be worn as an outward sign to others that you are a Mason. Wear your ring with the Compass points towards you.
2) Set the ring on your finger so that the legs of the compass face away from you.

So, which is it to be?

Personally, I believe the legs of the Compasses (compass is a navigational tool) should face toward you. I have no reason for this other than the fact that the ring is solely for my benefit, not for me to advertise the fact that I am a Freemason to all and sundry.

22nd Understanding why men of the 17th century desired to join a fraternity such as Freemasonry has often puzzled me; however, in London at that time there were many convivial dining clubs and fraternities. For example:

The Order of Jeopardy
The Society of Bucks
The Friends of Awakening Nature
The Order of Noah
The Jerusalem Sols
The Salamanders…to name but a few.

But there is in fact little doubt that during this period of time, 'conviviality' appeared to have been a prominent characteristic of many lodges.

In 1722, Freemasons had the dubious honour of being included in the English version of 'The Praise of Drunkenness' which obviously prompted that famous York Freemason Francis Drake, to declare in a speech, '… the pernicious custom of drinking…which we of our nation too much indulge…I wish I could not say that I have frequently observed in our own Most Amicable Brotherhood'.

23rd We are introduced to the Five Points of Fellowship in the Third Degree. However, in 1696 the Five Points of Fellowship was part of what appears to be a two Degree system, with some suggesting there was only one Degree. But whatever the case, present day, the Worshipful Master explains, 'They are Hand to Hand, Foot to Foot, Knee to Knee, Breast to Breast and Hand over Back'.

In 1696, the Master asked, 'How many points of the fellowship are ther?' The answers at that time was, 'fyve viz foot to foot Knee to Kn Heart to Heart, Hand to Hand and ear to ear. Then make the sign of fellowship and shake hand and you will be acknowledged a true mason'.

Subtle changes, but nevertheless, evidence the Five Points of Fellowship has long since been part of our ritual.

24th Can you recall when the Worshipful Master asked you the following question? 'How do you demonstrate the principles of your being a Mason to others?' and you answered, 'By signs, tokens, and the perfect points of my entrance.'

In the Edinburgh Register House MS (1696), Freemasonry's earliest recognised ritual document, the Master asks the same question:

Q. Are you a mason?

A. Yes.

Q. How shall I know it?

A. You shall know it in time and place convenient. Remark the fors[d] answer is only to be made when there is company present who are not masons But if there be no such company by, you should answer by signes tokens and other points of my entrie.

The point I am making is that this earliest recorded version of the ritual is not necessarily the earliest or first time it was used, therefore we can not only see the origins of some of our words, but the possibility that the ritual used then, had already been in use for up to one hundred years, thus making our ritual over four hundred years ago.

25th You are all familiar with the phrase from the Second Degree Tracing Board lecture where we learn that seven make a lodge perfect; seven has an allusion to the seven Arts and Sciences, and that King Solomon's Temple at Jerusalem was seven years and upwards in building, completing and dedicating.

When I heard this, I realised that there is nothing new under the sun, for I had read the phrase before in relation to the re-building of London after the fire of 1666. The Government of the day prepared three new statutes for the rebuilding of London and one particular statute took steps to increase the supply of labour, by suspending all local trade and encouraging an influx of workmen from outside London.

My point is that in doing so, it used the phrase 'for seven years or more' indicating the minimum length of time in would take to rebuild the city.

Now I am not saying that this particular reference was where that Masonic phrase originated, but the phraseology of our ritual must have come from somewhere and etymology teaches us that language always generates from known sources and is rarely ever invented.

26th

Can you recall on the night of our Initiation when the Senior Warden, having been commanded by the Worshipful Master to do so, bestows upon us our first apron with the words that it is: '...more ancient than the Golden Fleece or the Roman Eagle and more honourable than the Garter...?'

These words were not chosen by random as they were in fact highly respected contemporary civil Orders.

It was Philip, Duke of Normandy that founded the Order of the Golden Fleece in 1429. As wool was the predominate product of the lower European countries, the fleece was chosen as the emblem. It was considered as the highest of all civil Orders in Europe

In 1701, Frederick I of Prussia founded the Order of the Black Eagle. The number of knights was limited to thirty, exclusive of the princes of royal blood. The revisers of our rituals probably selected the reference to the Roman Eagle as it was the highest emblem of dignity, honour and power that famous empire could bestow.

According to tradition, in 1343, Edward III was dancing with the Countess of Salisbury when he picked up a garter that had slipped from her leg and placed it about his own. As at this time the king had been very successful in his campaigns, he instituted an Order of the Garter for rewarding his army favourites. After a series of changes by ensuing monarchs, the Order became known as the Most Noble Order of the Garter.

27th There are several types of columns and pillars referred to in Masonic teaching; this section deals with the pillars that support the lodge. The lodge is supported by three great pillars, which are called Wisdom, Strength, and Beauty.

Wisdom, illustrated by the Ionic column and found at the Worshipful Master's station in the East, helps contrive and conduct us in all our undertakings.

Strength, illustrated by the Doric column and found at the Senior Warden's station in the West, helps support us under all our difficulties.

Beauty, illustrated by the Corinthian column and found at the Junior Warden's station in the South, helps adorn the inward man.

Therefore, the Universe is the Temple of the Deity whom we serve; Wisdom, Strength, and Beauty are about His throne as pillars of His works, for His Wisdom is infinite, His Strength omnipotent, and Beauty shines through the whole of the creation in symmetry and order.

28th Have you ever wondered what ritual was practised in 1717, at the so-called revival of Freemasonry and the formation of Grand Lodge?

Well to be perfectly honest, but for a few exposures which set out some procedures and catechetical exchanges, we know very little and even then, as these were printed for monetary gain, we can only assume what is written is in fact, right.

What we do know is that the ritual we enjoy today was prepared and formulated in some form of unity by the Lodges of Promulgation and Reconciliation as part of pre- and post-Union preparations. We can also connect many of our practices, usages and traditions to the old documents and exposures, so on that basis alone, we do have some idea.

However, in 1717, there does not appear to be a Third Degree and there was some confusion over the terms like, Passed Master and Past Master. Certain ceremonies were carried out at Grand Lodge and not in private lodges. But whatever the case, the terminology and fable of that early period was not lost and resonates powerfully through the ritual we practice today.

29th

The life of an operative mason was well organised if the Fabric Rolls of York Minster are anything to go by. From 1352, we read the following under the heading 'Orders for the Masons and Workman':

> *The first and second masons who are called masters of the same, and the carpenters, shall make oath that they cause the ancient customs underwritten to be faithfully observed. In summer they are to begin work immediately after sunrise until the ringing of the bell of the Virgin Mary* [cannot find any reference to this but I guess it was probably about nine o'clock)]; *then to breakfast in the Fabric Lodge* [*logium fabrica* – lodge room or workshop]; *then one of the masters is to knock upon the door of the lodge and forthwith all are to return to work till noon; Between April and August, after dinner, they shall sleep in the lodge; then work until the first bell for vespers;* [Vespers is the sunset evening prayer] *then sit to drink until the end of the third bell, and return to work so long as they can see by daylight. In winter they are to begin work at daybreak, then continue as before till noon, and return to work until daylight is over. On Vigils [the eve of a festival or holy day as an occasion of religious observance] and on Saturdays they are to work until noon.*

30th Have you ever noticed on the Worshipful Master's Collar, a small dome in the centre on the V, stitched to the seam and covered in silver braid? You will find the same on any Past Master's Collar.

A Brother once asked what it depicted, and I was at a loss to answer, but it gave me another subject to research.

The results are quite interesting, because it actually represents nothing whatsoever. It is merely a means of drawing together the ends of the braid that meet at the seam.

Harry Carr explains that the dome was not introduced till after the standardisation of the regalia in 1815 and holds no other significance. Older portraits of collars display rings of metal or braid, stitched in the same place and used to hold the jewel.

So the lesson of the day is, not everything in Freemasonry has a symbolic meaning.

December

1st From about 1721, it became the custom for Grand Lodge to assemble at a tavern and process in full regalia to the nominated City Company Hall to hold their Assembly and Feast.

But 1741 saw the first mock procession, organised to bring the Craft into disrepute and a broadsheet of the time contained a poem describing the event. The chief antagonists were said to have been Esquire Carey and Paul Whitehead, who were said to be members of the famed 'Hell-Fire Club'.

The most famous attempt to embarrass the Society was the engraving of the procession by Mr. A. Benoist, which was published in 1742 and entitled, 'A Geometrical View of the Grand Procession of the Scald-Miserable Masons' – 'Scald' meaning shabby or lousy.

Unsurprisingly, Grand Lodge processions were discontinued in 1747, when the present-day restrictions came into force.

2nd Legend has it that in Co. Cork, Ireland, in or around 1711, Arthur St Leger (1695-1775), 1st Viscount Doneraile, was holding lodge meetings in his home, which at the time was undergoing some renovations. The bricks for the walls were stacked up hastily, particularly in the wall that adjoined the lodge room to the library, which was the next room.

Shortly before the lodge meeting started, Arthur's daughter, Elizabeth, was reading in the library. Eventually, she fell asleep only to be awoken by the voices from the meeting. Being curious, and seeing some of the bricks were loose, she listened and heard the complete ceremony.

Realising the importance of what she had heard, she crept from the room only to be confronted by the outer guard; the brethren were alerted to her presence and realised she had heard the ceremony. After some debate it was decided that they had no alternative but to initiate Elizabeth.

She was initiated that very evening, with the lodge being presided over by her father, as well as her brother, and future husband. So began the legend of the Lady Freemason, the Hon. Elizabeth St Ledger, daughter of Lord Doneraile.

3rd The name Solomon is a Hebrew name meaning 'peace'. As we know, Solomon was the son of David and Bathsheba, who succeeded his father as King of Israel.

Interesting, under the Kabbalistic interpretation of the name, it expresses the terms or symbolism of *Sol-om-on. Sol*, the rising sun, *Om*, the sun at its meridian, and *On*, the setting sun, equal to that of the three Principle Officers in Freemasonry.

The Kabbalah is an esoteric discipline or school of thought that originated from or within Judaism.

4th We have heard how Jacob's Ladder rests firmly on the Volume of Sacred Law in our lodges and reaches to the Heavens, and the angels of the Lord ascend and descend thereon.

The staves of the ladder we are told are many and they point out the several moral virtues, but have specific reference to the three principle virtues, which are Faith, Hope and Charity. This is because we should have Faith in the Great Architect of the Universe; Hope in Salvation; and to show Charity to all men. Here we look at Faith.

Faith is the foundation of justice, the bond of amity, and the chief support of civil society. We live and walk by Faith. By it we have a continual acknowledgment of a Supreme Being. By Faith we have access to the throne of grace; are justified, accepted, and finally received. A true and sincere Faith is the evidence of things not seen, but the substance of those hoped for. This, well maintained and answered in our Masonic profession, will bring us to those blessed mansions, where we shall be eternally happy with God, the Great Architect of the Universe.

5th One of the most amusing incidents I have ever witnessed was the time when I attended a lodge of seafarers, and those associated with the sea. The lodge's Opening and Closing Odes, were hymns favoured by sailors and even the Festive Board, was announced by the shrill tones of a Bosun's whistle.

The Initiation began at the same time as the most horrendous storm, with almost ear-shattering claps of thunder. Stalwartly, the Junior Deacon pressed on with the Candidate until he was joined by the Senior Deacon in front of the Master's pedestal.

The Worshipful Master began to speak, culminating in the words, 'Are you therefore willing to take a Solemn Obligation, founded on the principles I have stated, to keep inviolate the secrets and mysteries of the Order?'

As the Master finished speaking several drips of water, caused by a leak from the ceiling, dropped directly onto the head of the Candidate.

Obviously believing the water to be part of the ceremony, and undaunted by current satiation, uttered 'I am', before the Junior Deacon could indicate he needed to give a response.

What was even funnier was that the lodge decided not to inform the Candidate that the water was not part of the ceremony and therefore the poor chap was none the wiser until he witnessed another Initiation some months later.

6th One of the terms we frequently hear in Freemasonry is 'time immemorial'; the definition is quite simple: 'A time in the past that was so long ago that people do not have any knowledge or memory of it.'

In law, it has a different meaning: 'That a property or benefit has been enjoyed for so long that its owner does not have to prove how they came to own in'

In 1275, by the first Statute of Westminster, the time of memory was limited to the reign of Richard I, beginning 6 July, 1189.

In Freemasonry, it is sometimes used as a means to describe ritual practices, customs or traditions, whereby there is no evidence of how, where or when, they originated. This can sometimes give the false impression that the practice has been in use since time began, but it is wrong for us to assume this timescale.

We must remind ourselves that because we have no record of when a custom started, so we cannot automatically assume it is from a time of great antiquity and therefore give the impression that the Craft is older than what the records that are available, suggest.

7th In China, *c*.500BC, Mencius the philosopher wrote in the book called *The Great Learning*: 'A man should abstain from doing unto others what he would not they should do unto him, and this is called the principle of acting on the Square.'

There is an Israelitish legend that in the days of King Herod, there lived a famous Hebrew called Hillel who was said to have been one of Herod's Wardens during the rebuilding of the Temple in the time of Zerubbabel. The story goes that Hillel was asked by a stranger to teach him the whole of the Sacred Law while he stood on one foot. Hillel replied in just a few words, saying: 'What is hateful to thyself do not do unto thy neighbour. This is the whole Law, the rest is just commentary.'

In a similar vein, the Charge to the initiate says: 'To your neighbour, by acting with him on the square, by rendering him every kind office which justice or mercy may require, by relieving his necessities, soothing his afflictions, and by doing unto him as in similar cases you would wish he should do to you.'

Therefore, in Freemasonry, acting on the Square is defined as the duties we owe to our neighbour.

8th 1 Kings 6:8 tells us in reference to the winding staircase that, 'The door for the middle chamber was in the right side of the house: and they went up with winding stairs into the middle chamber, and out of the middle into the third.' So has the winding staircase any other significance in Freemasonry? Our ritual further tells us that:

> *...the Fellow Crafts were paid their wages in specie, which they went to receive in the middle chamber of the Temple. They got there by the porchway or entrance on the south side. After our ancient Brethren had entered the porch, they arrived at the foot of the winding staircase which led to the middle chamber.*
>
> And: *King Solomon afterwards caused it to be adopted as a pass word in a Fellow Craft's Lodge to prevent any unqualified person ascending the winding staircase which led to the middle chamber of the Temple.*
>
> And: *They then passed up the winding staircase, consisting of three, five, seven, or more steps.*
>
> Also: *After our ancient Brethren had gained the summit of the winding staircase, they arrived at the door of the middle chamber which they found open, but properly tyled against all under the Degree of a Fellow Craft by the Senior Warden, who demanded of them the Sign, Token and Word of a Fellow Craft.*

Without having any great single significance, many consider it to have what could be described as a compound symbol that is its significance brings together several separate symbols found in the three degrees. Each of these symbols has their own separate significance when used alone. Yet when brought together in a single symbol, it represents a most interesting lesson within the allegory.

Concentrating on the number of steps, which are: three, five and seven, they represent the three Degrees of Masonry. The Entered Apprentice begins his symbolic journey with three, the Fellowcraft, five and the Master Mason, seven.

The First Degree lessons are primarily intended to prepare the recipient for the mental, moral, and spiritual light that is to be achieved in the succeeding degrees.

In the Second Degree, the recipients' real intellectual journey begins as he enters the laborious task of self-improvement.

The Third Degree culminates in his ability to overcome his frailties, refine his conduct, perfect his character and seek eternal life in the mansion of the Most High.

Therefore, his Masonic destiny requires him to ascend the winding stairs, step by step, until he has reaches the summit, where the treasures await the faithful and obedient.

9th During that wonderful address known as the Explanation of the Second Degree Tracing Board, we are told in relation to those two great pillars that, 'They were formed hollow, the better to serve as archives to Masonry, for therein were deposited the constitutional rolls.'

As you know, there was no Freemasonry (as the Lecture implies) in those days and certainly no Constitutional Rolls.

10th St Barbara is the patroness of Builders and Architects and is the heroine of a romantic story brought to Western Europe by the Crusaders. Her father, so the legend goes, locked her in a tower to prevent the possibility of her marrying, but during her imprisonment she was converted to Christianity. During her imprisonment, she asked that a third window may be placed in the tower, but the builder betrayed her and told her father of her conversion. In his rage her father killed her which led to her martyrdom. Her symbol subsequently became the tower.

11th When we speak of King Solomon's Temple in the Second Degree, we refer to a Pillar that is situated on the right.

The ritual explains that the right-hand Pillar '...was so named after Jachin, the Assistant High Priest who officiated at its dedication.' However, the fact remains that it was not named after him and he did not officiate at the dedication of the Temple.

12th The Ornaments of the lodge are the Mosaic pavement, the Blazing Star, and the Indented or Tessellated Border. The Mosaic pavement is the beautiful flooring of a Freemason's lodge, the Blazing Star the glory in the centre, and the Indented or Tessellated Border, the skirt work round the same.

The Mosaic pavement may justly be deemed the beautiful flooring of a Freemason's lodge, by reason of its being variegated and chequered; this points out the diversity of objects which decorate and adorn the creation, the animate as well as the inanimate parts thereof.

The Blazing Star, or glory in the centre, refers us to the sun, which enlightens the earth, and by its benign influence dispenses blessings to mankind in general

The Indented or Tessellated Border refers us to the planets, which in their various revolutions form a beautiful border round that grand luminary, the sun.

13th The Bible tells us that the Ark of the Covenant, the Table of Shewbread and the furniture of King Solomon's Temple, were all made of Acacia, which the scriptures refer to as *Shitta* or in the plural sense *Shittim*. Its attributes include the fact that the wood is heavier than water, its ability to avoid attacks from insects or parasites and the sweet aromatic quality for which it is an ingredient in holy anointing oil.

Also referred to in early Masonic works as 'Cassia', it first appears in that form in Pritchard's *Masonry Dissected*, and later in Anderson *Constitutions* of 1738. Preston's *Illustrations of Masonry* uses both words.

In the Masonic setting, Acacia may be said to be emblematic of the immortality of the soul as the plant is evergreen. A sprig of Acacia appears on the top of the Third Degree Tracing board and we are told in the Traditional history that King Solomon sent out search parties:

> *Many days were spent in fruitless search; indeed, one class returned with out having made any discovery of importance. A second, however, were more fortunate, for on the evening of a certain day, after having suffered the greatest privations and*

personal fatigues, one of the brethren, who had rested himself in a reclining posture, to assist his rising, caught hold of a shrub that grew near, which to his surprise came easily out of the ground. On a closer examination he found that the earth had been recently disturbed. He therefore hailed his companions, and with their united endeavours re-opened the ground, and there found the body of our Master very indecently interred. They covered it again with all respect and reverence, and to distinguish the spot, stuck a sprig of acacia at the head of the grave.

14th Have you ever given a passing thought to the connection between Jazz and Freemasonry? Did you know that some of the greatest jazz musicians were Freemasons?

Here's just a few on that list:

Louis Armstrong – Jazz Musician
Glenn Miller – Orchestra Leader
Paul Whiteman – Orchestra Leader known as the 'King of Jazz'
William C. Handy – Composer known as the 'Father of the Blues'
Antoine Joseph Sax – Inventor of the saxophone
James 'Eubie' Blake – Composer and Pianist
Lionel Hampton – Orchestra Leader and Composer

Then there are:

Irving Berlin – Song Writer who wrote many of the jazz standards
Al Jolson – Starred in the first 'Talkie', the 'Jazz Singer'
Nat King Cole – Singer and Pianist
Roy Fox – Orchestra Leader

And others who built their careers in England:

Stanley Black
Joe Loss
Edmundo Ross
Geraldo

What talent and all Sons of the Widow!

15th Did you know that at a technical level, the simplest jazz chord gives us a suggestion as to why some say there are similarities between the Craft and jazz?

The simplest jazz chord is made up of the 1st, 3rd, 5th and 7th notes in the diatonic scale. In fact, it is essentially the use of the 7th note, which differentiates a jazz (or blues) chord from a classical chord, you simply flatten the 7th note. As the chord structure gets more complicated you flatten the 3rd note next and then the 5th and so on. I will leave you to draw the symbolic parallels between the 3rd, 5th and 7th.

But there is a good reason why there are seven notes in the diatonic musical scale. As you may know and appreciate, Pythagoras was a most important figure in early Freemasonry, and in mathematics; in fact, you can see his theory illustrated on the IPM.'s jewel. He and his followers believed that the universe was designed around hidden numeric relations and that its entire structure was governed by mathematical patterns.

They discovered mathematical relations between sounds and developed the concept of 'music of the spheres', that being the ratios between notes in the diatonic musical scale that we know today which, so I am told, actually mirrors the distances from Earth to the seven planetary oracles: Moon, Mercury, Venus, Sun, Mars, Jupiter and Saturn.

16th On that list of Masonic entertainers is the great Al Jolson, renowned for his great generosity and good works. For example, Al made a name for himself during the 1906 earthquake in San Francisco when he donated his time to sing in the rubble-filled streets to keep morale high. It was here he coined the phrase 'You ain't heard nothing yet'.

In 1913, Al was Initiated, Passed and Raised in the St Ceciles Lodge in New York under the name of Albert Jolson, along with several other entertainers. As his reputation as an entertainer grew, so did the distinguishing characteristics of a Freemason and he carried out great works of charity, which he always insisted were kept secret.

He gave generously to the building of a church for native Indians in California; he made a film for the Police Patrolman's benevolent fund, for the children of those policemen killed in service. As early as 1911, at the age of 25, Al was already noted for fighting discrimination on the Broadway stage and later in his movies and at a time when black people were banned from starring on the Broadway stage, he promoted the play by black playwright Garland Anderson, which became the first production with an all-black cast ever produced on Broadway; he became a folk hero amongst the black population of New York.

He brought an all-black dance team from San Francisco that he wanted to feature in his Broadway show and it was said that he was 'the only white man allowed into an all-black nightclub in Harlem'.

He once read in the newspaper that songwriters Eubie Blake and Noble Sissle, neither of whom he had ever heard of, were refused service at a Connecticut restaurant because of their race. He immediately tracked them down and took them out to dinner 'insisting he'd punch anyone in the nose who tried to kick us out!'

> *According to the St. James Encyclopaedia of Popular Culture:*
>
> *Almost single-handedly, Jolson helped to introduce African-American musical innovations like jazz, ragtime and the blues to white audiences...[and] paved the way for African-American performers like Louis Armstrong, Duke Ellington, Fats Waller, and Ethel Waters...to bridge the cultural gap between black and white America.*

Al gave of himself right up to the very end, when in 1950, he insisted on going to entertain the troops in Korea. At his own expense, he performed forty-two shows in a mere seven days, the strain was so much he fell ill and returned home and on 23 October 1950, Bro. Al Jolson died in San Francisco of a heart attack aged 64; the world had lost its greatest entertainer. He was posthumously awarded the Congressional Medal of Merit for his many overseas tours with the United States Services.

Bro. Al left over $3,000,000 to charity.

Two years prior to his death, he was number 2, 12 and 13 on the list of best album sales for 1948. Glenn Miller was at number 6 and 11.

17th As a child at Christmas, my parents would always play a compilation album of seasonal music and my favourite track was, 'Good King Wenceslas', by Glenn Miller. In fact, I so enjoyed his music I spent much of my pocket money on many of his EP's (Extended play) and LP's (Long play) records. It was not until some forty-five years later, while working on a lecture about Freemasons and big bands, that I discovered he was a Freemason.

Alton Glenn Miller was born in 1904 and recorded as missing in action in December, 1944. He was America's most famous big band musician, arranger, composer, and bandleader of the swing era.

He was one of the best-selling recording artists from 1939 to 1943, with songs like 'In the Mood' 'Moonlight Serenade' 'Pennsylvania 6500' 'Chattanooga Choo Choo' 'String of Pearls' 'American Patrol' and 'Tuxedo Junction'; many of the songs we know and love today.

Sadly, while flying to France to entertain U.S. troops during World War II, his aircraft disappeared in bad weather over the English Channel. It is believed that on their return from a bombing raid in Germany, a group of RAF aircraft flying at a high level, released their remaining bombs over the English Channel, as was their usual practice, to avoid landing with a dangerous payload. Flying in the other direction across the English Channel a thousand yards below, was the small plane carrying Glenn Miller. The belief is that the discharged payload hit Miller's plane.

One thing we know for sure, Brother Glenn Miller's music is legendary, enduring, almost comforting, as well as being thoroughly melodic and enjoyable, it has and will continue to live on.

As a footnote to this story, I now have my full Glenn Miller music collection on CD and some years back, I was privileged to meet and listen to John Miller, nephew of the famous band leader.

18th

In the film *The Glenn Miller Story*, Miller goes to a Harlem club where he listens to fellow Freemason Louis Armstrong.

Louis Armstrong was born August 1901 and died in July 1971; nicknamed Satchmo or Pops, he was a jazz trumpeter par excellence, and singer, born in New Orleans, Louisiana.

Coming to prominence in the 1920s as an 'inventive' trumpet and cornet player, Armstrong was a foundational influence in jazz, shifting the focus of the music from collective improvisation to solo performance. With his instantly recognisable gravelly voice, Armstrong was also an influential singer, demonstrating great dexterity as an improviser, bending the lyrics and melody of a song for expressive purposes.

He was also skilled at scat singing, which uses sounds and syllables instead of actual lyrics, just like Cleo Laine used to sing.

Renowned for his charismatic stage presence and voice, almost as much as for his trumpet-playing, Armstrong's influence extends well beyond jazz music and by the end of his career in the 1960s, he was widely regarded as a profound influence on popular music in general. His artistry and personality allowed him socially acceptable access to the upper echelons of American society that were highly restricted for a black man.

His Masonic membership has been disputed by some, as his lodge appears to be irregular, but, like most Masonic commentators, I am happy to refer to him as a Brother.

Among the many recordings and albums that Louis Armstrong released, there was an album dedicated to his great hero called *Satch plays Fats*, it was Armstrong's tribute to the great Fats Waller

19th Thomas Wright 'Fats' Waller was born in May 1904, and died December 1943. He was an influential jazz pianist, organist, composer, singer, and comedic entertainer, whose innovations to the Harlem stride style was the groundwork for modern jazz piano. Two of his best-known compositions, 'Ain't Misbehavin' and 'Honeysuckle Rose' were also inducted posthumously, into the Grammy Hall of Fame, 1984 and 1999.

Waller contracted pneumonia after a successful show at the Zanzibar Room, Detroit, during which he had fallen ill. He was returning home when he sadly died on a cross-country train near Kansas City, Missouri.

It was reported that more than 4,000 people attended his funeral in Harlem, which prompted Dr Adam Clayton Powell Jr. who delivered the eulogy, to say that Fats Waller 'always played to a packed house'. Coincidentally, as the train with the body of Waller stopped in Kansas City, so did another train with his dear friend Louis Armstrong on board.

The Thomas Waller Lodge No.49 was named after Fats Waller.

20th One of Thomas Waller Lodge, No.49's most famous members was none other than Nathanial Adams Cole, better known to us as Nat king Cole.

Brother Nathaniel Cole (1919-1965), became a great American singer and musician, but first came to prominence as a leading jazz pianist. Noted for his soft, baritone voice, he first performed with jazz bands. He was one of the first African Americans to host a television show and has maintained worldwide popularity since his death.

Cole was a very heavy smoker throughout his life and was rarely seen without a cigarette in his hand. He believed that smoking up to three packs a day gave his voice its rich sound and before any recording session, he would smoke several cigarettes in rapid succession. In 1953, after an operation for a stomach ulcer, he was advised to stop smoking but did not heed the warning.

In December 1964, he was diagnosed with lung cancer and died on 15 February 1965, at St John's Hospital, Santa Monica, California.

21st One of the many people Nat King Cole collaborated with during his career was fellow Freemason, Duke Ellington.

Edward Kennedy Ellington, known to us all as the 'Duke', was born on 29 April 1899, in Washington D.C. His father James and his mother Daisy, who was the daughter of a slave, were both pianists, she played parlour songs and he operatic airs. The young Ellington began taking piano lessons at the age of seven and continued his mother Daisy's practice, which was to surround her son with dignified woman to reinforce his manners and to teach him to live elegantly.

Young Ellington's childhood friends could not fail to notice his casual manner, easy grace and his elegant dress, which gave him the appearance of a young nobleman. Ellington later recalled when referring to his schoolboy friend, Edgar McEntree, 'I think he felt that in order for me to be eligible for his constant companionship, I should have a title. So he called me Duke'. The name stuck.

The 'Duke' became a member of the Social Lodge No.1, Washington, D.C., in 1932. He was also a 32° Scottish Rite Mason, and a member of the Shrine.

Duke was of course great friends and musical rivals with that other titled band leader and Freemason, Count Basie.

22nd William Basie was born to Harvey Lee and Lillian Basie in Red Bank, New Jersey. His father worked as a coachman and caretaker for a wealthy judge. Both of his parents had some type of musical background. His father played the mellophone and his mother played the piano and she gave Basie his first piano lessons. She took in laundry and baked cakes to sell, so she could pay the pay the twenty-five cents a lesson for him to further continue his piano instruction.

Not much of a student in school, Basie dreamed of a travelling life, inspired by touring carnivals which came to town. He finished junior high school but spent much of his time at the Palace Theatre in Red Bank, where doing occasional chores gained him free admission to performances. He quickly learned to improvise music appropriate to the acts. Though a natural at the piano, Basie initially preferred drums but at age fifteen, switched to piano exclusively.

Basie was a member of Wisdom Lodge No.102 in Chicago, Illinois

23rd One of the most enduring Christmas songs of all time was written for the film *Holiday Inn*.

Legend has it that Irvin Berlin wrote the song on a warm evening in 1940, while staying at the La Quinta Hotel, a favoured Hollywood retreat. He told his secretary, 'Grab your pen and take down this song. I just wrote the best song I've ever written—heck, I just wrote the best song that anybody's ever written!' He was right, the Guinness Book of Records, 2009, claims that it has become the bestselling song of all time and since its release, has sold well over 100 million copies.

Brother Irving Berlin was Initiated, Passed and Raised between 12 May and 3 June 1910, at the Munn Lodge, No.190, New York. He became a life member in December 1935.

24th At this time of year we often think of taking the family to a traditional pantomime; therefore I guess it would also be very remiss of me not to mention, at this point, some English entertainers who were Freemasons, and who starred in, and entertained us, in those Christmas pantomimes and of course, over the years on the television, at Christmas time.

From the Music and Variety Halls, we have George Robey, Harry Randall, Sandy Powell, Leslie Saroney, Nervo & Knox, Wee Georgie Wood, Harry Lester, Les Allen, Nat Temple, Lupino Lane, Nat Jackley and Billy Danvers.

From television, we have Dick Emery, Bob Monkhouse, Peter Sellers, Arthur English, Alfred Marks, Bud Flanagan, Billy Dainty, Bernard Bresslaw, Tommy Cooper and Roger de Courcey, to name but a few.

How lucky were we as children, to have such wonderful seasonal memories of many of the aforementioned well-known names; most of whom have now passed to the Grand Lodge above.

25th On this special day in the Christian calendar, celebrated throughout the world, I send you fraternal and seasonal greetings.

At the closing of the Convocation of a Royal Arch Chapter, the following words are used by the three Principles which are taken from Luke 2:14:

Zerubbabel:	Glory be to God on high.
Haggai:	On earth peace.
Joshua:	Goodwill towards men.

When I hear these words, I am always reminded of how the love, generosity and consideration we show for our fellow creatures at this time of year, should be enduring and remain with us all year long.

This is the message, the ethos and the principles that the whole of Freemasonry was founded and built upon.

26th The Deacon's Lament – Unknown

Oh, I wished I'd looked after my ritual, I wish I had studied that book.
I just might have got through a whole meeting, without having to take a sly look,
At the words printed so neatly and tidy, with capital letters and dots,
Inverted commas and rows of small hammers to remind me about them there knocks.

If I had been to a Lodge of Instruction and followed the Preceptors plan,

My signs might be more like a Mason and less like a tic-tac man.
A Past-Master once said with sarcasm, as his doffed his apron of dark blue,
You lay 'five to one' when the Lodge is begun and 'evens the field' when it's through.

Time was, when I was a Deacon, I was proud of my wand and my dove,
Initiation was due; I was in a real stew, so I wrote the words out on my glove
Now some Candidates are cool and collected, mine was all nervous and hot,
I must not boast, but his hands were like toast leaving my glove as an illegible blot.

As I thumped the Wardens shoulder, the ink stained his coat a bright blue,
He said 'Who have you there?' I just stood in despair he could see I did not have a clue.
I looked at my glove for the answer at those five fickle fingers of fate,
The blots faded away, left the words plain as day, 'All Cotton, Dry Clean, Size Eight.'

27th Here is a general guide to jewel-wearing, but please, if in doubt, consult your DC.

Past Master Jewels are worn at Craft meetings only for the duration of the period before honours are received. This jewel should not be worn with Provincial, London Grand Rank or Steward's regalia.

Founder's Jewels for Craft can be worn at Craft meetings; Founder Jewels for Royal Arch Chapters should only be worn at Chapter Convocations.

Permanent Grand Lodge Charity Jewels can be worn at Craft meetings.

Charity Jewels are valid for the year in which they were earned and can be worn at Craft meetings for that duration only. Charity Jewels are not worn after the close of that event.

Festival Jewels unique to the Province which issued them, can be worn at Craft or Chapter meetings within that Province for the duration of that Festival.

Quatuor Coronati Correspondence Circle Membership Jewel can be worn at Craft meetings.

Lodge and Chapter Centenary and Bicentenary Jewels are worn by bona-fide members only and are considered permanent jewels. The Chapter Centenary Jewel in not worn at Craft meeting.

Hall Stone Jewels are worn on a collaret by Masters of Hall Stone Lodges.

Royal Arch Chapter Jewels which are presented to all Companions of this Order should be worn at Craft and Chapter meetings, closest to the heart. No other jewel should be worn to the right or in front of this jewel.

Royal Arch Past Zerubbabal Jewels are worn at Chapter meetings only.

Jewels struck to commemorate new Grand Lodges, etc., are generally only worn at Craft meetings within the designated boundaries of that area.

Other general points of guidance:

It is the common practice these days, because of spiralling costs, of having Past Masters or Past First Principal Jewels entrusted rather than given. You should therefore be especially mindful of returning these jewels once promotion has been received. In such cases it is the general practice of having your name engraved on the jewel.

Jewels from any other Orders are not worn at Craft or Chapter meetings.

Jewels should never be worn on collars.

28th In a previous section we discussed the Landmarks of the Order and how the most plausible were suggested by the late

Masonic Historian, Harry Carr. We also learnt how the Landmarks were notionally, time immemorial.

Brother Carr lists four Landmarks relating to Belief, the V.S.L., Gender and Allegiance, all of which are listed in the *Old Charges* dating from c.1390; therefore these four qualify unequivocally as time immemorial.

The fifth Landmark, which relates to the immortality of the soul, was implicit in the religious belief of that period.

Therefore, these five Landmarks of the Order satisfy the criteria of being time immemorial.

29th The word *mystery* is synonymous with Freemasonry, and you will recall the Candidate at his Initiation comes, '...humbly soliciting to be admitted to the mysteries and privileges of Freemasonry.' While the Candidate for Exaltation during the Holy Royal Arch ceremony 'seek[s] to participate in the light of our mysteries.'

So what on earth are these mysteries?

It is quite simple really, if you look at the word itself. Bearing in mind we have inherited many terms and traditions from the trade organisation of Masons, so mystery refers to the skill of the workman or the mystery of his art. To the lay-man, any competent artisan, whose skill is evident in his work, is a mystery to another man. The term is better known to us these days as 'tricks of the trade', which are frequently shared. However, it is still within living memory of the many trade disputes regarding demarcation, at a time when tradesmen jealously guarded their skill.

We should also consider the term being synonymous with the message contained in the symbolism, which is a mystery to non-Masons and which Masons themselves moralise upon with different interpretations.

30th An imposter! An imposter! In 1847, a visiting American named Major General George Cooke L.L.D., who resided in England for a period, joined the Prince of Wales Lodge No.259. He became a great supporter of Masonic Charities and became Vice-President of the Girls' School and Life Governor of the Boys' School.

Before he returned to his native America, he was given the rank of Past Grand Warden and appointed the Grand Master's representative at the Grand Lodge of New York. A fund was even raised for the purpose of placing his bust on display at Freemasons' Hall.

However, not long after he returned to America, it came to light he was no more than a medical quack that hawked his wares in his home country. He was immediately stripped of his Grand Rank and expelled from Grand Lodge, who reimbursed the sums on money he had given to Masonic charities.

31st We always approach the New Year with real optimism and good intentions and sadly by the end of January we fail in most of our resolutions and are back to square one. That is not always a bad thing for at least we had good intentions; it is just that we often set ourselves lofty tasks that we cannot complete. The failure often demoralises us and that is when we get the January or post-Christmas blues.

To prevent this, I am trying something new this year; I learnt a new word recently and am introducing it into my mind set.

'Suboptimal' means something of less than or below the highest standard or quality, and I felt this year my approach to tasks, relationships and Freemasonry must never be suboptimal.

Freemasonry requires that we give of our best to the tasks that life apportions us. Therefore if we accept, that this New Year, we will put forward our very best endeavours in all we are asked to do, then having done our best, to the highest level of our talents and capabilities, then we can do no more.

All the belief systems in the world encourage us to achieve our potential and striving to achieve our optimal level in all we do, will restore the feeling of achievement, raise our self-esteem and help us achieve the feeling of control and stewardship in our life.

Postscript

Having reached the conclusion of this book, no doubt your head will be filled with various facts and information, which, by keeping this book to hand, you can constantly refresh your memory. There are however, several other methods you can use to collate your information.

Notebook – I constantly use a notebook to write facts, ideas or information that I need to retain for future reference. You might also include the source of the information, i.e. book title and page number.

Highlight – whenever I am reading a book, I frequently use a pencil to notate the relevant information that I wish to retain. I have also been known to use a yellow highlighter. The information can be transferred to your notebook at a later stage.

Laptop/PC/Tablet/Mobile Device – I also have much of my information stored electronically with copies available on all my devices. This method is safe as long as you always remember to copy your information to more than one device. This ensures you will never lose any of your information.

The more information you collate, the more you may wish to write about the subject for your own edification or to share with your lodge. Here are some handy tips to remember.

When gathering information, Provincial libraries, bona fide Masonic websites, books and magazines, will all contain information on the subject you wish to study. Always study more than one source to ensure you have a good overview of the topic from more than one opinion. Not all you read will be true, so be careful and verify your facts.

Always ensure you quote your sources and remember, to research or copy from one source is plagiarism, to research or copy from two sources is research.

Build an index of your work because many topics cross-reference with another and the easier you notate your work, the easier it will become for you to retrieve it at a later date.

Finally, Freemasonry is a long-established organisation; get to know your way around it. Respect the views of others, remember promotion in Freemasonry is not given on one's knowledge; therefore rank does not mean a higher or better knowledge. Keep you subjects simple, precise and to the point. Avoiding guesswork, assumptions, what if's and maybe's, as they might sound perfectly feasible to you, but your arguments will flounder without sound fact.

Good luck in your quest making your daily advancement.